To Anar
the Ba,
Porter. God bless you all!

The Catholic Mom's
PRAYER
COMPANION

♡, The Haddads
Michael, Heather,
Pierce,
Lincoln Hudson

The Catholic Mom's
PRAYER
COMPANION

A Book of Daily Reflections

**EDITED BY LISA M. HENDEY
AND SARAH A. REINHARD**

AVE MARIA PRESS AVE Notre Dame, Indiana

Founded in 1865, Ave Maria Press is a ministry of the United States Province of Holy Cross.

www.avemariapress.com

Paperback: ISBN-13 978-1-59471-661-4

E-book: ISBN-13 978-1-59471-662-1

Cover image "Canticle of Mary" © Jen Norton, JenNortonArtStudio.com.

Cover and text design by Katherine J. Ross.

Printed and bound in the United States of America.

Library of Congress Cataloging-in-Publication Data
Names: Hendey, Lisa M., editor.
Title: The Catholic mom's prayer companion : a book of daily reflections / edited by Lisa M. Hendey and Sarah A. Reinhard.
Description: Notre Dame, Indiana : Ave Maria Press, 2016. | Includes bibliographical references.
Identifiers: LCCN 2016018058 (print) | LCCN 2016018844 (ebook) | ISBN 9781594716614 | ISBN 1594716617 | ISBN 9781594716621 () | ISBN 1594716625 ()
Subjects: LCSH: Mothers--Prayers and devotions. | Catholic women--Prayers and devotions. | Devotional calendars--Catholic Church.
Classification: LCC BX2353 .C375 2016 (print) | LCC BX2353 (ebook) | DDC 242/.6431--dc23
LC record available at https://lccn.loc.gov/2016018058

INTRODUCTION:

The Catholic Mom's Prayer Companion

The little book you hold in your hands is a labor of love. If you had any idea of the machinations involved in its inception, its crafting, and its refinement, you would likely laugh out loud at the various layers of insanity, caffeine, and chocolate involved in pulling it all together. When our editor approached Sarah and me with the idea to craft a prayer book that would combine the voices of our *CatholicMom.com* community and be a daily companion for our readers, I was "all in."

Then, as Sarah will agree, the reality of more than eighty authors and the truth of 366 (because yes, we needed leap day) reflections kicked in. Countless times in the months we spent working on this project, my prayers for this little book sounded like they were coming from a petulant toddler instead of a mature empty nester. "Seriously?" I would challenge God. "Will we really pull this off?"

What you hold in your hands is confirmation that tiny miracles are possible. Sparing you any more details on our behind-the-scenes challenges, I simply want to invite you into these pages to make of them what best serves and supports you in your daily prayer life. You'll find here a marvelous mix of voices, perspectives, tones, and vocations. We hope that this prayer companion will invite you into a deeper relationship with God, our Blessed Mother, the Communion of Saints, and our beloved Church.

But we also hope that these simple reflections and prayers will draw us all closer to one another as sisters in Christ. The vocation of motherhood can sometimes feel isolating and beyond our emotional, mental, physical, and spiritual capacities. We moms look far too often at our flaws and hurdles and not frequently enough at our blessings or even those tiny miracles sprinkled through our days.

As you take a few moments each day to pray with these pages, envision yourself among a community of friends from around the world. Joining you in meditation are a housewife in the Midwest with little ones, an adoptive mom with teens, a working professional on the East Coast, a home-schooling mom in Europe, a single mother in Canada, and even this empty nester in California. Also with us are companions we will never meet in real life but who pause alongside us for a few moments of quiet each day because they too need the spiritual fuel provided to make the most of the "yes" they desire to give to God, their families, and our world.

While our to-do lists vary, our priorities are universal. We desire to become saints, to serve, to give, and to draw ourselves and our loved ones ever closer to God. In our busyness, we moms often neglect our own prayer lives while seeing to the many needs of our families. This little book is your encouragement that setting aside even a few moments of quiet prayer each day can be one of the very best gifts you can give to your family.

Saint Elizabeth Ann Seton, herself a Catholic mom, counseled, "We must pray without ceasing, in every occurrence and employment of our lives—that prayer which is rather a habit of lifting up the heart to God as in a constant communication with him." We moms are very familiar with this "constant communication"—prayers offered for teens as we match socks, for our husbands as we balance the checkbook, for aging parents as we endeavor to serve generations at both ends of life, for our babies as we beg for a night of sound sleep.

This busyness is why I love a second quotation of Mother Seton's that counsels us, "Be attentive to the voice of grace." Sometimes, in our haste to tackle our monumental and competing priorities, we miss those moments of grace that God gifts to us. The hand-drawn, misspelled love letter. The "This is good, honey," dinnertime compliments. The day without a single mishap or even the days that contain way too many unplanned distractions. In them all, there is a grace that signals the constancy of God's love for us if only we can quiet our hearts for a few moments to hear and give thanks for it.

Sarah and I hope that by providing you with a few simple lines each day we can help you to draw closer to that voice of God's grace. Use this book in whatever way and at whatever time most fuels you to thrive in your vocation as a Catholic mom. As you read, feel our presence alongside you. And we ask as you pray with these pages that you remember in your intentions all those who are a part of our *CatholicMom.com* community; we are united together in our mission to serve and lift up our domestic Churches.

May God richly bless you today, throughout this year, and throughout your life with joy, with peace, with companionship, and with grace.

LISA M. HENDEY

FOUNDER OF *CATHOLICMOM.COM*

January

THEME: RESOLUTION

A Year of New Days

For nothing will be impossible for God.

Luke 1:37

I love to flip the cover on a new calendar. Not yet coffee-stained or burdened under the scrawl of too many commitments, its pages hold the potential for vast possibilities. Staring at the unfilled dates that will soon be overflowing, I feel a fleeting yet brilliant modicum of control.

What a joy to look at a year full of days, to imagine, and to wonder! Our planned traditions, events, and activities are coming. And the many surprises, known only to God, which will soon grace these pages? Those are coming as well.

Today, sitting by my spangled Christmas tree, listening to the crackle of a winter's fire as my family slumbers upstairs, I will do what I always do: form resolutions and inscribe them in my new calendar. Admittedly, I often fall short of these self-inflicted goals. Yet the optimist in me recognizes the incredible grace of cooperating with God's perfect plan for my life, so I persist.

I love to imagine God smiling down on my little "resolved" memos. How often I struggle with the same shortcomings. How amazing that God, in his bounty, showers forgiveness time and time again, loving me through it all, even the messes. And how beautiful that in the dawn of every morning, each new year, such vast potential for growth, for discovery, for renewal, and for love unfolds before me.

Mother Mary, in celebration of your spotless fiat, this year will be my gift to my Creator, to my loved ones, and to our world. Draw me ever closer to your Son.

To Ponder: What spiritual, familial, and personal goals do you have for the coming year?

LISA M. HENDEY

JANUARY 2

Come, Holy Spirit

Acquire the Holy Spirit and thousands around you
will acquire salvation.

Saint Seraphim of Sarov

Saint Seraphim dreamed big. Honored by both the Roman Catholic (today) and Orthodox (January 15) traditions, this wonderworker emphasized seeking communion with God as the true purpose of life for every Christian. Saint Seraphim's life demonstrated that everything else was merely the means for "acquiring the Holy Spirit."

Wait! Didn't we acquire the Holy Spirit at Baptism, and weren't we sealed with the gift of the Spirit at Confirmation? Can't we acquire more of the Holy Spirit in the sacrament of Reconciliation or when we receive the Eucharist? A resounding "yes" to all of these.

How do we acquire the Holy Spirit when we are alone, frustrated, and confused?

A prayer that works anywhere, anytime: "Come, Holy Spirit!" This calms us and brings us into communion with God.

This is a prayer for clarity murmured first thing in the morning before you are sure what day it is or what you'll face. It's a prayer for perseverance when you find joy in what you are accomplishing until interruptions disrupt your every intention.

You can say this quick prayer in the middle of a traffic jam, an argument with your boss, or a bout with the flu—all means of acquiring the Holy Spirit.

Saint Seraphim doesn't promise that this prayer will change everything around you—just those in your growing circle of influence. Wait for it and watch it happen!

Come, Holy Spirit! Be my companion throughout the day and help me respond in a way that brings others closer to you.

To Ponder: We all have difficult people in our lives. How can invoking the Holy Spirit help you when you are with such people?

NANCY H. C. WARD

JANUARY 3

In Gratitude for the Small Things

Enjoy the little things in life because one day you will look back and realize they were the big things.

Anonymous

As we enter into the endless possibilities of the new year—a long-awaited graduation or dream job, a marriage or the birth of a child, a long-anticipated vacation or even retirement—this quote challenges us to acknowledge the grace and blessing of this very moment. We must be careful not to miss the beauty of the little things of today, for life can change in an instant.

Ours changed in an instant when my husband fell and severely injured his knee. For weeks he was confined to the upper floor of our two-story home. As I assumed the new roles of being a caregiver and a room service attendant, I found myself missing our former life together: our weekly date nights, leisurely walks, even grocery shopping together; I longed for all of those little things to return to my life.

In this new year, I invite you to find great joy in the ordinary things in life, for each is a gift from God. Savor your morning cup of coffee, tuck a love note into your children's lunches, carve out time in your busy schedule for God and just sit. Breathe in and savor the blessings of the day.

Lord, fill my heart with joy and gratitude for the people, places, and events in my life.

To Ponder: Reflect on your own life. What small things can you be grateful for today?

DR. MARY AMORE

Start with a Heart for God

And we know that in all things God works for the
good of those who love him, who have been called
according to his purpose.

Romans 8:28

Do you ever wonder how it is that we are supposed to be able
to faithfully weave together taking care of our families and
using our gifts outside the home? Saint Elizabeth Ann Seton,
the first native-born American saint, sets a fantastic example.

Although best known for establishing the first free Catholic school system and the first congregation of religious sisters
in America, Saint Elizabeth was also the biological mother
of five children and the foster mother of six. Quick math
says that she had *eleven* children in her care before indoor
plumbing, refrigeration, or microwaves had been invented!

What secret did Saint Elizabeth possess that allowed her
not only to care for such a large family, but also to establish
not one, but two Catholic institutions in a social and economic age dominated primarily by Protestant men?

I propose that her "secret" lies not in some great per-
sonal-professional balancing act, but in her enduring love
for God. Because of this all-consuming love, God was able
to redeem the many challenges of her life: losing her mother
at age three, the rejection of her stepmother, early widow-
hood (at age twenty-nine), and the death of two of her own

children. These trials gave Saint Elizabeth a heart for the orphan, the sick, and the dying, and it was this heart that willingly said "yes" when called to serve God outside as well as inside her home.

Father, thank you for all the circumstances of my life.

To Ponder: What could you do to fall more deeply in love with God? How might this help you serve God both inside and outside your home?

HEIDI BRATTON

JANUARY 5

Tying the Knot

Love is trinity.

Venerable Fulton J. Sheen

Whenever I present the subject of marriage to my group of teens, I always begin by handing each of them a rope and getting them to pair off. "You have thirty seconds," I say, "to take two pieces of rope and braid them together—and no knots!" Frenzied fingers and laughing ensues. I then hand each pair a third rope. A timed race begins again and ropes are twisted into braids with ease. Now they may "tie the knot"!

"A threefold cord is not quickly broken" (Eccl 4:12). In strong marriages, God is the central piece around whom a couple's lives are braided. Without him, we quickly fall apart. It was this way from the beginning, when God called the first man and first woman into communion with each other and with him.

As the creator of marriage, God strengthens couples to witness to his love in the world with a love strong and faithful to the end. The task can seem as challenging as braiding two ropes, which is why we must remember the third. How many times I have begged God to throw us the third rope of his presence and save us! Then we set about the work of re-braiding. He teaches us about the sacrifices necessary to weave our separate wills into his own. This joy is a foretaste of the eternal marriage in heaven where we will be one with God.

Holy Trinity, you want our marriage to image your love in three persons. Teach us to turn to you in all things.

To Ponder: Marriage truly tests just how selfless we can be. Do you need to ask God to "throw you a rope"—or to help you re-braid what has been divided?

CINDY COSTELLO

JANUARY 6
EPIPHANY OF THE LORD

Overwhelmed with Joy

Always remember this: life is a journey.
It is a path, a journey to meet Jesus.

Pope Francis

The blessing of seeking is in the finding of the gift hidden under wraps, the answer to the question, the destination at journey's end. Epiphany celebrates the "showing" of Jesus, the Son of God. Jesus was the Messiah of Israel, but also the Christ to the Gentiles, a Savior for all.

Scripture describes the wise men from the East yearning to meet this child king. Aided in their pilgrimage by the appearance of a star, their travels were an outward expression of an inner journey: they were seeking God.

"And there, ahead of them, went the star that they had seen at its rising, until it stopped over the place where the child was. When they saw that the star had stopped, they were overwhelmed with joy" (Mt 2:9–10). This was more than simple relief after concluding a long journey; the wise men's joy sprung from a personal encounter, the fulfillment of the longing at the center of every human heart.

"Upon entering the house, they saw the child with Mary his mother, and they knelt down and paid him homage. Then, opening their treasure chests, they offered him gifts of gold, frankincense, and myrrh" (Mt 2:11). After kneeling before Jesus, the wise men bestowed lavish treasures upon him. Yet his presence bestowed on them the greatest gift of all.

Jesus, may I seek you and greet you with overwhelming joy!

To Ponder: Did you know the word *monstrance* (the elaborate container that holds the consecrated host) comes from the Latin *monstrare*, "to show"? Why not make a small pilgrimage seeking the presence of Jesus in eucharistic adoration?

PAT GOHN

New Resolutions

The way you live your days is the way you live
your life.

Annie Dillard

The Ignatian practice of "examen" is a kind of daily review of
the day. It gives us an opportunity to step back and examine
the various moments, to rejoice in our strengths and humbly
acknowledge the weaker areas in need of improvement.

In and out of the confessional, it's important to live each
day intentionally, to examine our consciences, to resolve to
resist temptation, and to thank God for the graces he sends
to help us. It's important to take time to think about our own
personal and spiritual goals, to ask, "What goals does God
have for me?" As you begin a new year, take time to humbly
examine the following areas in your life:

- How can I deepen my prayer life?
- How can I make more time for silent prayer with God?
- What small acts of kindness can I do for my family and spouse?
- Do I make enough time for simple fun and relaxation as a family and for myself?
- What do I need to detach from or do less of?
- What can I do more of?
- What hinders me from serving my family as best as I can?
- How can I love my spouse more?

- How can I help my spouse love me more?
- What helps life flow more smoothly for myself and my family?

Lord, lead me and weave me into how you envision me. Grant me the grace to refocus on you as my ultimate resolution and goal.

To Ponder: What do you believe God is asking of you, in this current stage and situation in your life? What plans might he have for your future?

ERIKA MARIE

JANUARY 8

Doing Something More

Rejoice in hope, be patient in suffering, persevere
in prayer.

Romans 12:12

Every year I create a long, daunting list of ways I want to improve my life, grow in virtue, and get rid of something—it might be weight, clutter, or bad habits. One year when I looked at my list, I resolved to take a different approach.

I took my list to my spiritual director and asked him, "What should I focus on first, Father?"

"Focus on God and your relationship with him," he responded.

And so, I resolved to begin each day with a simple morning offering—giving everything to God before it even happened, uniting my crosses to the cross of Christ, and asking

God for his grace and strength rather than relying on my own. Father said it should only take five minutes, and I was shocked by the simplicity of it. That's it? What about the rest of my list? Father told me it could wait.

In the grand scheme of resolutions, mine did not seem like much. But my simple offering to God made all the difference. Almost immediately, I noticed a change in my mind and heart. My attitude improved, and I felt more joyful, even in the midst of chaotic and frustrating situations. And, in time, the other things on my list started falling into place. By offering everything to God first, it became clear what to do next.

Thank you, Father, for hearing my prayer, accepting my simple offering, and responding in love according to your holy will.

To Ponder: At the beginning of this new year, what is one resolution you can make that focuses on your relationship with God?

SARAH DAMM

JANUARY 9

Encourage One Another

God gives power to the faint, and strengthens the powerless.

Isaiah 40:29

It's the same thing every year: I put "exercise" on my resolutions list . . . and run out of energy after the first week. Whenever my kids see "exercise" on my to-do list, they always put little comments in the margins, such as, "You can do it, Mom!" Somehow, that makes getting to the gym less of a trial.

On the days they've left notes for me, they come home from school and ask, "Did you work out, Mom?" All hearts are lighter (and in my case, healthier) if the answer is "yes." The reverse is also true. Words of encouragement are powerful motivators.

This is true for kids as well. Sometimes I can whisper in my son's or daughter's ears, "I have faith in you." And those words fill that child with something buoyant. Knowing "someone else believes in me" carries greater weight than rewards or bribes.

God also believes in us. He points out opportunities for us to shine and be an example to the world, a person in whom God delights because he or she brings God to others. Resolve to strengthen your own willingness to listen to God and be that source of encouragement for others, and to obey the call to act. God waits in joyful hope for us to listen and to obey.

Lord, give me the strength I need this day, to encourage those around me. Help me to make healthy choices so that I might have the strength I need to share my gifts.

To Ponder: Is there someone in your life who needs a word of encouragement?

SHERRY ANTONETTI

HOUSEPLANT APPRECIATION DAY

Let's Take an Honest Look at Ourselves

Remember this, my friends: there are no such things as bad plants or bad men. There are only bad cultivators.

Victor Hugo, Les Misérables

How are your houseplants doing? Mine are still alive but a bit shriveled. They need some care and a little better cultivation.

Cultivating change, whether in our plants or in ourselves, is a big and often thankless job. We don't enjoy making those changes because some bad habits give us immediate pleasure—guilty pleasure, but pleasure nonetheless. So we make excuses. We may even blame others for our bad habits. We forget to consider what's best for us in the long run: stronger or healthier bodies, more loving relationships with God, family, or others. Maybe we just want to start sharing our talents or resources a bit less selfishly. It isn't difficult to come up with what we know in our hearts that we ought to do. What's difficult is the actual "doing."

Jesus, help me realize that my pride, fear, and laziness can keep me from looking at myself honestly. Help me to commit to change myself for my own greater benefit and the benefit of those I love.

To Ponder: Which of my houseplants—or my habits—needs to be cultivated? What's one thing I can do to make that change?

KAYE PARK HINCKLEY

JANUARY 11
NATIONAL MILK DAY

Honoring Our Lady of La Leche

Mary thus learns that the Most High has ever borne
a Son in his bosom, and that this Son has now chosen
her bosom as dwelling place.

Hans Urs von Balthasar

The image of Our Lady as a breastfeeding mother is one filled with consolation and maternal affection. It's no wonder that the devotion honoring Mary as Our Lady of La Leche ("Our Lady of the Milk") is one of the most ancient and widespread of devotions. In Rome's Priscilla catacombs, the tender depiction of a nursing Madonna adorns one of the walls, while across the Mediterranean Sea stands the Milk Grotto, where Mary is said to have hidden to breastfeed Jesus during the Slaughter of the Innocents.

The construction in Spain of a shrine dedicated to Our Lady of La Leche was overseen by King Philip III in the early sixteenth century, and, soon after, missionaries and Spanish settlers brought their fervor for the Blessed Mother to the New World. In Saint Augustine, Florida, these settlers built the first Marian shrine in the United States, dedicating it to Nuestra Senora de la Leche y Buen Parto ("Our Lady of the Milk and Happy Delivery").

Countless women have, through the intercession of Our Lady of La Leche, been granted the gift of motherhood, obtained good health for their children, or overcome obstacles to breastfeeding. The maternal heart of Our Lady of La Leche is readily touched by the prayers of her children.

Our Lady of La Leche, draw me close to your Son through my daily duties. Help me to mirror your motherly virtue to the souls in my care.

To Ponder: Are you hurt, stressed, afraid? Go to Mary. Could anything be more comforting than nestling in your heavenly Mother's lap?

CELESTE BEHE

JANUARY 12
THE BAPTISM OF THE LORD

Hearing the Father's Voice

This is my beloved son, in whom I am well pleased.

Matthew 3:17

On the last day of the Christmas season, the Church invites us to reflect on the Baptism of Our Lord. Jesus's baptism reveals to each of us our own baptismal destiny: to hear the Father's voice resounding within us, saying, "You are my beloved daughter; in you I am well pleased." And yet, so often the Father's voice is drowned out by the voices of the world as we are driven into the isolation of our own deserts to stand against the voice of the tempter.

Here, too, we are called to imitate Christ, who confronted the evil one with the Father's thundering pronouncement— beloved Son!—still sounding in his ears. Ignoring the voice that bellows, "Prove your worth by what you can do, what you possess, and what people think of you," Jesus first reveals his compassion, suffering with us over the taunts and lies of the world that insist we are merely the sum of our power, possessions, and popularity.

God's voice of infinite love, on the other hand, communicates a very different message. Do we really believe in his unconditional love and mercy? Are we convinced that we are God's beloved daughters, whom he knows and loves personally, passionately, purposefully, and persistently? Every day, there are a myriad of voices that challenge us to doubt this fundamental truth. Whose voice will we listen to today?

Father, may I be alert and attentive to your voice, which proclaims your unconditional love for me. Please silence the voices in me that oppose this truth.

To Ponder: When you close your eyes in prayer, can you hear the Father's voice saying, "You are my beloved daughter"? If not, what voice and message do you hear?

JUDY LANDRIEU KLEIN, M.T.S.

Communicate Gently

Let's communicate with friends and loved ones with
clarity, tact, and charity.

Anonymous

Family dinners, block parties, and work lunches offer great
chances to build relationships . . . or not. The ability of people
to connect with or reject one another, especially concerning
matters of politics and faith, can have alarming results!

In Saint Hilary of Poitiers' day, people quarreled about
the divinity and humanity of Christ. Saint Hilary spent his life
helping to ease such tensions, although this fourth-century
bishop in the region we now call France was born to pagan
parents. He studied himself into the Catholic faith through
the sheer reasonableness of it and defended the faith against
Arian heresies.

Saint Hilary was married and had a daughter before he
entered the Church. Many a dinnertime conversation must
have unfolded as this scholar grew in faith. He learned well
the art of gentle persuasion, gaining a reputation as a courte-
ous and clear communicator. Can you imagine being remembered for such traits sixteen hundred years after your own
death? If people misunderstood points of faith, he offered
patient corrections. If they erred in interpreting teachings,
he engaged people in respectful debate.

In our lives, chances to practice the art of gentle communication are many. Like Saint Hilary, we can ask for God's
graces to be charitable in word and example.

Dear Lord, thank you for the people in my life, even ones who are argumentative or rub me the wrong way. Help me to pray for them, and to shine forth God's love through every contact.

To Ponder: Recalling recent Christmas and New Year's celebrations, how often did you embody the tact and courtesy of Saint Hilary? Did you insist on having your own way in conversations?

MARIANNA BARTHOLOMEW

JANUARY 14

Eating Frog

If it's your job to eat a frog, it's best to do it first thing
in the morning. And if it's your job to eat two frogs,
it's best to eat the biggest one first.

Mark Twain

Sometimes, it's the dishwasher I'm dreading . . . all those little plastic cups in the top rack that have flipped over and filled up with grainy, soapy water during the rinse cycle. They're just waiting for me to unlatch and open the door to unload them.

Sometimes, it's the laundry. Because I didn't get it out of the dryer the night before (I was just too tired), it's lurking behind the door now, the wrinkles multiplying with every hour I delay.

Whatever the task is that I'm dreading most, I can be sure of one thing: putting it off will not make it easier or more pleasant. I know I need to get my day off to a strong start. Tackling one of these jobs is a good way to do just that.

The best way to get my day off to a strong start, though, is to offer it to Jesus—first thing, frogs and all. And so, cup of coffee in hand, I invite Jesus into my day and ask him to use it for his glory, whatever amphibians may present themselves.

Dear Jesus, help me to remember to seek you first, before the tasks of the day, no matter how important they might be.

To Ponder: What "frogs" do you anticipate today? Take a moment to invite Jesus into your day and to rest in his presence before you take on any tasks that might require extra energy to complete.

ABBEY DUPUY

JANUARY 15

On Ordinary Time

We know that winter is just another step in the cycle of life. But standing here among the people of Punxsutawney and basking in the warmth of their hearths and hearts, I couldn't imagine a better fate than a long and lustrous winter.

From the movie Groundhog Day

Is there a more lowly time of year? The sparkle of Christmas is long over, and the glimmer of hope that is Candlemas is still a few weeks away. I would appreciate it more if it were Lent. At least in Lent the dull and dreary seems to have meaning and purpose.

But it is what it is—a day in *Ordinary* Time. I'll be so glad when that's over!

Actually, over the past couple of years, that's become one of my pet sayings: "I'll be glad when that's over!" I said it so frequently for a while that my husband offered to put it on my gravestone. Imagine the chuckles!

And yet, as a philosophy of life it's also kind of sad. Imagine if I spent the remainder of my life just waiting for something to be "over" and not living the joy of *right now.* Sure, "now" doesn't always seem all that inviting. On the other hand, life is what we make of it.

So today I'll get out of the warm covers, enjoy the company of my family, make plans for something we can do outside or inside. I'll organize and put away my Christmas things and start thinking about getting ready for Lent. Then I'll spend a little time looking at the Valentine crafts on Pinterest while appreciating a long and lustrous winter.

Jesus, make my heart like unto thine.

To Ponder: What's one thing you can do to help you better appreciate the time you are in *right now*?

ELENA LAVICTOIRE

JANUARY 16
NATIONAL RELIGIOUS FREEDOM DAY

Put Out into the Deep

Freedom consists not in doing what we like but in having the right to do what we ought.

Saint John Paul II

On this date in 1939 the detective radio drama *I Love a Mystery* debuted. The motto of the show was, "No job too tough, no adventure too baffling." Midway through January, New Year's resolutions can seem tough and baffling, and we worry about not being able to keep them. And yet, Thomas Aquinas reminds us why we made them in the first place: "If the highest aim of a captain were to preserve his ship, he would keep it in port forever."

Resolutions are our way of seeking to better ourselves and to be the person God wants us to be. John Paul II encourages us, "Do not be afraid. Do not be satisfied with mediocrity. Put out into the deep and let down your nets for a catch." These words stir a desire to be resolute in our pursuit of holiness. Saint Cyril reminded those preparing for Baptism that Jesus put down his nets first: "You have been caught in the nets of the Church. Be taken alive, therefore; do not escape, for it is Jesus who is fishing for you."

Resolution originally meant "reduce to a simpler form." What could be simpler than to entrust your resolutions to God? He has already caught you.

I surrender to you, Jesus.

To Ponder: Saint Paul says that surrendering to God is "our spiritual act of worship" (Rom 12:1). Give yourself to God, and he will make a saint out of you. Are you ready for the adventure?

MARGARET KERRY, F.S.P.

Resolving to Find the Peace Within

Do not lose your inner peace for anything
whatsoever, not even if your whole world seems
upset. If you find that you have wandered away
from the shelter of God, lead your heart back to him
quietly and simply.

Saint Francis de Sales

Don't you sometimes feel like leaving everything and just
getting away? Housework, laundry, bills, children, husband,
and, for many women, a job outside the home all constantly
call for your care and attention. Peace is a luxury for a wife
and mother.

As a young man, Saint Anthony gave his considerable
wealth to the poor and went to live as a hermit in the nearby
Egyptian desert. Maybe you think Anthony got off easy, but
simply being alone is no guarantee of finding peace. Peace
is always elusive.

Traditional artwork often depicts Anthony being attacked
by hideous demons. They may be real but most certainly they
also represent his internal demons—the faults, sins, and dis-
ordered desires that, no matter how far you run, you never
escape. Anthony did battle with them in the solitude, the
vast, lonely landscapes of his heart, and he triumphed.

Peace can't be dependent on your situation because
your situation will never be perfect. Peace comes from a

heart given totally to God, a heart that trusts in God, a heart aligned with God's will. Resolve to place God in the unmoving center of your heart, allowing other cares and desires to revolve around him. There you'll find peace.

Jesus, give me the strength to love you above all else and to continually give you my heart.

To Ponder: Are you seeking God's peace or the world's? Do your circumstances or your love for God rule your heart and actions?

MARC CARDARONELLA

JANUARY 18

Talking for Two

Marriage is an act of will that signifies and involves a mutual gift, which unites the spouses and binds them to their eventual souls, with whom they make up a sole family—a domestic Church.

Saint John Paul II

When was the last time you had a meaningful conversation with your husband, the kind of talk that draws you closer together as a couple? I'm not talking about a basic exchange of facts about the kids, the house, or work, but a heart-to-heart dialogue that is part and parcel of sacramental marriage. Without such conversations, the demands of work and family life make it far too easy to lose track of the other half of yourself: your spouse.

In twenty-five years of marriage, there have been times when our need for conversation has been perfectly synchronized, and times when we needed to give this area special attention. For example, when I returned to school I would get frustrated because I couldn't talk to my husband about what I was learning. He hadn't read what I was reading. But because I wanted to talk with him about this area of my life, if he seemed interested in a particular subject, I began to read aloud to him to share the wealth of the learning process with him. Then we would discuss it. It really strengthened our marriage! Just like spending time in prayer each day revitalizes my relationship with God, taking time in conversation with my spouse revitalizes my relationship with him.

Dear Father, thank you for the gift of my spouse, my other half. Help us to grow in your grace and love, that we may together attain the vision of you in heaven.

To Ponder: Are you spending time in conversation with your spouse or just exchanging information?

KATIE O'KEEFE

JANUARY 19
NATIONAL POPCORN DAY

The Little Things

Hearing nuns' confessions is like being stoned to death with popcorn.

Venerable Fulton J. Sheen

Whenever I read that quote from Fulton Sheen, I can't help but think of a similar saying, "Raising children is like being pecked to death by chickens." Each expression hints at the suffocating weight of many little things, like the combined weight of millions of tiny snowflakes that add up to a suffocating avalanche.

A snowflake, a chicken peck, and a kernel of popcorn: individually, each of these might be a unique delight, a laughable annoyance, or a hint of a snack. Often, however, little things in our lives multiply and persist until they overwhelm us. Watching a child discover the wonders of gravity as he knocks a cup off the table is cute—the first time. It gets old quickly. And yet it continues, again and again. Those repetitive frustrations and annoyances can build up like the wall of a tomb.

What then? Most of us don't want to remain in such a cold, uncomfortable place. We are tempted to escape, but in the tomb is our humility. After all, it is our own little, repetitive sins that put Christ in his tomb.

Father, I hurt you by my many repetitive faults. When I feel like I am buried in little things, all I want is to escape. Help me to stay in the moment and instead rest with your Son, our savior Christ Jesus, in the precious sanctuary of his tomb.

To Ponder: What are the little things that seem to be pressing in on you today? Spend a minute or two meditating on how much Jesus had to relinquish when he let himself be buried for our sins.

ERIN MCCOLE CUPP

Preparing for Battle

The devil strains every nerve to secure the souls that belong to Christ. We should not grudge our toil in wresting them from Satan and giving them back to God.

Saint Sebastian

Today is the feast of Saint Sebastian, a martyr in the early Church. While he was serving in the Roman army, Sebastian's practice of Christianity was discovered, a crime punishable by death. Under Emperor Diocletian, Sebastian was tortured with arrows, but miraculously, none killed him. A Roman woman nursed Sebastian back to health and he returned to defending the faith. Later, when Sebastian criticized the emperor for his cruelty to Christians, the emperor ordered Sebastian to be beaten to death.

Saint Sebastian suffered not one but *two* different intense efforts to kill him. How did he withstand that kind of cruel punishment?

Perhaps he prepared for the real battle by daily denying himself. Then this habit of self-denial would have readied him to fight when his name was called. Like him, we must learn to deny ourselves small things, such as the second piece of cake or hitting the snooze button. We must attempt to do the hard thing every day so that if and when our time for martyrdom comes, we will be up to the task like Saint Sebastian. Today, we live in a world of excess, a world where we can get what we want, how we want it, whenever we want it. To develop self-control and learn to tell ourselves "no" is an important skill if we want to be followers of Christ.

Saint Sebastian, you are the patron saint of soldiers. Help me to become a soldier for Christ, to deny my own self in service of him.

To Ponder: What is one area of your life where you need to implement self-denial or self-control? What is one thing you can do today to make yourself battle-ready?

COLLEEN MURPHY DUGGAN

JANUARY 21

God Reigns

Have no anxiety at all, but in everything, by prayer and petition, with thanksgiving, make your requests known to God.

Philippians 4:6

My family received an unexpected and unpleasant surprise. I guess you could call it that. It wasn't necessarily a bad thing, but it came out of left field and meant a lot of extra work. So I did what I usually do in those circumstances: I made a list. And as I began writing down my new to-dos, which would be piled on top of my old to-dos, not to mention the daily round of chores it already took to keep our family fed, clothed, and (mostly) on time, I started to worry.

Right then, my five-year-old brought me a school paper and asked me to read the sticker her teacher had put on it. It said, "God reigns." The significance was not lost on me. But just to make sure I *really* got the message, the Holy Spirit used the spiritual equivalent of a two-by-four to the head: the first reading that day was the story of Joseph being sold into slavery in Egypt, and how God used even that for good, to save Israel from starvation.

At the time, when Joseph was first carried to Egypt in chains, there was no way he could have foreseen the end of his story. Still, in the middle of his afflictions, with no way to know how it would end, Joseph trusted in God. And that trust eventually saved his family and helped bring about, in time, the greatest blessing the world has ever known.

Jesus, I trust in you!

To Ponder: What "surprises" or worries are you now experiencing that could be opportunities to trust God more?

JAKE FROST

JANUARY 22

The Breath of Life

Every child begins the world again.

Henry David Thoreau

Before Dave and I married, we wondered if we were ready for the awesome responsibility of raising children. Would we be good parents? How would we know what to do? Would we push too hard, or not hard enough? During my first pregnancy, we went to a class and I read many books. And then, ready or not, Ryan came.

The first time Ryan had hiccups, his tiny body shook so hard that I consulted Dr. Spock's compendium for a diagnosis. At three months, Ryan cried so hard one afternoon that I called the ambulance only to have the emergency personnel diagnose it as a heavy dose of gas. Clearly we did not know a lot. But while there was no manual, there were paternal and maternal instincts. Eventually we would learn that love is the best guide.

Every birth is an invitation to a glorious love story. Father Ted Hesburgh, my mentor and friend at Notre Dame, would often say that God expresses his deepest confidence in the human race when he entrusts us with children. Made in his image, endowed with unique gifts, our children take us out of ourselves to love deeply and unconditionally. Through them, we see the world with greater tenderness and experience daily the miracles of growth in body, mind, and spirit. The joy they bring is beyond words, and I see in my sons God's grace and presence. Into our marriage, God breathed life and shared with us his greatest treasure made in his image and fashioned from our physical beings. What greater partnership between God and couple is there?

Dear Lord, let us never take for granted your greatest partnership with us, our children, made in your image and from our physical beings!

To Ponder: Is there someone who needs your support, your mothering? How can you tap into God's gift of your motherhood to bless someone else today?

DR. CAROLYN Y. WOO

Say Yes

Most people know the sheer wonder that goes with
falling in love, how not only does everything in
heaven and earth become new, but the lover himself
becomes new. It is literally like the sap rising in the
tree, putting forth new green shoots of life.

Caryll Houselander, The Reed of God

The story of a marriage has many beginnings: our first
meeting, our first date, and a hundred other discoveries and
epiphanies leading up to the wedding day. Including, of
course, the day we got engaged.

On that Easter Monday, I had the day off from work.
Since it was surprisingly sunny for March, I went for a long
run before my boyfriend came over for dinner after work.
As soon as he arrived, I couldn't stop babbling about my
afternoon. Suddenly and slyly, he slid a ring box out of his
pocket and popped the question right there on the couch. I
couldn't stop crying or laughing! Even though we had talked
about marriage for months, I was completely surprised. Ten
years later, I can't think about that day without a joyful heart.

Today is the feast of the Betrothal or Espousal of the
Blessed Virgin Mary. Even though the traditions of her time
were different and the circumstances of her marriage unique,
Mary still teaches us what it means to be a loving spouse.
Despite the surprises life threw at her, she trusted God and

she trusted Joseph. Together they became the faithful family that God asked them to be. May we, too, trust in our yes.

Holy Mary, Mother of God, pray for our marriages and keep our love strong. Guide our hearts toward God and help us to grow in joy together.

To Ponder: What is your favorite part of your engagement story? Share a memory from that day with your children tonight over dinner.

LAURA KELLY FANUCCI

JANUARY 24
SAINT FRANCIS DE SALES

Rest

To eat little, work hard, have lots of concerns on our mind, and then to refuse to give our body sleep is to try to get much work out of a poor, emaciated horse without letting him graze.

Saint Francis de Sales

This quote from Saint Francis de Sales makes me laugh, but it reminds me of something serious: we women have a tendency to neglect ourselves as we struggle to meet the demands of our vocations as wives and mothers. It can be hard to sleep at night, but it's even harder to make ourselves go to bed when the laundry is piled high and the bills are coming due.

Saint Francis offered spiritual direction to women with the utmost affection, gentleness, and wisdom, knowing their hearts were often overburdened by too many tasks and too little time. But he reminded them that the projects and worldly concerns of this lifetime—he called them "trifles"—will not, in themselves, make a bit of difference in the world to come. In heaven, only the gentle patience with which we offer our efforts to God will matter.

Jesus, please bring peace to my heart. Help me to sleep soundly each night and to give myself and my loved ones a fresh start every day.

To Ponder: How often do you forget to tend to your own needs in order to get something done? Our lives are sacred to God, so you need not prove your worth to anyone. Prioritize prayer time and bedtime into your routines, and ask God to give you a spirit of joyful trust in his love for you and your family.

LISA MLADINICH

JANUARY 25
THE CONVERSION OF SAINT PAUL

Highway to Heaven

Heaven is filled with converted sinners of all kinds,
and there is room for more.

Saint Joseph Cafasso

Have you ever missed a turn in traffic because of all the noise coming from the back of the minivan? Of course not. Your kids are perfect, too—just like mine. Right? It's easy to get down on ourselves and on our parenting, especially when the other Catholic families we see at Mass or games or school functions seem to have it all together.

Saul seemed to have it all together, too. He was so eager to prove himself as an "up and comer" that he was hunting Christians down and calling for their execution. All that changed, obviously, when Christ appeared to him (Acts 9).

I've often asked myself, "Why did you appear to Saul, Lord? I mean, this is the guy who was murdering Christians. Why would you choose that guy to do your work?"

Put simply, even though Saul's car was headed in the wrong direction, at least it was moving. It's a lot easier to change direction and turn the wheel if you're moving than it is if you are in park, unwilling to move.

The next time you are distracted by the "saint-makers" in the car seats behind you and have to hang a U-turn, remember Saul. You may not feel like a very good Christian some days. You may feel like you are making all the wrong decisions and headed in the wrong direction—but at least you are trying; at least you are moving. Keep driving . . . toward heaven.

Lord, help me to find peace in my failures and rejoice that your perfect love never gives up on this imperfect heart!

To Ponder: Do you feel like you are failing as a mom most days? Do you easily get down on yourself? Can you see the Lord rejoicing over his choice to send you children? He believes in you more than you do!

MARK HART

Challenge and Change

A dead thing can go with the stream, but only a
living thing can go against it.

G. K. Chesterton

When I was a school counselor, I often mused about the days
when my future children would become academic prodigies.
It was never a question in my mind, and the possibility of
anything otherwise didn't exist for me at the time. Then I
gave birth to two girls with very different special needs and
my perspective changed dramatically. Societal perceptions
and expectations of academic success suddenly melted into a
more definitive, Catholic concept for me and our family: lifelong learning. I realized the necessity of viewing my children
primarily as *humans* before attempting to squeeze them into
standards that really don't account for the unique individuality of our humanity.

Lifelong learning is about challenge and change: God
challenges us, and we are changed. There is no one-size-fits-
all approach to learning. We all exist on a spectrum of gifts
and talents. Some of us are more or less talented than others,
and this is *good.* It is how God designed our individuality so
that we all contribute to the universal call of the Church: to
be extensions of Christ—his hands and feet—to the world.
The call isn't to be *perfect,* but rather to offer our imperfections
to God with great love, so that *his light* may shine through
our lives.

Thank you, heavenly Father, for creating me with the flaws and foibles of imperfection. I embrace them and offer them to you so that you may teach me how to love myself, my family, and you more fully.

To Ponder: We often compare ourselves to others without realizing it. What are some ways you can celebrate your differences—and even your imperfections—in a way that glorifies God?

JEANNIE EWING

JANUARY 27
SAINT ANGELA MERICI

Seeing with the Eyes of the Heart

Look at everything as though you were seeing it
for the first time or the last time. Then your time on
earth will be filled with glory.

Betty Smith

Those reared on Catholic education owe a deep debt of gratitude to those religious sisters who taught us. These women suffered much, received little, and gave so much to the Church and its future generations—most of them with great kindness and love.

Saint Angela Merici was one such sister. As a young woman Angela lost her sight during a trip to the Holy Land, and this blindness deepened the vision of her heart. When she regained her sight, she saw more clearly how education, particularly education for women and the poor, was necessary for unlocking their human potential. So when Pope Clement VII offered her a leadership role with a religious order of nurses, she turned down that honor to go work with educating the poor.

Saint Irenaeus is credited with saying, "The glory of God is man fully alive!" Saint Angela saw more in the lowliest women and poor made in the image of God. Mothers have a unique opportunity to nurture learning in their own children, teaching them how to love God and love neighbor.

God, thank you for the Ursuline Sisters and all those who worked tirelessly to educate the poor because they saw them as your beloved own.

To Ponder: How do we look upon the poor or uneducated? Do we see them in the motherly and nurturing ways like Saint Angela? How do we resist turning a blind eye and instead raise our children in solidarity with the lowly with a clear view of the world's greatest needs?

JAY CUASAY

JANUARY 28
SAINT THOMAS AQUINAS

When Our Human Senses Fail

Down in adoration falling,
This great Sacrament we hail,
O'er ancient forms of worship

Newer rites of grace prevail;
Faith will tell us Christ is present,
When our human senses fail.

Saint Thomas Aquinas, Tantum Ergo

Today we celebrate the immense talent and goodness of Saint Thomas Aquinas. Beholding Jesus in the Eucharist, Aquinas wrote, "Faith will tell us Christ is present, when our human senses fail."

Yes, our human senses tell us the Eucharist is bread and wine. It looks, tastes, smells, and feels like bread and wine. But our senses are failing us. When senses insist "bread and wine," faith claims "Flesh and Blood." Though I have no experience with the taste of human flesh, my tongue is pretty sure the Eucharist tastes like bread. Nonetheless, Jesus himself demands that we *literally* gnaw on his flesh. Saint John (6:54–8) uses the Greek word for *eat* that describes the way animals gnaw on their food.

My senses fail me not only when contemplating Jesus in the Eucharist but also in many other mysteries of life. Sometimes I look directly at a situation and have an immediate, natural instinct to judge what I see: "That's the ninth time my husband has lied to me about that. I'm done." My sense of betrayal tells me exactly how I should act. Faith suggests otherwise: "Forgive seventy times seven times."

Jesus is present in every moment of our lives, even times when we feel ashamed, hurt, and abandoned.

Lord, give me the faith to believe you are with me, even when I don't sense your presence.

To Ponder: How has the Lord accompanied you in your life? How is he with you now?

GRACE MAZZA URBANSKI

JANUARY 29
NATIONAL PUZZLE DAY

Puzzles of Faith

Our culture has filled our heads but emptied our hearts, stuffed our wallets but starved our wonder. It has fed our thirst for facts but not for meaning or mystery. It produces "nice" people, not heroes.

Peter Kreeft

Puzzles are entertaining and they challenge us. Within the Catholic faith, we have some giant puzzles. They challenge us, but we're not necessarily meant to figure them all out. We have some big mysteries of faith, including the Trinity, the Incarnation, the Eucharist, and Our Lord's passion, death, and resurrection for our sins.

I certainly don't have a phenomenal understanding of the mysteries of our faith.

God made the entire universe in just six days, and sometimes it's all I can do to get my kids out the door with their lunches, signed permission forms, and matching socks. Jesus suffered to take on the sins of the world, while I grimace at tiny inconveniences and break feeble resolutions to pray more or complain less the moment it becomes "too hard." Within the tabernacle of every Catholic church in the world he waits for us, and we barely genuflect as we shuffle into the pew, fighting distraction through every prayer.

We can't understand how God has done these things. We can only keep reading and asking and praying and watching him reveal himself to us through our daily lives. We need to trust, choose to believe, follow him in faith, give up trying to have all the answers, and let him be our God of the universe and God of our hearts.

In humility, Jesus, I ask you to guide me, increase my faith, and show me how to honor and bless you with the gifts you have given me.

To Ponder: Which mystery of faith intrigues you the most and challenges you to be a better Christian?

MONICA MCCONKEY

JANUARY 30

His to Love

Take God for your spouse and friend and walk with Him continually, and you will not sin, will learn to love, and the things you must do will work out prosperously for you.

Saint Teresa of Avila

One of the greatest blessings I have in my husband's love for me is how *all-encompassing* that love is. Sometimes I tend to see and judge myself as a conglomerate of functions: the Christian Rhonda, the mothering Rhonda, the working Rhonda, the sinning Rhonda, etc. Instead of seeing me as the sum of my talents and faults, my husband instead takes me as an integral whole. He loves me because, as he says, "God gave you to me."

I am loved simply because I *am* and because I am his to love.

Realizations like this help me appreciate the graces that flow through the sacrament of Matrimony. On a far greater scale than any human love, Our Lord also loves me because I *am* and am his to love.

Often my pride, scrupulosity, and criticalness stem from a tendency to judge myself by my accomplishments or failures rather than my innate dignity as a human person. But God loves me with a devotion whose "flames are a blazing fire," to borrow a phrase from the Song of Songs, and that love is not contingent on how good or accomplished I am. I cannot earn his love. He loves because he is love, the source of love itself.

Thank you, Lord, for accepting and loving me as I am today. Help me to grow in the knowledge of your love so that I might in turn grow more in love with you.

To Ponder: Have you lately been critical of yourself or others? If so, what concrete acts can you take to restore your faith in God's unconditional love for yourself and others? Take a moment to write down your resolutions.

RHONDA ORTIZ

Accepting the Load

The chief thing is to take the burden on one's shoulders. As you press forward, it soon shakes down and the load is evenly distributed.

Saint John Bosco

Sometimes bad habits form when we fall into a rut of doing our work poorly. One week of skipping the washing of our family's sheets can quickly become two, then three, then six months. Jobs that require extra time and effort are all too easy to label as simply "impossible to complete during this time of my life" and pushed aside, usually with a harrumph and some candy.

If we're lacking the energy or motivation to do our work better, we could look to Saint John Bosco's mother for some inspiration. When John was just two years old, his father, Francis, died, leaving his mother, Margaret, alone to care for John, his two older brothers, and their homestead. Instead of feeling sorry for herself, Margaret took up her new responsibilities and helped her boys to do the same. She taught them that work was a privilege and taking joy in their duties would help lighten the load.

Saint John Bosco, please pray for my fortitude in forming and keeping better work habits.

To Ponder: Is there one job that I've been putting off or doing poorly? What needs to change—externally or internally—in order for me to do it well?

MEG MATENAER

February
THEME: LOVE

Remembering the Enslaved

He has sent me to proclaim liberty to captives and recovery of sight to the blind, to let the oppressed go free, and to proclaim a year acceptable to the Lord.

Luke 4:18–19

Today, on National Freedom Day, we commemorate Abraham Lincoln's signing of the joint House and Senate resolution that became the basis for our country's Thirteenth Amendment outlawing slavery. While it's hard to think back to a day when men, women, and children were regarded as property and treated so despicably, we forget that around the world far too many still live in conditions of slavery.

The Gospel teaches us to follow Christ's example of love for all. Yet in our comfortable circumstances we sometimes forget the trafficked, the impoverished, and even those enslaved by substances. As we enter into a month-long celebration of loving expressions, of hearts and roses, we must open our eyes to modern-day slavery if we are truly to love as Jesus did.

Today also provides a good moment to ponder those things that enslave our own hearts, minds, or bodies: the negativity we can't escape, the bad habit that leads to sin, the impurity that stains our minds and souls. Jesus is waiting to set us free. Liberty, total freedom that is lasting and offered without condition, is ours in and through Christ.

Lord, help me to act on behalf of all who dwell in modern-day slavery. Liberate me from the things that bind me in sin.

To Ponder: Against what struggles do you feel powerless or oppressed in your own life?

LISA M. HENDEY

FEBRUARY 2
PRESENTATION OF THE LORD

The Sorrow of Loving

. . . and a sword will pierce your own soul, too.

Luke 2:35

So many of the frustrations and sorrows of motherhood come from watching our children do things wrong and wondering if we could have prevented those problems. But what about the sorrow that comes when our child is doing everything right?

We can't blame bad parenting for the sorrows that befell the Holy Family. Mary was preserved from sin, and while Saint Joseph may not have been sinless, he was certainly devout, reverent, and trustworthy. We mothers sometimes imagine our mission is to protect our children from every possible misfortune. But the reality is that every person is going to encounter suffering in this fallen world, no matter how good, holy, or wise we are.

Motherhood makes us able to experience a kind of sorrow we would otherwise never know: standing by watching our heart of hearts experience pain that we absolutely cannot prevent and are helpless to alleviate. That sorrow doesn't have to be meaningless. In offering our heartbreak to God, we can literally change the world. Our prayers, in the form of our faithfulness to God in the darkest possible moments, even as we may be feeling lost and abandoned, are powerful. Thus we can each receive that ability, modeled by the Blessed Virgin, to intercede for others.

Dear Jesus, when I am alone and brokenhearted, take my sorrow and use it to help others.

To Ponder: What is the "sword" in your heart today? Who is it you are helplessly watching suffer? Give thanks for the ability to remember and pray for those who so desperately need your prayers.

JENNIFER FITZ

FEBRUARY 3

Daily Lessons Make Broad Lessons

Faith is what someone knows to be true, whether they believe it or not.

Flannery O'Connor

When I was a child one of my favorite ways to spend time was with my great-grandparents, my mother's mother's parents. With three other children in my family, my mom was happy for me to go over to their house, so I did frequently. I would walk over ready for the adventure of the day. Sometimes I walked with my great-grandfather to the store to buy the Italian newspaper or get some vegetables for dinner. Other times I watched the end of my great-grandmother's soap opera with her before we would start dinner. They had so much patience and time to spend with me, and I loved being with them, no matter what we did.

On Saturdays, I learned how to clean bathrooms and make beds with very tightly pulled sheets. Sometimes we cooked and I was allowed to use the curved knife with wooden handles, a *mezzaluna*, to chop vegetables for soup. As I grew older, my great-grandmother taught me how to sew on her Singer sewing machine. It may only have had one stitch setting, but it got the job done and we made beautiful clothes together.

My great-grandparents taught me many practical things that I am grateful for to this day. They also taught me the value of family, love, dedication, and perseverance. Their example was a life lesson I will never forget and hope to emulate always.

Thank you, Lord, for the gift of family and friends who have taught and nurtured me in my life; help me to reach out to others in the same way.

To Ponder: Who has taught you the life skills you use every day? Are you still learning from others? Thank them and let them know how they have impacted your life.

DEANNA BARTALINI

Heroes to Heal Our Divisions

I am definitely loved and whatever happens to me, I am awaited by this love. And so my life is good.

Saint Josephine Bakhita

February brings us Valentine's Day with love in the air. In the United States and Canada it is also Black History Month. It would be nice to think that race is a nonissue today. Yet racial tensions rage openly in various cities for months on end. Color lines still have the power to hurt. Studies tell us it is not only our neighborhoods; our churches are also split largely along racial lines.

In a month where the focus is on love, it might be time to ask ourselves as mothers how we are teaching our children to love people who don't look like them. One place to start might be by celebrating remarkable people with a different racial background than your family. Our children need heroes who don't look like them. Something very good will have happened when white children have black heroes, black children have Asian heroes, Asian children have Hispanic heroes, and so on. Compassion for one's neighbor is good. Admiration might be better.

Sainted and not, heroes aren't hard to find. In honor of Black History Month, I'll suggest Saint Josephine Bakhita, former slave and servant of the poor, as a worthy hero for any mother or child. There's nothing quite like her for getting my head on straight when I think I've got it bad.

Dearest Jesus, open our hearts and eyes to the many faces of your children. Teach us to love like Saint Josephine Bakhita loved.

To Ponder: How are you giving your children opportunities to see the common humanity we share as people? What heroes of other races and cultures can you and they learn from and emulate?

MICHELLE JONES

FEBRUARY 5
SAINT AGATHA

More Beautiful than Barbie

The human body bore in itself, in the mystery of creation, an unquestionable sign of the image of God.

Saint John Paul II

There my wife stood, naked and unashamed . . . and nine months pregnant, ankles swollen, back aching, and "retaining more water than a dam" (to quote her). I helped her ease into the tub for a much-needed bath and break from the kids. No sooner did she begin to wash than I heard her loudly utter, "Well, now this is just depressing." I turned to see my wife laughing with tears streaming down her cheeks. Our older daughters used the same tub earlier and had left a half-dozen Barbie dolls—all completely naked—sitting upon the side of the tub staring back at my very pregnant wife.

At that moment, my wife never looked more beautiful to me. She was a picture of self-sacrifice, visibly uncomfortable and completely self-effacing even in her nakedness. We laughed hilariously. We mocked the ridiculousness of Barbie's figure, the divinely inspired glory of the female form, and the fact that no force on earth is more powerful than hormones—except grace.

On this feast of Saint Agatha, patroness of women and victims of breast cancer, let us pause to thank God for the female body, its life-giving force, and its inestimable beauty.

Lord, thank you for the gift of womanhood, and for all you reveal to us about your love through a mother's bodily sacrifices.

To Ponder: Have you ever subjected yourself to unrealistic expectations from a man or unnecessary comparisons with other women when it comes to body image? As your body has changed with age and motherhood, do you find it more difficult to "love" your exterior self? The Lord rejoices in his Mother and in all mothers. Remember that he loves you from the inside out.

MARK HART

FEBRUARY 6
MARTYRS OF NAGASAKI

The Martyrdom of Motherhood

[For] love to be real, it must cost—it must hurt—it must empty us of self.

Saint Teresa of Calcutta

I have always been fascinated by stories about Christian martyrs. Their courage. Their self-denial. Their deep love for Christ. Blessed Oscar Romero once coined the phrase "the martyrdom of motherhood." Certainly many mothers die to themselves for love of their children. I need only to look at my own mother to see this kind of love.

What really inspires me is how my mother has given of herself over and over again. We four children have all been able to count on her, no matter what. There was the time my brother was far away in prison and he had no visitors. She traveled for hours many times to visit him and stood by him through his journey to healing. When my sister was put in a nursing home hours away, Mom again traveled to visit her and worked night and day to get her moved closer to home. She was with my sister when she died.

These days Mom is caring for her friends. She moved one friend into an assisted-living facility and oversees her care. She visits another friend who has cancer and sits with her through chemotherapy treatments. Mom is eighty years old.

I do not need to read about famous Christian martyrs. I need only to look at my own mother and hope I will someday love like she does. A love that is real.

Dear Lord, help me to give my life every day for love of others and for love of you.

To Ponder: How would you define love that is real and self-emptying? In what ways do you love until it hurts? Reflect on those who have loved you unconditionally.

COLLEEN SPIRO

The Big Impact of a Small Note

The word that is heard perishes, but the letter that is written remains.

Anonymous

Being a mother is hard work. There was a joke going around the web where a man comes home from work and stuff is everywhere. It looks like someone has broken in and trashed the house. Food is spilled on the counters and floor and the kids are playing outside with no clothes on. He frantically runs upstairs and finds his wife in bed, reading a book. "What's going on?" he asks. "Well," she replies, "every day you ask what I do all day. Today, I didn't do it."

That little joke pretty much sums up a mother's life. You spend all your time and energy doing work that is difficult and boring and no one notices until you haven't done it. As a mother, compliments are few and far between. Some of my most treasured possessions are notes from friends and family.

One day my stepmother sent me a card telling me what an awesome job I'm doing home-schooling the girls. My stepsister sent me a heartfelt note on Mother's Day one year. My daughters have made me many beautiful cards and drawings. On rough days, I can read them over and feel valued again.

Dear Lord, thank you for the blessings you have given me. Please help me to work joyfully for you. Show me someone I can reach out to who may need a kind word.

To Ponder: Is there a woman you know who could use a bit of encouragement? If not, take a moment of silence and see if there is someone God has in mind. Take five minutes to write her a short note and put it in the mail.

JEN STEED

FEBRUARY 8
SAINT JOSEPHINE BAKHITA

Freeing Ourselves with Forgiveness

If I were to meet the slave-traders who kidnapped me and even those who tortured me, I would kneel and kiss their hands, for if that did not happen, I would not be a Christian and religious today.

Saint Josephine Bakhita

We think of forgiveness as a difficult thing, that if we stop holding on to why we are angry and relinquish our claim to righteous wrath we may have nothing to show for it but a renewed vulnerability. So we hold on to our anger and our puny resentments, and we think we are building a good sort of life.

How good can life be, though, if we truncate the amount of love we allow into it? When we close a door to forgiveness we reduce the whole theater of love in which we are meant to live and move and have our being. We know forgiveness is an instrument of grace, and where grace is permitted to flourish, God may be trusted to fulfill his plans for us, which are that we might "live life to the full" (Jn 10:10).

Forgiveness costs us nothing; in return for our willingness to offer it, we gain freedom and power over the very thing that has too long kept us burdened. Bakhita's gratitude for her life of freedom and ministry inspired her to great love; her forgiveness was the greatest expression of her freedom.

Saint Josephine Bakhita, help us to appreciate the grace-filled mystery of our whole lives.

To Ponder: If we believe God is love and we trust in that love, what do we really risk if we move toward forgiveness? If you could have a "do-over" from the past, who would you want to forgive? Or, consider someone you have forgiven and imagine what love would be missing from your life today if you had not.

ELIZABETH SCALIA

FEBRUARY 9

Lenten Hope

Praised be You, my Lord, with all your creatures,
especially for Brother Sun,
Who is the day and through whom you give us light.
And he is beautiful and radiant with great splendor
And bears a likeness of You, Most High One.

Saint Francis of Assisi, "Canticle of the Creatures"

February is the cruelest month. By now we've had it with the unending landscape of black, brown, gray, and white. We've had enough of winter weather that keeps us housebound, that prevents our children from enjoying outdoor playtime, that requires us to keep tabs on mittens, snow boots, and warm hats. The snow we eagerly anticipated at Christmas has turned into a burden, and we long to see a trace of green on those bare tree branches.

In the middle of all this, Lent starts. In the middle of winter, when we feel like the season that demands so much from us will never end, the Church adds in a time when we're expected to sacrifice—and we already feel like we're giving until it hurts.

There's hope, though. Lent is actually all about hope, even joyful hope. Even the name of Lent, in English, is about hope. The word "lent" comes from the same root as the word "length." It refers to that glimmer of hope we feel when we suddenly realize that the days are getting longer—it's not dark before dinnertime!

In the depths of winter, that little bit of extra sunlight each day is a gift. It's hope.

Lord, when I am overwhelmed by a difficult season, help me to find hope in the little things and to appreciate the gifts you offer me, both big and small.

To Ponder: Where do you find hope during the tough seasons?

BARB SZYSZKIEWICZ, O.F.S.

More to Love

Love now becomes concern and care for the other.
No longer is it self-seeking, a sinking in the
intoxication of happiness.

Pope Benedict XVI, On Christian Love

My husband objects to the Hallmark-driven nature of Valentine's Day, arguing that a forced show of romance every February 14 is no substitute for real romance all year long. I don't mind that, since I'm not a flowers-and-chocolate kind of gal anyway.

Valentine's Day has turned into a nationwide celebration of passion, but true love can't be limited to that. Love, or romance for that matter, isn't a kind of mutual narcissism, where we tell each other how magnificently sexy we are and tell the rest of the world it can go fly a kite.

True love between husband and wife is about friendship and shared family life, too. Instead of closing ourselves off from others, married love opens us up to others, including our kids. Marriage and parenthood teaches us that our love is bigger than just the two of us. So every Valentine's Day, instead of treating each other to some grand gesture, my husband and I take our six kids ice skating. We show them that holding hands as we skate across the ice can send our hearts racing, kissing on the lips is okay because we're married, and our love for each other is inseparable from our love for them. Passion is great, but there's more to love.

God, please help my spouse and me to love each other more each day and to show our children what healthy married love looks like.

To Ponder: Children form ideas about marriage by watching their parents. How do you treat your spouse when your children are watching?

KAREE SANTOS

FEBRUARY 11
OUR LADY OF LOURDES

Worthy of a Miracle

Our God is the God of surprises.

Pope Francis

When I was a child, the story of Our Lady of Lourdes was wonderfully mysterious. There were the appearances of Mary to Bernadette, the miraculous spring: it was a story that gave me shivers of the best kind, like a ghost story without a ghost.

Although I still recognize the miraculous aspects of the apparition of Lourdes, other parts of the story resonate more strongly now. I'm struck by the fact that the Queen of Heaven would show up in a barren, rocky dumping ground. I'm moved that Mary would appear to an impoverished teenage girl instead of the clergy or the town's elite. I'm awed by the strength of Bernadette, the shy girl who stuck resolutely to her truth no matter how many powerful people pressed her to recant.

Lourdes proves that our own expectations of the world around us often miss the mark. God sees what we don't and challenges our preconceived notions of what—or who—is worthy of a miracle.

Lord, help me to recognize that your grace appears everywhere, even in places I don't expect.

To Ponder: Who are the "Bernadettes" in your life—the last people whom you would expect to have a close encounter with heaven? Challenge yourself to see them as God sees them.

GINNY KUBITZ MOYER

FEBRUARY 12

The Heart She Held

We need no wings to go in search of Him, but have only to look upon Him present within us.

Saint Teresa of Avila

Her head pounded and anxiety gnawed at her heart. Disciplining her two sons was never an easy task. She was now alone in the kitchen, but the unpleasant after-school moment still kept company. She unzipped her youngest son's backpack, and something fluttered out. It was a red construction-paper heart with the words "I love you Mommy" written crudely across the front. The tears that had been pricking the backs of her eyes now blurred her vision, but she could still see the shape of the heart she held—God's reassurance that he was by her side through the difficult moments of motherhood and a confirmation that her sons still loved her in spite of, or perhaps because of, her efforts to form their character.

Dear God, please help me to recognize your presence even in the most challenging moments of my day.

To Ponder: Whether it is in a beautiful sunrise, the perfect cup of coffee, or a morning snuggle from a child, God is always revealing his love to us. How can you be more open to the subtleties of his presence today?

CHARISSE TIERNEY

FEBRUARY 13
WORLD RADIO DAY

The Eternal Life of Misspoken Words

Words which do not give the light of Christ increase the darkness.

Saint Teresa of Calcutta

I am reminded of a discussion I once had with a talk-show host friend of mine about how radio can be much more forgiving to your unwise choice of words than print media is. At least, that's the way it used to be before the days of MP3s and podcasts. Our on-air words were spoken and gone. People didn't remember them like they did when things were in print. Whether that's still true in the Internet age can be debated.

But one thing is for sure: the fleeting nature of the spoken word does not seem to apply to the ears of children. There are times when one of my children will quote me and say, "Remember that, Mom? Remember when you said that?" Sometimes I do and sometimes I don't. And sometimes I wish I didn't.

So what do we do about all those things we wish we'd never said? This may sound crazy, but I say a prayer that they might be forgotten, and I make a resolution to be more careful what I say because it is clear that those words have a lasting effect.

Dear Lord, give me self-restraint so all my words will be for your greater glory and none will bring harm.

To Ponder: How are some ways you can make sure every word you speak helps bring the light of Christ into the world?

SHERRY BOAS

FEBRUARY 14
SAINT VALENTINE

Looking for Love in All the Right Places

There is a terrible hunger for love. . . . The poor you may have right in your own family. Find them. Love them.

Saint Teresa of Calcutta

When I was nineteen years old, I spent fifteen minutes alone in the chapel with Mother Teresa of Calcutta. I was a seminarian in her congregation of priests, the Missionaries of Charity Fathers, in Tijuana, Mexico. She was in town for an ordination. As part of her visit, each seminarian had the opportunity to meet with her privately to talk and to pray.

I walked into the chapel to find Mother Teresa seated close to the tabernacle, quietly passing her Rosary beads through her fingers. I sat facing her, and she took my hands in hers and looked into my eyes. She smiled and asked my name.

I expected to talk about my vocation and holy things. But she wanted to talk about my family. Mother Teresa—a woman recognized the world over for her faith and her service to humanity, a woman who had picked up countless people from the streets and cared for them so that they could die with dignity—wanted to talk with me about my *family*.

At the time I didn't understand it. But today I do. Family is where we learn to love.

On Valentine's Day, let's look for love where we know it can be found. Love is usually right there under our noses in the messiness and awkwardness of family life.

Jesus, help me to recognize you truly present in the members of my family, and help me to love you in them.

To Ponder: Sometimes those we are closest to can be the most difficult to love. How can you practice learning to see Jesus in the members of your family?

JEFF YOUNG

Love Takes Courage

You know, sometimes all you need is twenty seconds
of insane courage. Just literally twenty seconds
of just embarrassing bravery. And I promise you,
something great will come of it.

We Bought a Zoo

I am married to one of my best friend's brothers. She was
my friend before I met him, and although I love him now, I
wasn't, let's say, *sold* on him at first. He first saw me at his
cousin's wedding in August and I found out that he had
asked about me. This completely scared me, and I kept my
distance, leaving the room if he would walk in, until March
or April of the following year. By the spring I had noticed
something was changing in him, and that Easter he went to
Franciscan University for the Easter Vigil celebration. It was
then that I saw his Catholicism flourish and I quickly fell for
him. Shortly after, his sister told me that he had been set up
on a date with a mutual friend. This did not sit right with me.
I knew I had to let him know I was interested in getting to
know him more. My twenty seconds of courage came when
I called my now sister-in-law and told her she could tell her
brother that I was ready for him to take me out. He called
me almost immediately and within a few weeks we were
officially courting.

*Father, please help us to always have the courage to continue to
show our spouses and our family that we are actively pursuing
them.*

To Ponder: What is one twenty-second action of insane courage that you can do for your spouse today to show him your love?

COURTNEY VALLEJO

FEBRUARY 16

More

If you really want to love Jesus, first learn to suffer,
because suffering teaches you to love.

Saint Gemma Galgani

The stores are filled with discount Valentine candy and already tempting us with Easter treats. It seems as if Lent is simply an opportunity to sell fried fish. We are constantly barraged by our consumerist society telling us we need more to be happy. They tell us that we deserve to be happy all the time. This is a serious struggle, because as Catholics we must embrace suffering. When we suffer, we find Christ there with us. When we suffer, we can move beyond simple earthly pleasures to true joy and glory.

In our culture, Lent takes effort. It can be a struggle to sacrifice instead of focusing on what we want. But when I think of a mother telling her hungry child that there is no food, it is easier. So this Lent, I offer my small sufferings but also will try to sacrifice more. I will try to sacrifice to the point of suffering.

When I look with the eyes of love at the poor, as brothers and sisters rather than as a demographic, I see how much I could live without: desserts and snacks, haircuts, TV, extra clothes, relaxing baths, beds, appliances, free time, and so much more. All are opportunities for Lenten sacrifices that help us love better.

Jesus, help me to know that my desire for more can only be filled by you.

To Ponder: Think through your typical day. What sufferings do you face that could help you unite with Christ and his love? What luxuries have you taken for granted that you could sacrifice this Lent?

KATE DANELUK

FEBRUARY 17

A Love Beyond Mom's

For great is his steadfast love toward us,
and the faithfulness of the Lord endures forever.

Psalm 117:2

I asked my first-graders how long they thought God would love them, and one little girl said, "I think God will love me until my hair is so gray and my face is so wrinkly even Mom wouldn't recognize me anymore." Her friend replied, "Nope, he will love us even longer and bigger than that."

When I try to wrap my mind around the magnificent love of the Father, I have to think back to the three moments in my life when the doctor laid a miracle in my arms. They were my babies, my gifts, my blessings, and each was the most captivating thing I had ever experienced. I remember being overcome with a love so huge it washed over me like a tidal wave. My commitment to them and my adoration of every tiny little part of them was instant and everlasting. They are young adults now, but each time they pull in the driveway I have that same feeling all over again.

As enormous as my love for my children is, I know the love I have for them is only the teeniest sliver of love compared with the love the Father has for me each time I call out his name. His kindness is everlasting and his love is never-ending.

Loving Father, please help me remember your love is your gift to me. It is not deserved and it cannot be earned; it just is.

To Ponder: What prevents you from accepting the enormous love of the Father? Imagine what your days would be like if you recognized the depth and width of his love for you. Contradict any negative thoughts about yourself with an affirmation of the Father's love.

SHERI WOHLFERT

FEBRUARY 18
BLESSED FRA ANGELICO

Dazzling Gifts

Fra Angelico's art is centred on Christ. . . . He displays, before our dazzled eyes, the rich mysteries of the Incarnate Word.

John Saward, The Beauty of Holiness and the Holiness of Beauty

When we humbly offer our talents to God, he blesses them with his love and makes them bear beautiful fruit. A Dominican monk of the early fifteenth century, Brother Giovanni of Fiesole was affectionately known as "Fra Angelico"—the Angelic Friar. A kindly soul who tenderly served the poor and cared nothing for honors or admiration, Blessed Fra Angelico was an artist of glittering reputation. Yet, his humility and sanctity impressed the popes of his time even more than his spectacular paintings. Offered the archbishopric of Florence by Pope Nicholas, he turned it down, recommending a holy friend in his place.

In all things, Fra Angelico worked in cooperation with the Holy Spirit. Before lifting his brush to paint, he would always kneel devoutly in prayer. His paintings are not mere images but glorious meditations on spiritual realities. His ability to authoritatively depict scenes of great power and holiness is a testament to the purity and sanctity of his own soul.

As mothers, we are raising up beautiful works of art to heaven: our precious children. But to joyfully live out our vocations and attract our loved ones to the Catholic faith, we need the daily habits of silence and openness to the Holy Spirit. When we humble ourselves to ask for help, God blesses our small efforts and makes them masterpieces of his love.

O Jesus, help us to grow in faith, hope, and love, so that our lives will shine with your glory.

To Ponder: Do you take time to pray at the start of each day?

LISA MLADINICH

The Lost Earring

God our Lord would have us look to the Giver and
love him more than his gift, keeping him always
before our eyes, in our hearts, and in our thoughts.

Saint Ignatius

Splashing water on my face, the little girl came up from
underneath the pool's surface with a frantic expression. "Can
you help me?" she cried. "I lost my earring!"

To my nine-year-old self, there was nothing more annoying than having my afternoon swim interrupted. Couldn't
she see that I was busy doing important stuff like practicing
my underwater somersaults? I moved away into the deep
end. Relentlessly, she pursued me. "Please, they were my
favorite earrings. Can you help me?"

Around and around the pool we went, in a game of cat
and mouse, until exasperated, I pulled myself out of the pool
and plopped down on the hard plastic beach chair. My mom,
who had been watching the whole exchange, pulled her sun-
glasses down and looked me straight in the eye.

"Chaunie," she said. "Didn't you see Jesus in that little
girl? Would you have helped him?" Years of Catholic schooling and nothing strikes action into the heart like a good dose
of mother's guilt. Mortified, my eyes flashed over to the shallow end of the pool, where the little girl now drifted forlornly,
having given up the hunt.

Resolutely, I climbed back into the pool and paddled
my way over. "Hi," I said. "I'm sorry about before—can I
help you find your earring?" And much to my surprise, the

hunt became not the tedious chore I had been expecting, but actual fun, as we splashed and giggled and dived together. And wouldn't you know it? In that great, big, deep pool full of people—we found one sole glittering earring.

Dear Jesus, help me to always search for you in the hidden moments, in the times I am not expecting it.

To Ponder: Have you passed over an opportunity to see Jesus in a situation that may have not seemed worthy of your time? How can you always strive to see Jesus in everyone—and teach your children to do the same?

CHAUNIE MARIE BRUSIE

FEBRUARY 20

Hidden Blessings in Sacrificial Love

True love hurts. It always must hurt. . . . A mother who gives birth to her child suffers much. It is the same in religious life. To belong fully to God we have to give up everything. Only then can we truly love. The word "love" is so misunderstood and so misused.

Saint Teresa of Calcutta

It hurts to love when we don't feel love in return, when we are enduring heartache, when we are contradicted, or when we are utterly exhausted. The culture would have us believe that love should always feel warm and fuzzy, and if it doesn't, we ought to move on.

Mother Teresa pointed out that true love always hurts in some way. We can't run away from the pain that we sometimes encounter when caring for our family, but we can make a decision to embrace it and recognize that it is within the mystery of loving sacrifice that miracles happen. God will grant us the graces we need to love with his love. We should ask for those graces often.

Dear Lord Jesus, please grant me the graces I need this day to love with your love and to offer my hurt to you so that you will transform it all into beautiful blessings for my family.

To Ponder: How do you feel when you are given a hurtful comment in response to your sincere act of love? Do you react negatively or do you pause to pray? Difficult moments can be wonderful opportunities for grace when we turn to the Lord.

DONNA-MARIE COOPER O'BOYLE

FEBRUARY 21

Surrender Prayer

More things are wrought by prayer than this world dreams of.

Alfred, Lord Tennyson

By the end of an exhausting day, when the shadows of evening pull at my heartstrings, I sometimes wonder if all my straining efforts, ardent prayers, and fulfilled to-do lists make any difference. It is in that twilight time between hectic day and exhausted night that fears of failure loom largest, dimming everything I have done into mere shadows of the morning's hopes. Dinner needs to be served, tired kids need to be put to bed, those last demands of the day need to be accomplished, and the just-mopped floor is streaked already.

Yet it is then that my prayer can reach its most profound depth. It is then that I throw myself into God's arms in childlike surrender, knowing that he loves me more than I can comprehend, that he sees all my fantastic and futile efforts, and that he really does understand and appreciate them. When no one else comprehends the struggle it took to manage that last algebra problem, to scrub that never-clean-for-long-enough floor, or to humble myself in silence when others strike out, he sees and he appreciates. He loves and he rewards in his own generous way. He tucks me into dreamland, he comforts me with rest, and he draws the sun and my spirits forth once more to meet the newest day.

My God, my surrender to you is my most ardent prayer, and in that prayer I am most refreshed.

To Ponder: In the trials of an ordinary day, can you lift your soul for that utter surrender—trusting all the while that God loves you for it?

A. K. FRAILEY

FEBRUARY 22
SAINT MARGARET OF CORTONA

Steps to Sainthood

You learn to speak by speaking, to study by studying, to run by running, to work by working, and just so, you learn to love by loving. All those

who think to learn in any other way
deceive themselves.

Saint Francis de Sales

"Lord, make me a saint."

Kneeling before the crucifix, in the still quiet of the church, the words felt brave upon my tongue, and yet I was compelled to pray them. In weeks prior, I had been reading inspiring biographies of Saint John Paul II, Saint Teresa of Calcutta, Saint Gianna, and Blessed Charles de Foucauld. Reading examples of such modern saints as these and seeing their photographs make them come alive. When I contemplate the details of their lives, lived out in a modern world very similar to my own, sainthood seems all the more attainable, even for a small soul like me.

We should pray to become saints, but even more, we need to practice the art of loving in order to become better at answering God's call to holiness, one small step at a time. As I prayed in the church that evening, I considered those things that challenge me as I work toward holiness; most of them were people. I am a sinner. The people God put in my life for me to love sometimes bring out the worst in me, like impatience, selfishness, anger, pride, and jealousy. But the best way to learn to love better is to practice loving better . . . starting right now.

Make me a saint, Lord. One person at a time.

To Ponder: God made you to be a saint. How can you better love the people God places in your life and grow to see them as aids to holiness instead of obstacles?

DANIELLE BEAN

Polycarp Parallels: Martyrdom Then and Now

To die for Christ, my young friends, is to live.

Saint Jaime Hilario Barbal

By about the year AD 160, Polycarp was already an old man of eighty-six years. He was the bishop of the Church in Smyrna, which is modern-day Izmir in Turkey.

Imagine this: Polycarp not only knew but also had been a last disciple of Saint John. This was one reason he was greatly revered as a teacher and Church leader. He was also a friend of Saint Ignatius of Antioch, and he was an unapologetic defender of the truths of Catholicism.

These are the words of that saint: "Stand fast, therefore, in this conduct and follow the example of the Lord: firm and unchangeable in faith, lovers of the brotherhood, loving each other, united in truth." Polycarp died in a blaze of sweet-smelling smoke, thrust through by a lance of hate and intolerance.

We also have had the sweet experience of beloved Saint John Paul II, an apostle of Mother Mary. An apostle of evangelization. His words: "It is Jesus that you seek when you dream of happiness; he is waiting for you when nothing else you find satisfies you; it is he who reads in your heart your most genuine choices, the choices that others try to stifle."

He, too, was called to martyrdom: a complete surrender to love and to a life-ending palsy. Yet even in his final days, put him in front of a group of witnesses or dreamers and John Paul II would lift himself from his drool and bring the dream of certain victory to all around him.

Saints Polycarp and John Paul II, pray for us.

To Ponder: If you wonder what you are called to, the parallels of irony have placed you here today reading this. How can you embrace the martyrdom you are called to today?

DEACON TOM FOX

FEBRUARY 24

Boasting in My Weakness

My grace is sufficient for you, for power is made perfect in weakness. So, I will boast all the more gladly of my weaknesses, so that the power of Christ may dwell in me.

2 Corinthians 12:9

A fun mom I never was. We cooked, baked, read storybooks, and went to the park, but I did not wrestle or run or do anything remotely like exercise.

Just give Charon his lost coin and send my rocking chair across the River Styx.

Yet, on the heels of raising five children, my sons blessed me with three Herculean grandsons, and I realized the need to focus on my waning strength, stamina, balance, and posture.

Nothing says fun like a body on the floor, preferably one with inert potential.

Welcome to my living-room floor, where prayers for potential—that cannot be found in my own strength—are breathed low. I lie on the floor, inert at best, focusing on my breathing, my flex, and my stretches.

And to three little boys, Grandma becomes a mountain, a bridge, a boat, or a car.

Yet all I really am is an inert body with potential.

So begins a God-given blessing: a May-May who is potentially fun, even when inert on the living-room floor.

It's a start.

Lord, help me to know my weaknesses and my strengths. Allow me to lie inert in your presence and breathe in the potential that I am only capable of because of you.

To Ponder: How do you gather the breath to pray in a lifetime of busy motherhood? Find and practice a complete inert trust that God will provide the time and space.

CAY GIBSON

FEBRUARY 25

Love Lessons
from Adult Children

Love is patient . . . It does not insist on its own way.

1 Corinthians 13:4, 5

Watching my adult children from afar has taught me about letting go. Each lesson has been like pulling teeth.

It took our son many years to find his trajectory. The process was messy, frustrating, and sometimes heart-wrenching to witness. While he never got into serious trouble, I wondered if he would ever find his way out of the maze he had created. I tried walking the tightrope of being supportive without getting overly involved and fell off many times. For both our sakes I had to back away and leave him be. And it hurt, but now I can rejoice. The process worked and he is finally on his way.

Unlike her brother who shares too much, our daughter prefers to keep her thoughts to herself. She'll act first and then announce the results. I won't hear from her for a couple of weeks or more. I miss her terribly. But when she calls, I rejoice. There is often pleasant news of changes in her life, and I can share in her joy of accomplishment. Each phone call is a pleasant surprise and a cherished moment. That sense of longing for her, though never totally fulfilled, is actually a good feeling.

It took ten years to learn to let go of my children. Now I have two more adults whom I can call "friend."

Love is not possessive; love is letting go.

Lord, I thank you for stretching my heart to the limit and beyond because of your gift of my children.

To Ponder: What have your children taught you about love?
SUSAN BAILEY

The Hard Work of Happily Ever After

Fairy tales are more than true, not because they tell
us that dragons exist but because they tell us that
dragons can be beaten.

G. K. Chesterton

When my girls were small, they loved fairy tales about dashing princes who did battle for princesses. When my younger daughter was two, she met Cinderella at Disney World and literally trembled with excitement over meeting her "favorite." Fairy tales have familiar themes that center on family, true love, and the classic promise of "happily ever after."

Real love—and the marriages that are a part of that—isn't like fairy tales, for even if you find your Prince Charming, life isn't always happy. There are times of hurt and pain, the kind that makes you wonder why you're hanging on. But that's a part of the battle that husbands and wives take part in, and when those battles are fought well, they're won for true love.

Our children have seen their parents struggle through difficulties together. They've seen their father do great things for us out of love—just like the princes who battle dragons for princesses in fairy tales. His "dragons" are long days at work, long drives to go to weddings and funerals, or late nights spent helping his daughters sort out the troubles of teenage life. But these battles are real, and seeing him fight them prepares them to find their own true love—the man who will fight those kinds of battles for them.

Lord, help me to show my children the benefits of working through the struggles of family life.

To Ponder: Family life isn't always easy, but it's always worth fighting for. Have you shared the battles you've fought for your family with your children? Do they know how you got to "happily ever after"?

CHRISTINE JOHNSON

FEBRUARY 27

My Father's Tear: A Final Gift of Love

In marriage, a man and woman freely choose to make themselves irreplaceable to each other. . . . [This] prepares them to receive the fruit of their union, a new person, as a gift of equal value and dignity to each of them.

William E. May, Getting the Marriage Conversation Right

The moment of my father's death was one of the most haunting of my life. Holding hands at his bedside, my sister—my only sibling—and I felt our collective hearts lurch as he gasped and took his last breath. Though sad and shocked, I also felt a wave of sweet consolation and gratitude wash over me. For even while his spirit left the room, holiness entered, and a gift came in the form of a single tear in my dad's eye. Perhaps science has an explanation. Maybe it can be waved off simply as a physical response to death. But to me, Dad's tear contained a message. He hadn't been able to communicate with us in those last days, but we'd stayed near, singing, praying, and offering our love in whatever ways we could. Surely Dad would have wanted to reciprocate, and through his tear in that last moment of his life, he did. *I love you*, I heard, deeply in my heart. *I love you too, Daddy*.

Eternal Father, thank you for the irreplaceable circle of love you've given me, both through my family of origin and the family I helped create with my spouse. Each person you have brought into my circle to love and receive love from is a unique and unrepeatable treasure.

To Ponder: What final gift has been given to you? What gift do you hope to leave someday?

ROXANE B. SALONEN

FEBRUARY 28

God's Love

Human love and the delights of friendship, out of which are built the memories that endure, are also to be treasured up as hints of what shall be hereafter.

Father Bede Jarrett, O.P.

"God loves you." No truer words were ever spoken. But there is so much more to it than that.

God doesn't just love you; God *is* Love.

Thus, all acts of love that you experience—a child's big hug, an unexpected gift from a loved one, a random act of kindness from a stranger—are ways God reaches out to you in love. The warmth of the sun, the smell of autumn, the beauty of fresh fallen snow, and the reawakening of spring flowers are God's doings to give you hints of his love. The love you experience, that you feel, and that you give is a wonderful gift from God. It is a hint of the fullness of love you will one day experience in heaven.

Here's a truth even more awesome: God couldn't love you any more than he does now. Even if you were the perfect person you desire to be, God wouldn't love you any more. He loves you not because you are good but because he made you. Even your most messy self he sees as beautiful because you are. He created you in his own image and likeness to be his very own child. He couldn't love you more.

As Saint John says, "We have come to know and believe in the love God has for us. God is love, and he who abides in love abides in God, and God in him" (1 Jn 4:16).

Heavenly Father, thank you for loving me. Help me to show others your love.

To Ponder: How can you help God show his love for others today?

KELLY GUEST

Prayer

Ask and you shall receive.

Matthew 7:7

Jesus told a story about a judge who wanted an obnoxious widow to stop bugging him, but God appears to want us to bug him and keep bugging him. Why? Perhaps because he is a loving Father and likes being with us even when we come just to ask him to open his wallet. The problem is that we often ask for the wrong things because we misidentify what will really make us happy.

So before talking to him, which is a dimension of prayer, we need to listen to him, which is an even more important dimension of prayer. We were given two ears and only one mouth for a reason.

But how do we listen? One privileged way is through scripture. These words are food for our souls. Most of us don't eat once a week, but daily—several times a day, in fact. So we should gather up the manna of God's word at least daily, maybe even several times a day.

There are scriptural, bite-sized snacks called the psalms that have been the backbone of prayer for nearly three thousand years. They are God's word through which he speaks to us, but they happen to be cast as prayers we can use to speak with him. That kills two birds with one stone. And they cover everything that we could possibly want to say to God: "Thank you." "Why are you doing this to me?" "Help me!" There are even a few asking God to smash our enemies!

If you have time for three snacks a day, you have time for at least three psalms a day.

Jesus, the psalms were your prayers. Show me how to pray them with you.

To Ponder: At what moments in the day could you pause and pray a psalm?

DR. MARCELLINO D'AMBROSIO

March

THEME: SANCTITY

Blessing the Busyness

Jesus is happy to come with us, as truth is happy
to be spoken, as life to be lived, as light to be lit, as
love is to be loved, as joy to be given, as peace to be
spread.

Saint Francis of Assisi

For many years, my favorite "chapel" had four wheels, lots
of bumper stickers, and too many cookie crumbs littering
the floor to count. As we drove to our local Catholic school
each day in that mom-mobile, the boys and I would begin
our days in prayer.

Don't get me wrong: these weren't pious Latin recitals.
Often we were rushed and distracted in our intercessory
petitions on behalf of loved ones, anticipated tests, or world
events. But pray we did, together and on the move. Even
my own frequent yet sincere "God, give me patience and
energy" pleas emanating from the front seat gave me hope
that our life—so often messy and out of control—could be
sanctified. Certainly we aimed for more formal prayer and
frequent Eucharist together. But I love to think that those
school morning rituals taught us all to begin our days by
loving and communing with God and one another. I believe
Jesus smiled upon our little prayer time, recognizing that in
giving even the craziness of those mornings over in love, we
drew ever closer to him and to one another.

*Jesus, help us to recognize that in loving, in serving, and in joyfully
giving of our gifts, we give our hearts and lives to you.*

To Ponder: Are there simple moments in your day, even amid the busyness, that can be sanctified through intentional moments of prayer with your children?

LISA M. HENDEY

MARCH 2

Everything Is Providence

Do not be afraid to abandon yourself unreservedly to his loving Providence, for a child cannot perish in the arms of a father who is omnipotent.

Saint Margaret Mary Alacoque

A few years ago I had the privilege of living in a lay Catholic community, which was started by a little nun in Italy and now has sixty-five houses around the world. Living in this community changed me in so many ways, as it taught me to live my days with joy and embrace both the daily crosses and the resurrections that make up the fabric of our lives.

Yet one charism of the community that changed how I viewed God was that we lived off divine providence—radically and completely. We literally lived off the groceries that people would bring to our doorstep. Although we worked and prayed hard, we made no money for ourselves nor asked for anything but only *trusted* confidently in God's provision.

For over a year I would watch God provide for us in the most miraculous of ways. We would need eggs, milk, stockings, meat . . . and as we prayed and trusted, what we needed would show up before our eyes. Sometimes what we needed and prayed for did not arrive at the time nor in the form we expected, but we learned that this, too, was God's providence, for through it God was teaching us to go without, detach, let go, learn patience, or simply trust more.

Through this experience I began to see in a very real way that God is a father who provides. He knows our needs. He has counted the hairs on our head, and everything—all that is happening in our lives as well as all that is not—is his providence.

Thank you, Lord, for providing for all my needs. I trust that all that is happening in my life as well as all that is not is your providence.

To Ponder: Do you trust that God knows your needs and will provide for you?

KARA KLEIN

MARCH 3
SAINT KATHARINE DREXEL

On Loan

Take, Lord, and receive all my liberty,
my memory, my understanding,
and my entire will,
All I have and call my own.
You have given all to me.
To you, Lord, I return it.
Everything is yours; do with it what you will.
Give me only your love and your grace,
that is enough for me.

Saint Ignatius of Loyola, Suscipe

Be careful what you wish for!

Saint Katharine Drexel, a wealthy and faithful young woman from Philadelphia, once visited Pope Leo XIII. She had been pouring money into missions for Native Americans and begged the pope to send more workers to the missions she funded. The Holy Father surprised Katharine by suggesting she offer her own life in service.

Katharine's parents, generous philanthropists, had always stressed that their wealth was on loan to them; they must put all they had at the service of others. That selfless outlook cultivated a habit of generosity in Katharine. When the time came to offer all she had, she was ready.

A Morning Offering Prayer
Here I am, Lord.
You have given me all I am, all that I have.
I now return to you my day and everything in it.
Accept my offering. I place it in your heart.
Unite it with the gift of yourself in the Eucharist,
where you show me how to pour myself out for others.

To Ponder: How do you start your day? Try writing and praying a morning offering of your own.

GRACE MAZZA URBANSKI

Frank Conversations with God

*Daughters, I would have you exhibit manly strength
in this quest for holiness.*

Saint Teresa of Avila

Saint Teresa of Avila, great mystic and Doctor of the Church, is a woman of psychological insight and profound spirituality. We couldn't find a better guide for holiness of life. Teresa is known for her visions and locutions (audible messages from God); however, her most valuable contributions relate to everyday growth in the spiritual life. Teresa believed all are called to prayer but understood the differences in temperament and vocation meant that people would live a prayer life differently. She taught her own father, Don Lorenzo, to become a man of prayer in the midst of his secular life.

Women who are busy mothers and/or working professionals may be tempted to limit their spiritual growth. Teresa says we need a *muy determinatada determinación*, very tenacious determination in prayer. She knew that none of us prays without effort and practice. Eminently practical, she tells us that we need courage and decisive action to pray. How did she define prayer? Nothing more (or less!) than a frank conversation, frequently, with one whom we know loves us.

We may find it hard to believe that the Lord wishes us to pray in this familiar way, but this is at the heart of spiritual growth. Knowing the Lord personally, allowing the Lord into our lives as friend and guide, is the surest way to persevere on the journey toward holiness.

Lord, give me the gift to see myself as a woman of prayer. Give me that determination and desire for intimacy with you that will nourish me for holiness of life.

To Ponder: What does holiness mean to you? Have you begun this journey?

JULIE L. PAAVOLA

MARCH 5

Love without Measure

Intense love does not measure; it just gives.

Saint Teresa of Calcutta

In a few months, my husband and I will celebrate our thirty-fourth wedding anniversary. Our wedding day seems like a lifetime ago. Several of our friends and relatives who married around the same time are no longer together or are on their second or third marriages.

These same relatives and friends have asked us, "What's your secret?" Well, there really isn't a "secret." Our devout Catholic faith tells us to be selfless and to sacrifice for the other. That's it. For example, every morning, I try to wake up with this thought: "What can I do to make my husband's life easier today?" It's incredible how many things come to mind.

He is now retired, but my husband worked sixty to eighty hours per week as a high school teacher for twenty-six years. When our children were small, I sometimes felt like a single mother because of these crazy hours. However, he gave up a promising artistic career to take a financially stable teaching job to make it possible for me to stay at home to raise our children.

Intense love really does not measure; it does not keep score. It truly gives.

Lord, help me not to keep score in all my relationships.

To Ponder: What can you do today for your spouse to make his life easier?

ELLEN GABLE HRKACH

MARCH 6

Take a Penny Walk

Perfect love of God means the complete union of our will with God's.

Saint Alphonsus de Ligouri

The month of March is a good time for a penny walk. First, you'll have to put on your walking shoes. Then, you'll need to find a shiny penny. All set? Let's go outside!

Walk to the nearest corner. Flip the penny, and see which side lands up. If it's tails, make a left. If it's heads, make a right. Keep walking to the next corner, and when you get there, flip the coin again to find out which way to turn. Continue in this manner, flipping the penny at every corner and following its direction. Now you're on a penny walk!

A penny walk is good therapy for an individual with controlling tendencies because it can help to subdue that person's compulsion to plan her—and everyone else's—next move. Going on a penny walk demands that a person let go of her own will and turn her steps in a direction that she may not have wanted to go.

Walking with God requires resignation, too. Submitting to the divine will means allowing God to direct your footsteps along the path he's chosen for you. A beautiful expression of trust in God's will can be found in the Divine Mercy chaplet, where we pray that we should "with great confidence submit ourselves to your holy will, which is love and mercy itself." Complete resignation to God's will is difficult, but it's a certain path to sanctity.

Dear Lord, please help me to remember that the road you choose is the one that will lead me to heaven. Teach me to unite my will to yours, even when it hurts.

To Ponder: Are you ready to follow the GPS: God's Perfect Strategy?

CELESTE BEHE

MARCH 7
SAINTS PERPETUA AND FELICITY

Reflecting His Holiness

For I am the Lord your God; sanctify yourselves
therefore, and be holy, for I am holy.

Leviticus 11:44

We who are seeking personal holiness usually have an idea of what we think holiness should look like and feel like. It should look like someone in quiet repose in a Spartan room for hours on end, yes? It should feel like gladly praying endless Rosaries while wearing a hair shirt, right? Well, maybe, but maybe not. While the call to holiness is universal, answering that call is very individual. This is why, even after participating in many holy endeavors, our soul can still feel deflated, and so we frantically look for the next "holy" thing to pump it up.

Authentic, personal holiness, however, is not something we can manufacture but something more like our being a mirror of God's own holiness. Saint Paul points this out in holy scripture by writing, "He saved us and called us to a holy life, not according to our works but according to his own design and the grace bestowed on us in Christ Jesus before time began"(2 Tm 1:9).

We cannot earn or accomplish holiness as if it were a college degree, but when we seek God for his own sake and dispose our wills to his will, our lives do begin to reflect more of his holiness. Singing hymns in the shower or listening to a child learn to read can be ways of growing in holiness if through them we experience God's purpose and grace.

Father God, thank you for being holy and helping my life to mirror yours.

To Ponder: What could you do today to better reflect God's holiness? It could be something as ordinary as walking through the woods and wondering at God's creation.

HEIDI BRATTON

Steps to Sanctity

There is no duty, however menial, that cannot be
retrieved for sanctity.

Venerable Fulton J. Sheen, Those Mysterious
Priests

Earlier today, I was faced with a monumental choice. A choice
that, depending on which way I chose, could very well have
put me one step closer to heaven or hell.

There was a scrap of paper on the floor, you see, eight
inches from the trash can. I had just tried to toss it out as I
rushed past the trash can, but due to my less-than-stellar
basketball skills, I had once again missed my mark. So then
I had to make a choice. Ignore the paper, knowing that in
about three hours my daughter would be sweeping the floor
and the paper would wind up where it belonged anyway, or
let out an exasperated sigh, bend over, and harshly toss the
scrap into the can.

But then I was reminded I had a third option: to offer the
moment up to Our Lord as an act of love.

"It is a little thing," I reasoned, "but it means so much.
Therefore, I do this for love of you," I prayed as I picked the
scrap up and tossed it into the trash. No one noticed. No one
would have cared. But Our Lord saw that tiny act, and I pray
he was consoled.

Victory! And one step closer to sanctity.

*Lord, keep me ever mindful of the many little acts of love I can offer
you during my day.*

To Ponder: The only time we are ever given to grow in holiness is the present moment. If you said the words "For love of you, Lord" before every small action or choice you made, how might this change your heart over time?

CASSANDRA POPPE

MARCH 9
SAINT CATHERINE OF BOLOGNA

Shine Forth
Your Talents and Faith

If we let him, God will use our education, talents,
and faith to uplift the world.

Anonymous

We shuffle our children from school to soccer, from piano to catechism classes. We would love our bright kids to solve higher math problems, run a 5K, show artistic flare, *and* draw closer to God.

Parents in fifteenth-century Italy also craved well-balanced children. Young ladies such as the noble Catherine of Bologna learned to speak and write elegantly, to embroider and stitch fine seams, and to sketch and oil paint. As for faith, Catherine entered a convent to begin formation for religious life at age fourteen.

Her talents flourished even as a cloistered nun. Catherine's painting of the Blessed Mother and Child still inspires with its silver stars adding a heavenly glow. She also wrote clearly on the spiritual life in her *Treatise on the Seven Spiritual Weapons Necessary for Spiritual Warfare.*

Always "do good," wrote Saint Catherine, but remember we can never succeed alone. We should trust God and not fear the battle against evil, either "in the world or in ourselves." Meditating on Jesus's life, especially his passion and death, and remembering that we, too, must die, will draw us closer to God. Keep heaven firmly in view, reminded Catherine, and if we keep holy scripture in our hearts, it will "guide all our thoughts and actions."

Dear Lord, thank you for Saint Catherine of Bologna, patroness of artists. Help us to be like her in drawing on our talents and faith, leaning on you to do good each moment.

To Ponder: Even as a cloistered nun, Saint Catherine of Bologna's gifts and holiness shone forth. How can we learn from her life and reflections, letting God work through us to uplift the world?

MARIANNA BARTHOLOMEW

MARCH 10

Holy Diversity

God arranged the members in the body, each one of
them, as he chose. The eye cannot say to the hand,
"I have no need of you," nor again the head to the
feet, "I have no need of you."

1 Corinthians 12:18, 21

Can't personalities be onerous? I like to cut to the chase. No perfunctory e-mail greetings or small talk for me. A certain woman at church phoned me weekly with profound concern about children's programs, someone's marital affair, the pastor's manners, the organist's hammer toe, freezing rain, and the possibility of spring onion chicken for the parish potluck.

I got caller ID just so I could screen her infernal, eternal conversation—mostly it was gossipy, and I despise gossip—but she just cornered me, all smiling and emoting and squeezing and *relaaaating*, at church or by the beets at the grocery. I stayed out of her vicinity. I never met her eyes. Once, I avoided the doctor's office when I saw her in the waiting room. She finally stopped approaching me, and I thanked Jesus Christ, Son of God, for having mercy on me.

Soon after, I saw a breathtaking video on the planet. Seahorse darting, seed sprouting, child racing, peony flowering, sun rising, nebulae swirling, elephant charging, baby bubbling, newlyweds dancing, whale breeching, vein pulsing, Africans dancing, elderly weeping.

How lovely it all is. Diverse. Intricate. Inventive. How deliberate. All of this on one earth? Maybe he *loves* every differentness? Maybe he loves that it's all dependent on the rest? I called she-who-loves-to-*relaaaaate*.

What is she bringing me, Lord?

To Ponder: Are you refusing what God is attempting to offer you through a particular someone? In what small way can you open yourself to that person today?

SONJA CORBITT

Apples and Wine

The way I see it, if you want the rainbow, you gotta
put up with the rain.

Dolly Parton

John Chapman, also known as "Johnny Appleseed," is legendary. Roaming westward from Pennsylvania to Illinois in the early nineteenth century sowing seeds, he planted orchards that sustained the early settlers.

But the apples he cultivated were a far cry from the Red Delicious apples we pick up at the grocery store or farm market. Most of the apples that grew on those trees were made into cider. Given the state of refrigeration in the nineteenth century, not all of that cider was kid-friendly. Rather, much of it was hard cider, drunk daily by young and old alike.

These settlers weren't party animals corrupting their children with forbidden fruit; they drank the cider because the local water supply was dangerous. Not only did Johnny Appleseed help these people establish homes, but he also played a part in keeping them alive.[2]

When we go to Mass and receive Communion, young and old alike can receive Communion from the cup. This wine isn't just any wine. It is the Precious Blood of Christ that we receive in memory of the sacrifice he made for us. The wine has been transformed into a gift of life we can barely imagine, given to us by a God who loves us so much he wants us to spend eternity with him. This Blood of Christ not only strengthens us in our day-to-day lives, but also promises us there is so much more beyond the here and now.

Lord, when I receive your Body and Blood, I pray that it will strengthen me and give me life beyond what I can imagine in the midst of my day-to-day life.

To Ponder: When you feel you are drowning, do you look for God's rainbow?

LISA LAWMASTER HESS

MARCH 12
NATIONAL PLANT A FLOWER DAY

A Quieter Life

Always we begin again.

Saint Benedict of Nursia, The Rule

The gardens were gone. After twenty-five years of caring for them, they were torn out in less than two. I could no longer care for a landscape filled with flower beds and vegetable gardens. An auto accident decades earlier had damaged my spine, and trauma-induced arthritis had advanced to where it limited many of my activities. Friends and neighbors had come during the past two summers and salvaged perennials and small flowering shrubs from among overgrown weeds.

My lot is small, but now with empty beds and expanded lawn, it looked huge and barren. I had thought of my gardens as a sacred place of sorts. It was a place where I prayed and conversed with Our Lord.

There was so much to pray about back then. A lot of time was spent weeding out and pruning back; my spiritual life grew in pace with the gardens.

Things are different now. I'm quieter and my prayers reflect the simplicity and confidence of later life. It's a time of increased solitude that's not empty but rather fuller and condensed.

It was the first spring since The Great Dig Out. The nearly empty border beds shifted the way I looked at my yard. I felt a familiar tug at my gardener's heart—begin again, mindfully and simplistically. Moments later I headed to the local greenhouse to buy a few potted roses. I planned to resurrect Mary's garden on a smaller scale.

Thank you, Father, for helping me to be attentive and embrace a quieter life.

To Ponder: Often we must let go of what is familiar. In what ways can you begin again? What is something new can you plant in your changed life?

MARGARET ROSE REALY, OBL., O.S.B.

NATIONAL GOOD SAMARITAN DAY

The Amazing Consequences of Unconditional Kindness

As I have done for you, so you must also do for others.

John 13:15

To be a Christian in this world means to take the emphasis off of ourselves and to place it on another. Unfortunately, our American culture encourages self-indulgence over and above the needs of another.

One day when my children were very little, Joey an infant and Lauren four years old, we went shopping all day in the heat of summer, and my last stop was at a privately owned store. After shopping, when I got into my car to go home, it wouldn't start. By now it was nearing dinnertime, my son was crying from hunger, and I was out of formula. My husband was on a business trip, so I had no one to help me. Going back inside the store I told the shopkeeper my plight. Without missing a beat, he said, "Hold on," and went into the back room. He came out with the keys to his car, instructing me to take my hungry children home. I thanked him profusely for his amazing act of kindness toward me and my children.

It's been thirty years since this happened, and I still have not forgotten the kindness of that shopkeeper. In every way, he was my Good Samaritan, and his actions inspired me to do for others what was done for me.

Jesus, you washed the feet of your disciples. Help me to willingly serve others in your name.

To Ponder: Have you ever been the recipient of an unconditional act of kindness? Have you offered this type of kindness to another? Which of these acts of kindness touched your heart in a most profound way and why?

DR. MARY AMORE

MARCH 14
NATIONAL POTATO CHIP DAY

The Best Food for Your Soul

Foolish is he who follows the pleasures of this world, because these are always fleeting and bring much pain. The only true pleasure is that which comes to us through faith.

Blessed Pier Giorgio Frassati

Why is it that I can eat a whole bag of potato chips in one sitting but I struggle to squeeze a single serving of vegetables into my whole day? I know potato chips aren't good for me. I know they don't fuel my body the way it needs to be fueled. Yet, I still gravitate to them like a piece of metal to a magnet.

When I manage to eat the vegetables that I should, they often taste better than I remembered. Sure, they're not salty or crispy (and not even the least bit greasy) like a good potato chip, but they have their own appeal: the sweet crunch of a carrot, the fresh coolness of a cucumber, the creamy sweetness of a baked butternut squash. And after I eat them, I don't feel sluggish or guilty.

It's really not all that different from the temptations I face in my search for holiness. Time and again I gorge myself on the empty spiritual nutrition of worldly pleasures. Maybe it's junk food or shopping or gossiping with friends, but it all leaves me spiritually malnourished. I know that if I spend my time living the corporal and spiritual works of mercy and striving for a life of virtue, I will fill myself with the best food for my soul. All too often, though, I settle for the temporary pleasures of the physical world that leave my soul hungry for real spiritual food.

Holy Spirit, give me the wisdom to recognize the spiritual food that will feed my soul and the strength to choose it over the temporal food of this world that only leaves me feeling empty.

To Ponder: What are the "potato chips" that you're feeding your soul? How can you change your habits to include lots of opportunities to consume what your soul truly needs?

LAURA B. NELSON

MARCH 15
SAINT LOUISE DE MARILLAC

Corral Mom

How good it is to trust God! Turn to Him often.

Saint Louise de Marillac

When my sons were infants, I lovingly strapped them into a car seat, "bouncy" chair, or swing. I always put them down to play in a playpen or play-yard fence set up on the family room floor. When working in the yard, my toddler would be close by in that same play yard. After the birth of my first son, we added a fenced-in play area in the backyard. I even purchased an expandable nylon outdoor sports complex to provide a safe environment for them to play while preventing them from chasing a ball into our busy street.

Forget helicopter mom: I am corral mom. If not for a dog allergy, I probably would have acquired a sheepdog to help me keep my kids safe when they were outside my fences and nettings. Their safety was and remains my primary concern and at the top of my prayer list.

Then there came the day when they were no longer containable. That joyous time when I knew exactly where they were, whom they were with, and what they were doing was over. Ah, I miss those days. My sons and daughter are first and foremost God's. I can't imagine he cares less about their well-being than I do. God is trustworthy, loving, and faithful. Reminding myself of this helps disperse fears and strengthen my trust in the Lord, especially with my "heart with legs," also known as my children.

Dear Lord, today I pray to not only say the words "I trust you," but to also actually trust you.

To Ponder: What is your greatest fear regarding your child(ren)? Are you willing to say it out loud today and then place it in God's loving hands?

ALLISON GINGRAS

The Test of the Vows

To love another person is to see the face of God.

Victor Hugo, Les Misérables

Marriage is hard. If yours isn't and you somehow have been blessed with a perfect union, feel free to stop reading. For the rest of us, those marriage vows get tested, sometimes daily. We all hope for the better, richer, healthier days, but somehow end up with a generous helping of worse, poorer, and sicker. Two imperfect people say "I do" and end up with a less-than-perfect union. It's really not surprising, is it?

Love is often much more of a choice than a feeling. I will choose to love my spouse today. I will choose to serve and honor him. I will choose to see the face of God in him. That last one isn't always easy. It can be difficult to see God in any person, much more so in someone you've lived with for many years. You've seen him at his worst. You know all his faults and shortcomings. But maybe, if I take off my glasses, cloudy with my own imperfections, I can take a closer look. Maybe I can focus on the good and the beautiful and the reasons why I married him in the first place. Perhaps I can see that glimmer of the divine that lives in his heart and rejoice in the presence of God.

Dear God, please help me to see your face in all those I love, especially my spouse.

To Ponder: Have you and your spouse been going through a rough patch lately? Perhaps instead of focusing on the negative, you could make a list of all his good qualities.

PATRICE FAGNANT-MACARTHUR

MARCH 17
SAINT PATRICK

Vision to Persevere

I pray to God to give me perseverance and to deign that I be a faithful witness to him to the end of my life for my God.

Saint Patrick, The Confession of Saint Patrick

Saint Patrick's Day is more than the "wearin' o' the green," cooking Irish stew, or enjoying merriment in parades or with a good pint. Saint Patrick is a saint precisely because he knew and loved Jesus above all. 'Tis the very love of God that sustained him daily.

Long before Patrick became a bishop, he suffered poverty as a slave, enduring separation from those he loved. In captivity he turned to God in prayer. God gave him a dream of one day preaching the Gospel in Ireland.

Faith gives us the vision to persevere.

Every Christian must persevere in the quest for holiness. Like Saint Patrick, we face obstacles, trials, and sufferings. Yet as saints-in-the-making we must keep our eyes fixed on Jesus, "the pioneer and perfecter of our faith" (Heb 12:2).

Imagine God's constant nearness and protection as you pray Saint Patrick's *Lorica*:

Christ with me, Christ before me, Christ behind me,
Christ in me, Christ beneath me, Christ above me,
Christ on my right, Christ on my left,
Christ when I lie down, Christ when I sit down,
Christ in the heart of every man who thinks of me,
Christ in the mouth of every man who speaks of me,
Christ in the eye that sees me,
Christ in the ear that hears me.

Jesus, let me envision your presence in my life the way Saint Patrick did.

To Ponder: What phrases of the *Lorica* speak to your heart? Find the full prayer online. Keep it handy when you need God's hope or protection.

PAT GOHN

MARCH 18
NATIONAL AWKWARD MOMENTS DAY

Rediscovering
Your Spouse

To maintain a joyful family requires much from both the parents and the children. Each member of the family has to become, in a special way, the servant of the others.

Saint John Paul II

Today is National Awkward Moments Day, a funny way to bring up a subject that is, well, awkward.

The empty nest has introduced a number of changes in my life. I discovered a kind of shy awkwardness with my husband. At first it was a little disconcerting, but it turned into something sweet, even endearing. After thirty-plus years together, we found ourselves looking across a wide table, now set just for us. We hadn't quite figured out how to cook for two again, and we weren't quite sure about having conversations that didn't involve schedules, drop-offs, and pickups.

It was quite liberating. And silent.

Happily, our morning routine became an opportunity to linger over a cup of coffee, maybe even two, before setting off for work at an unhurried pace. Over time, we found our rhythm again, and now laugh at the transition to being a couple with adult children who come for visits.

This new phase in our lives provides us with the gift of presence to each other. We're rediscovering the things that delight and surprise us, like gifts of flowers or movies, and what was once awkward has become an opportunity to shower each other with loving service.

Lord, help me to joyfully serve my husband with love.

To Ponder: Sometimes we take our loved ones for granted. We forget that love, especially in marriage, is a daily action. What simple action can you take today to connect with your husband? A date night? Sharing a favorite dessert?

MARIA MORERA JOHNSON

SAINT JOSEPH, HUSBAND AND WORKER

Patron and Protector

I ask for you the grace to be ever closer to your
children, allow them to grow, but be close, close!
They need you, your presence, your closeness, your
love. Be, for them, like Saint Joseph.

Pope Francis

In 1847, Pope Pius IX proclaimed Saint Joseph as the patron and protector of the universal Church. Why?

Because Saint Joseph—the husband of Mary and the foster-father of Jesus—was and is a just man. Far from being a saint on a pedestal or a man removed from the struggles of daily life, Joseph was a real husband and a real father. He worked daily to support his family. He cared for his wife, Mary, and he raised his son, Jesus. He was the head of the Holy Family.

We glean precious little of Joseph from the scriptures. The Gospel writers record not even a single word of his. But we do know he was a just man who accepted with courage the will of God even when it was beyond his comprehension. Joseph led, provided for, and protected Jesus and Mary. Whom better could Pope Pius IX have turned to for help in protecting the universal Church?

Joseph is a man of silent strength, a man of faith and prayer, a man of absolute dependence on God. When I feel confused and overwhelmed, I turn to Joseph. I ask him to be the patron and protector of my family, my domestic Church.

Joseph, husband of Mary and foster-father of Jesus, help me to trust and depend on God like you did.

To Ponder: Are there times in your life when the best and strongest thing to do is to keep silent? How might you best prepare yourself for those times?

JEFF YOUNG

MARCH 20

Won't You Be My Neighbor?

I have really never considered myself a TV star. I always thought I was a neighbor who just came in for a visit.

Fred Rogers, host of Mr. Rogers' Neighborhood, *born on this day in 1928*

I once heard Cardinal Dolan share a story from the early years of his priesthood when he served as an associate in a parish. The pastor of that parish asked then Father Dolan to go with him while he visited some parishioners' homes one day. Back then, neighborhoods were organized by religion and ethnicity, and as the pastor drove along the street in the Catholic neighborhood, he knew well the families living in each home. As he passed each house, the pastor would mention things like, "Mrs. Smith just had a miscarriage, Jesus, have mercy"; "Mr. Hill is having job struggles, Jesus, have mercy"; "Sally just became engaged to Johnny, Jesus, have mercy"; "Grandma Bea fell and injured her wrist, Jesus, have mercy."

I wonder if that still happens anywhere these days. For my part, when I drive down my suburban neighborhood street, while I recognize many faces, I don't know what's on my neighbors' hearts. We are more mobile and our neighborhoods are more transient than in generations past. Accordingly, it's imperative to be all the more intentional about building community within them. Chances are good that some of your neighbors are in great need of Jesus's mercy, and may not even recognize as much.

Dear Jesus, help me be a sign of your mercy to those in my neighborhood.

To Ponder: Is there a particular family in your neighborhood to whom you feel called to reach out? Consider stopping by for a neighborly visit and strike up a conversation.

LISA A. SCHMIDT

MARCH 21
WORLD DOWN SYNDROME DAY

God's Plans Versus My Plans

God's gifts put man's best dreams to shame.

Elizabeth Barrett Browning

I had a perfect life in the summer of 2000: a solid Catholic marriage and two beautiful daughters ages three and seven. I was home schooling and working part time teaching English at a college, yet I wanted more. I wanted another baby and, generously, God granted me one. Attending Sunday Mass halfway through my pregnancy, I heard him tell me, "Your baby has Down syndrome." Then, in the Communion line: "I want you to accept this child as a gift from my hand when you receive me." Amid tears, I said, "Yes."

Looking back, I realize that God was calling me to a call within the call of motherhood, a call to mother a child with special needs. I did not consider myself equipped for a challenge like that, but those who knew me did. Fourteen years later, with many lessons learned, I am starting to understand what God and my friends saw in me: I am raising a daughter who has Down syndrome and autism with complex needs. I am writing, advocating, and planning a retreat for mothers on this same journey. It is a testament of what God can do with even a reluctant and fearful yes.

Dear God, your plans are so often even better than my dreams. May your gifts to our families teach us to see people as you do, enjoy the joyfulness of each day, and not take any accomplishments for granted.

To Ponder: What challenge is God offering you at this time? How are you responding?

LETICIA VELASQUEZ

Learning through Laughter

He is a sane man who can have tragedy in his heart
and comedy in his head.

G. K. Chesterton

What a beautiful concept: realizing that we need not let the weight of the world weigh us down but rather sometimes we just need to "lighten up."

It is easy during the heavy times in life to turn our attention to God. Don't get me wrong. This is good; we should turn to him in times of need. In fact, sometimes God's mercy is packaged in such a way that it is our suffering that brings us to him.

But do we take notice of God in our lives when things are going smoothly and happiness abounds? It is in moments of laughter when we should be most aware of God's presence.

Laughter is endearing. It is said to be the shortest distance between two people. There is something about laughing with another that draws us closer to that person, establishes a sense of trust, and builds confidence.

Just think of Sarah's reaction in the book of Genesis as God informs Abraham that Sarah, in her old age, will bear a child. The second she laughs, she is drawn closer to God. She laughed out of doubt, but her confidence in God grew as the child in her womb grew, and her trust in the Lord intensified as the pains of labor intensified and she bore a son. Abraham must have wanted this beautiful lesson to span generations, for he named the child Isaac, which in Hebrew means "laughter."

Lord, help me recognize you in the laughter around me.

To Ponder: So often we quickly turn to God when we need something. How often do you *instantly* thank him for the blessings in your life? Next time you laugh, just say, "Thank you, Lord!"

KELLY M. WAHLQUIST

MARCH 23

Remembering to Rely on God

We are not human beings having a spiritual experience. We are spiritual beings having a human experience.

Pierre Teilhard de Chardin

Too often, I find myself racing through my days, usually on autopilot. Work responsibilities, my children's needs, home responsibilities, and extracurricular schedules have me rushing from one activity to the next without much thought. I only snap out of this mode when I realize that I am lacking proper focus. Stress mounts when my eyes, heart, and mind fall off of Our Lord. We may not see our tasks as part of the overall sanctity of our lives as mothers in the daily minutiae of life.

I usually look for any opportunity to snap back into a reliance on Christ. When I had to face disgruntled members of an association that I managed, years ago, I remember pausing while walking through the banquet room doors to what might have been a contentious meeting. I opened the door and paused for a few seconds. I envisioned Christ walking in before me. This was my form of prayer. I needed his help; I invited his help by a simple gesture. Not surprisingly, we settled on an agreeable solution that day. This prayer lasted just a few moments. The power of this prayer was that I acknowledged that Christ was with me, even at a work meeting. I relied on him at that very moment.

Lord, help me today to keep you in my heart no matter where I am and what I am trying to do. Be with me and help me to recognize the sanctity of my daily life in union with you.

To Ponder: How can you remind yourself of the sanctity of your life as a woman in your daily tasks?

MEG BUCARO

MARCH 24

Character Defects and Family Life

Deeds speak louder than words.

Assiniboine Proverb

I'm not proud of the many times I've gotten angry and yelled at my kids. Often the trigger was them dawdling or misbehaving while we were trying to get out the door for school. Shortly after my outburst, we would get in the car and begin our morning prayers.

Times with your family can be your biggest challenge area for growing in sanctity. Home is where you let your hair down. You are sloppier there when it comes to having your character defects on display.

It's hard to keep it together everywhere. It can be particularly difficult keeping your behavior in check at home with those you love. Frankly, without prayer, the Eucharist, and the Sacred Heart of Jesus, it is an impossible task.

While it seems hypocritical to pray before or after a lapse in behavior, I suggest this is actually God's design for the domestic Church. He picked a flawed first pope to lead his Church. Why would he select you, with your failings, to help lead your family? Because you are the perfect fit. Your loved ones see you slip. Then they see you pray. Then they see you try again. All the while you are at regular confession and attending Mass. You say you are sorry and ask for their forgiveness.

Your humble struggles with sanctity laced with prayer are a gift to your family.

You are a model of God's mercy and a realistic picture of what growing in sanctity really looks like for your family. This inspires those you love not to give up when discouraged and instead to follow the course you lead . . . quite imperfectly.

Jesus, help me to become more like you so that others will find you through me. Help me to not get discouraged, but rather to use each failure as an opportunity to receive the mercy of your Sacred Heart, to grow in humility, and to model that no one has to feel she needs to be perfect in order to strive for God's perfection.

To Ponder: Are you taking full advantage of prayer, the sacraments, and others to help you modify your not-so-attractive behavior?

CHRISTINA M. WEBER

MARCH 25
THE ANNUNCIATION

Questioning God

And Mary said, "Behold, I am the handmaid of the Lord; let it be done to me according to your word."

Luke 1:38

When I reflect on the angel Gabriel announcing to Mary that she has been chosen to bear the Son of God, I am reminded of another story in which the news of a child is announced by an angel. It is a story with striking similarities but vastly different outcomes.

Zechariah was an elderly priest of the Temple whose wife, Elizabeth, was barren. In his angelic visitation, Zechariah is told that his lifelong prayers have been answered. Not only will his wife bear him a son, but he will be great before the Lord. Zechariah questions the angel, wanting to be certain. After all, he and his wife are old.

Maybe as a priest, Zechariah should have known better than to question God. Perhaps he was afraid of disappointment. In any case, because of his hesitancy to believe, Zechariah is struck mute until the child is born.

Mary, in contrast, demonstrates the faith of a child. She also questions the angel, but it's not out of disbelief; it's more out of a desire to understand. It's as if she's saying, "I don't really get it, but I'm in."

Mary, help me to open my heart as you did to the angel Gabriel. Not just in big decisions but in the small day-to-day opportunities I am presented. May I learn to be an obedient servant like you.

To Ponder: How do you respond to God's prompting, especially when it doesn't always make sense to you? With the skeptical heart of Zechariah or the obedient heart of Mary? Choose a situation today where you can give someone a yes when you'd rather say no.

ELIZABETH FICOCELLI

MARCH 26
SAINT MARGARET CLITHEROW

Worth the Price

My cause is God's, and it is a great comfort to me to die in his quarrel: flesh is frail, but I trust in my Lord Jesu,[3] that he will give me strength to bear all troubles and torments which shall be laid up on me for his sake.

Saint Margaret Clitherow

During the Elizabethan era, English Catholics were savagely persecuted. In defiance of the law, a young wife and mother, Margaret Clitherow, secretly held Masses in her home. The penalty for harboring Catholic priests, and especially for celebrating Mass, was death, and she eventually paid the ultimate price.

In fact, her execution was especially brutal because she refused to take her case to trial. In a trial, the jury, her own family, and her neighbors would all be compelled by law to cooperate with her unjust punishment, so she staunchly refused all hopes of leniency out of concern for their souls.

Love for Jesus in the Eucharist can empower our ordinary lives, inspiring a hunger for holiness and the courage to live only for God.

Jesus, help me to be joyful, no matter what I suffer out of love for you. Fill my heart with courage each time I receive you in the Blessed Sacrament, and make me a valiant witness to your love.

To Ponder: Are you challenged by the dogma of the real presence of Jesus in the Eucharist? This week, ask Saint Margaret to intercede for you as you prepare your heart before holy Communion. On the days when you cannot receive, ask her to help you to treasure the presence of Jesus in your heart.

LISA MLADINICH

MARCH 27
WORLD THEATER DAY

Many Roles

All the world's a stage, and all the men and women merely players: they have their exits and their entrances; and one man in his time plays many parts.

William Shakespeare, As You Like It

Did you ever want to be an actress? Who among us can say that we never pictured ourselves dressed in a stunning gown, walking the red carpet, and then finally mounting the steps to the podium? Did you even practice your speech? "I'd like to thank the Academy . . ."

Alas, we grew up, and most of us found our future to be very different from those theatrical dreams. We passed on the gown and picked up the mom jeans. The carpet's color can be described best as "needs shampooing." Still, you are in a role that you've auditioned for your whole life and probably didn't even know it. In fact, you were *born* to play this role. Seriously! Your cast members were selected especially for you, to challenge you and make you shine exactly as brightly as you were born to shine. And when you shine, so do they. And if Jesus is the light of the world, let your light shine.

Father, I trust that you planned my role for me before the world began. That alone is a precious gift—an award of its own. Help me to see the moments where, with your grace, I have won the joy of pleasing you by serving others.

To Ponder: Where do you shine most brightly? In your role as wife? Mother? Child of God? If you were to make an "acceptance speech," whom would you thank?

ERIN MCCOLE CUPP

Glimpsing Eternity

*For me, prayer is a surge of the heart; it is a simple
look turned toward heaven, it is a cry of recognition
and of love, embracing both trial and joy.*

Saint Thérèse of Lisieux

When I think of this date, I am reminded of the days leading up to my son's unexpected birth. He came a little earlier than expected, but just before being labeled an April-Fools' Day joke. The days blend together so smoothly in my memories, but the pain of the labor and birth were only manageable through prayer. The song "Endless Is Your Love for Us" played over and over in my heart as I internally prayed Hail Marys in my mind. In a sort of prayer-like trance I found God through Our Lady.

On a daily basis, I must turn to God and Our Lady in prayer. On the days when I read scripture or pray a morning offering, the rest of the day seems to fall into place. As a home-school teacher, I long for the good days. I become frustrated much easier when I rely solely on myself. God asks and waits for us to turn to him for help. His help makes life so much sweeter. By relying on God during trials, it is much easier to be aware of joy in the everyday moments. Life is more simple and bearable with God's joy and love.

Thank you, God, for your unending love. Help me to recognize the blessings in my life as much as the trials in order to see how much you adore me.

To Ponder: What trials in your own life have brought you closer to God? When you are going through the trials, do you feel God's presence through prayer?

TANYA WEITZEL

MARCH 29

It's Okay to Start Over

Progress means getting nearer to the place you want to be. And if you have taken a wrong turning, then to go forward does not get you any nearer. If you are on the wrong road, progress means doing an about-turn and walking back to the right road; and in that case the man who turns back soonest is the most progressive man.

C. S. Lewis, Mere Christianity

My friend Melissa entered nursing school at age forty-six. A recently divorced stay-at-home mom of three boys, she reluctantly and courageously started over. She was eager to begin her new journey, but part of her felt like a failure. After all, she wouldn't be in this position of launching a new career if her marriage hadn't fallen apart.

Why is it exciting to embark on a new career path at age twenty-six, but it's something to be embarrassed about at age forty-six? I think it's because we don't like to admit that we've made a wrong turn on the imaginary road to fulfillment. It would certainly be easier to keep moving forward in a familiar struggle and to blame our limitations on mistakes of the past. It takes far more faith and courage to turn our lives upside down in an effort to find our way again.

That's what I admire most about what Melissa did: she was humble and obedient in making the more difficult choice. And it ultimately led to a more rewarding life for her and her boys.

Lord, please give me the courage and faith to answer your call, even when it means taking a step backward.

To Ponder: In what ways have you made a wrong turn in your life? Is it time to turn around and get back on track?

THERESA CENICCOLA

MARCH 30

Your Kids Are Your Neighbors

Then the righteous will answer him, "Lord, when did we see thee hungry and feed thee, or thirsty and give thee drink?"

Matthew 25:37

I've heard the above verse read from the ambo at least once a year for as long as I can remember, along with many like it about feeding the hungry, clothing the naked, comforting the sick, and, in general, loving my neighbor as myself, and they've always left me a little anxious. After all, the people I call my neighbors are the people who live in the other houses on my street, and they all seem to be getting along pretty well. If they are hungry it doesn't show, when they are sick they don't tell me, and I've certainly never seen any of them naked. Does this mean I need to go out combing the highways for neighbors to feed, comfort, and clothe?

Or, at least, that's how I felt until just recently, when my eldest turned eighteen and I paused to reflect on nearly two decades of parenthood. What have my wife and I been doing all that time? We've been feeding hungry kids, comforting them when they were sick, and keeping them in clothes that fit. It hit me, then, just how much the family is a school for holiness, and how it gives us every opportunity to practice Christ's teachings in a setting where natural love can help us along. There's so much we are already doing that we can offer up to God.

Jesus, you have taught me to serve my family in love. Thank you!

To Ponder: Your family members aren't the only "neighbors" you can find under your nose. Who else has God put in your life that you're already serving with love?

WILL DUQUETTE

MARCH 31

Doing God's Will

True holiness consists of doing God's will with a smile.

Saint Teresa of Calcutta

I try to do God's will. I honestly do. This would be easier if God sent an e-mail with detailed instructions every morning, but to date that has not happened. So, I muddle through, turning to God in prayer, trying to read the signs he sends in scripture, spiritual reading, and conversations with family and friends.

I think what is hard, especially for moms, is that while we may dream of doing great things for God, God's will for us is often to simply serve our families with love and kindness and, yes, with a smile. The love part is relatively easy. As I tell my children, even in the moments when they are not particularly likable, I always love them. Kindness is a little harder to come by, but still doable. A smile—well, that one I need to work on.

As I do the dishes; clean the floor; wash clothes; make breakfast, lunch, and dinner; and act as taxi driver, I don't always feel like smiling. On many days, these chores are done grudgingly. Yet, these little tasks are God's will for me for this stage of my life, and my holiness depends on my doing them willingly, and even with joy.

Dear God, help me to serve both you and my family well, with a smile. Help me to realize that even the little things can be a great gift to you.

To Ponder: What is the one task on your to-do list that you find the hardest to do with a smile? Make a concerted effort today to offer it to God and to do it with a joyful heart.

PATRICE FAGNANT-MACARTHUR

April

THEME: RENEWAL

APRIL 1
APRIL FOOLS' DAY

Rich Fools

But God said to him, "You fool, this night your life
will be demanded of you; and the things you have
prepared, to whom will they belong?" Thus will it be
for the one who stores up treasure for himself but is
not rich in what matters to God.

Luke 12:20–21

In recent years, April Fools' Day has become a cultural phenomenon. Celebrities, corporations, and news agencies get in on the act of playing harmless pranks and hoaxes. Although the holiday seems to have come into vogue in the nineteenth century, "fools" were prevalent even back in Jesus's day. Luke's twelfth chapter relates Our Lord's parable of the rich fool who thought that storing up material goods would be his ticket to happiness.

We live in a modern society that tries to trick us into believing that wealth, status, and physical beauty give us the keys to the kingdom. It's easy to get caught up in the mindset that "more" is better. Today, we're reminded not to fall for the joke. Our renewal comes in being "rich" in the things that matter most to God. While the rest of the world might be looking to "rest, eat, drink, and be merry," we know that the true prize is yet to come.

God, give me the conviction, strength, and discernment not to be fooled by popular wisdom. May my true renewal come in better knowing, serving, and loving you, today and always.

To Ponder: What are some ways in which you've been fooled by "what everyone else is doing"? What changes do you need to make this month to find true renewal through your faith in Jesus Christ?

LISA M. HENDEY

APRIL 2

Getting Support, Giving Support

"Home again, home again, jiggity-jog!"

"It's the end of the line, that's all she wrote! That's all you get for a nickel!"

Gram and Gramp

Their cheery voices rang out at the end of every car ride. It didn't matter where we had been—the grocery store, church, out to breakfast at McDonald's—my grandparents ended every trip the same way. Gram said her part first, and right on cue, Gramp chimed in with his line. I could rely on this silly couplet, no matter what; it was as reliable as the sun's rising.

When we lived with my grandparents after my father's death, these little rituals provided stability and comfort. We had many traditions: riding bicycles at the city park, making pies on Thanksgiving morning, going fishing on the river, riding in Gramp's Mustang with the top down after eating lime sherbet at our local ice cream shop. The consistent care and love my grandparents poured into my life created a solid place to stand after the loss of my dad. Although my mother found herself facing the challenging task of single parenting, she had her parents behind her for support.

The thing is, we're not meant to raise our children alone. We need help and backup from important people in our lives. The bonds of family can transcend biology; as Ruth was for Naomi, we can be family for those in our parishes and communities who face difficulties or need extra care. As family in Christ, we are called to support each other.

Jesus, help me to see those around me in your family who need help. Help me also to ask for help when I need it and to be willing to trust others.

To Ponder: Who is your lifeline when you need support for parenting? For whom can you be a lifeline today?

ABBEY DUPUY

APRIL 3

The Grace of This Season

Stay with me the world is dark and wild,
Stay a child while you can be a child, with me.

"Stay," from Into the Woods

Life is movement. When my Jewish wife and I moved from the Northeast to Florida, we experienced disorientation because the leaves never changed there and wintry Christmas lights on palm trees looked equally strange.

We've moved to several other places since then. With a growing child, life accelerates. Seasonal and liturgical markers begin to blur. Our child's leisurely early years started to fly by with each grade.

This sense of time moving quickly points to the difference between our chronological experience of time and "*kairos* time," the "newness" of God. This time of year we have Easter and spring to remind us of new life, but we also have tax season's financial weight and impending school-year finals to agitate us.

Let us not simply embrace this moment as this year's version of "better than the last" soon to be washed away by the rest of the year in a blur. Let us remember that every day God's reign is life-giving and everlasting. Every day is an opportunity to experience *kairos* time. We should not wait until Easter to experience this. God stays with us and lives out this promise *now*.

Creator, who brings forth each new season, Bring us to new life, not merely a repetition of another cycle. Help us find the rhythm of our flow and to know its source.

To Ponder: Is this time of year just about resetting our clocks or cleaning our houses for the next season? Or can we take the time to embrace the grace of *now* in the true spirit of renewal, which is the fullness of new life?

JAY CUASAY

Asking Forgiveness

My tongue and my heart have run wild without
restraint, causing misery to others and shame
to myself.

Saint Ambrose

It was desperation. I was taking my six children to the local
pet store on a day off from school. Why? Because it was close
to home and free. My children had been begging for a pet.
As I was barely maintaining sanity while caring for humans,
a pet was not an option, but I was hoping that perhaps they
would enjoy looking at hamsters safe in their homes. Perhaps
I dared to hope for a half-hour of entertainment on a long
winter's day.

As we got into the minivan, my oldest, age eight, loudly
decided that she didn't want to go. Her younger siblings
jumped on the bandwagon. My feelings of defeat quickly
turned to anger. It wasn't a great plan, but I was trying. As
we drove, I colorfully expressed my frustration using words
such as "immature" and "ungrateful." There were lots of
tears, but we arrived.

As six happy faces watched the mice in fascination, my
momentary joy turned back to anger . . . at myself. I had
achieved my goal but at what cost to their little eyes and ears?
Would they remember the fun or Mom's meltdown? What
kind of model am I to my children?

As we were watching the cats up for adoption (and I
hoped they weren't getting any ideas), my daughter apolo-
gized. I don't have the best track record of biting my tongue

when I am overwhelmed, but I do (often) ask for forgiveness. Perhaps this is what they are learning!

One can hope. And we arrived home with just the original seven of us—a victory.

Jesus, help me to forgive myself first.

To Ponder: How can you keep the peace when you are doing your best but others aren't appreciating your efforts?

TRISH BOLSTER

APRIL 5

Begin Again

Remember, every saint had a past and every sinner
has a future.

Bishop Robert Barron

Every spring, a beautiful miracle occurs. Green seeps back into the grass, the first bright flower heads poke out from under their ground covers, warm winds dance through the land, and rumbly storm clouds awaken the hibernating world with their invigorating rains.

While the winter winds howled, the seeds of spring quietly simmered underground, growing, waiting. The liturgical season of Lent is a contemplative hibernation of sorts. We detach in order to allow our souls to rest while the Holy Spirit plants his seeds in us, waiting, hoping.

Easter marks a springtime for our souls as we awaken from our Lenten slumber, refreshed and renewed. We have withstood the purification of Lent and are ready to renew our commitment to live in loving service with Christ.

In this time of renewal, we have the chance to begin again. Our souls have been cleansed, tested, and purified. We walked the path of Calvary and bore the cross with Christ, and now we are ready to "stand up, take your mat, and walk" (Jn 5:8). Every day, we are given this opportunity for renewal as we fall over and over again. Yet Christ continuously encourages us to get up and try, try again. Likewise, we must extend this same mercy to others, remembering that we too are given many chances for improvement and that we are all a work in progress.

Holy Spirit, as the spring rains give life to the land, pour down your grace on me and renew in me a pure heart. When I fall, give me your strength to get back up and begin again.

To Ponder: How will you renew yourself to Christ, your spouse, and your family?

ERIKA MARIE

APRIL 6

A Springtime Renewal of Heart

The goal of our spiritual life is to become a new person in Christ. It is not enough just to be a "good person" or to be "nice." We are called to be saints.

Father James Farfaglia

I love the way Easter comes just as spring is beginning. Emerging from the winter of Lent, the liturgical celebrations call for a newness of heart and spiritual renewal while all around you the landscape bursts with color and new life.

In the parish where I worked as RCIA director there was a large flowering shrub near the side entrance of the church. Like clockwork, it bloomed every year just before Easter. As the RCIA candidates and I walked from the parish center to the church preparing for the Easter Vigil, we were greeted by the sweet fragrance of its blossoms. It was a reminder of life emerging from dormancy, a metaphor of the spiritual renewal the candidates would experience by joining the Church.

Easter is a time of renewal for the whole Church. Like Lazarus, Jesus calls us out of spiritual tombs where we lie dead, wrapped in the burial clothing of our sin. But Jesus is not a resuscitated corpse like Lazarus, he is a new kind of man—divinely charged, Spirit-infused. At Easter, we are invited to become that same kind of new person, someone infused with the Holy Spirit and operating from that vital center where God dwells in our hearts.

Lord, create a new person in me. Resurrect me from the tomb of my sin and help me to live through you.

To Ponder: What is holding you back from living a new life in union with the resurrected Christ? What is holding you in the tomb and preventing you from experiencing renewal?
MARC CARDARONELLA

Today's Good News

Jesus wants evangelizers who proclaim the Good News not only with words, but above all by a life transfigured by God's presence.

Pope Francis, Evangelii Gaudium

Who is on God's list of people for you to evangelize today? Pope Francis encourages us to proclaim God's Word by the way we live. You can allow God to be God, living in your heart and working through you wherever you are, or you can do the sidestep dance and be miserable.

Do you know that when you read scripture and pray you are in God's presence, where he can transform you more and more into his image? What will be your response today during the trials of sickness, financial worries, children acting out, and the overwhelming minute-by-minute demands of motherhood? Are you tempted to focus on yourself? Your needs? Or is the Holy Spirit inspiring you to become the good news?

In the midst of today's battle, whatever the struggle, respond by choosing to trust God. Tell him that today you are going to trust in his great love. Tell him you desire to live in his presence so he can transform you. Persevere in proclaiming to him, yourself, and everyone around who he is to you by the way you live today. Let his loving presence overflow from within you. Allow him to live, act, breathe, see, and do through you and your little spot on earth.

Lord, give me the grace to see your Holy Spirit at work in the little ways of my life. Help me cooperate with the Spirit in every little way so that today I can live out God's purpose of why I'm here.

To Ponder: What's the next thing you can do to become the good news today?

NANCY H. C. WARD

APRIL 8
SAINT JULIE BILLIART

Bringing It to God

One should fear nothing, but trust in the Lord. Let us leave all to the good God. He will draw us out of our difficulties if it is his will.

Saint Julie Billiart

Kneeling before Jesus in the Blessed Sacrament, my head bowed and my heart filled with anxiety, I prayed. There were many thoughts racing forward, vying to be heard. We were just weeks from flying to China to bring home our daughter, and there were still so many loose ends. The paperwork, packing, and schedules for our sons, while cumbersome, were all within my power to complete. The travel expenses, however, loomed out of my control.

Even after twenty years of marriage, we did not enjoy financial stability. A combination of marrying young with no sound instruction on managing a budget, accumulating a mountain of debt, and staying at home with my kids without accounting for the lower income had left us financially strapped. The tears softly rolled, each a prayer for assistance or at the very least peace in this seemingly impossible and dire situation.

Suddenly, I felt a touch on my shoulder and something slipped into my hand. I turned to see an acquaintance exiting the church. In my hand was over a hundred dollars. Although the money did not cover the impending bill, that moment Jesus revealed that he was listening and that it would all work out. Regardless of the outcome, we were being called to trust and not worry.

Jesus, I love that I can come to you in the Eucharist.

To Ponder: What prayer looms heavy on your heart? Which one feels impossible and causes you to lose sleep? Have you considered bringing it and all your worries, anxieties, and poverties to Jesus in the Eucharist?

ALLISON GINGRAS

APRIL 9

Healing Our Sight

It is I. Do not be afraid.

John 6:20

When I shared with my spiritual director about the various "storms" that had recently erupted in my heart—kids, parents, the world, taxes—she suggested that I meditate upon Jesus walking on the water in the midst of the storm.

Reading each Gospel account of the story, I was struck by the fact that as Jesus came closer to his disciples, they began to be afraid (Jn 6:19). Exhausted from rowing against the wind in the darkness, they lost sight of reality and mistook Jesus for a ghost. Even after Jesus commanded Peter to walk on water, the apostle was swamped with fear. "O you of little faith," Jesus responded (Mt 14:31).

Faith is more than simply believing in God; it is the ability to see God and reality as they truly are. Faith empowers us to perceive our lives through the lens of God's perspective, trusting that God is for us, with us, right beside us. Jesus told the terrified disciples: "It is I." Translated literally as "I am," this name of God means, among other things, "I am here standing by, ready to be of assistance."

When we're focused on real or imaginary ghosts, the remedy for our little faith is the healing of our sight. What we need is the grace to see reality through God's eyes, so we may catch a clear glimpse of the Lord who is right next to us, ready to save us.

Jesus, increase my faith and help me to clearly see you beside me in the midst of every storm.

To Ponder: What storm are you facing now that is clouding your vision of Jesus? What might this situation look like from God's perspective?

JUDY LANDRIEU KLEIN, M.T.S.

Renewing Ourselves through Our Relationships with One Another

The ultimate purpose of marriage is not to make us
happy but to glorify God.

Nancy Leigh DeMoss

Evangelization cannot happen outside of a face-to-face
encounter because evangelization ultimately happens
through a lasting, loving relationship. Our bishop was speaking to the DREs of our diocese, but I couldn't help but see
the connection ten-fold in the margins of marriage and in
the folds of family.

Marriage allows closeness and flexibility between the
people involved in a relationship. It also helps us to intentionally balance our lives. Married couples must balance the
"I" and the "we." They balance the time apart and the time
together and must balance the separateness and the connectedness of their relationship.

They reconnect. They renew. They recommit. They do
this daily through Christ because Christ is the perfect family. It is in his guidance that we are made whole, that we
are made one. Outside of him we are all separate people in
search of completeness. Proverbs 16:3 reminds us that we will

only find success when our plans are committed to the Lord. That's a good curve for us all to follow.

We are uniquely individual, and specific help must be given specifically per couple. That is where our prayers, our goals, our conversations, and our relationships have to be intentional and specific.

Dear Father, remind me daily to be perfect as you are perfect. Remind me daily that outside of you, we are incomplete. Remind me that we can only succeed and bring our family to heaven through our relationships with one another.

To Ponder: Do you look to scripture to help you set the bar and move toward heaven as the goal for you and your spouse? Where have you allowed yourself to become sidetracked while moving toward the rewards he has promised you?

CAY GIBSON

APRIL 11

Giving Grace Away

I could easily have created men possessed of all that they should need for both body and soul, but I wish that one should need each other and that they should be my ministers to administer the graces and gifts that they have received from me.

Saint Catherine of Siena, The Dialogue

Throughout time, God has been telling us we need other people. We need others so we can give to them what God has given us. For many of us, the primary person we give to is our spouse. I have had a spouse much longer than I have not had a spouse. We have raised our children and, most days, life is wonderful. But there are other days when I need to remember all God has given me so I can give that to my spouse instead of the caustic comment, careless shrug, or uncensored scream.

It isn't easy, this giving to others. It's easier to take from God and keep it for ourselves; we need it to deal with our own troubles. But if I love God as much as I profess, then I am compelled to give the grace away. And I can, knowing that there is more grace, because as much as I love God, his love for me is immeasurable. His grace is poured out for us when we ask. I often ask for the grace to give whatever God wants me to give to others.

Father, thank you for all those in my life you have given me to minister to, especially my spouse, family, and friends.

To Ponder: How do you give to others what God has given you? Who needs you to share God's grace with them in a more tangible way?

DEANNA BARTALINI

Passing Down a Sacred Ritual

This is why the work of family is worth going through. There are moments of grace and satisfaction too deep for words.

Jon Carroll, "Without a Net"

My daughter Meredith gave me a most unexpected gift on Mother's Day.

Mother's Day had become problematic since I lost my mother. My mom and I had shared a special ritual of visiting the beautiful and historic Mount Auburn Cemetery in Cambridge, Massachusetts, to take in the spring migration of colorful songbirds and to view the flowers. Meredith had never expressed any interest in birds, but she is the keeper of the flame when it comes to family tradition. For Mother's Day, she took me to Mount Auburn where we savored memories of Grandma.

We happened upon a robin's nest full of little ones. There were several turtles at Willow Pond sunning themselves, including a baby on top of its mother. A tom turkey, all fluffed and fanned out, strutted his stuff in front of three females. He was fat and haughty-looking and the ladies paid him no mind at all. We took time to read the gravestones. They told stories of families of old, which fascinated Meredith. She does not find death to be morbid; she is blessed in that way.

Her gift to me took effort and sacrifice. The sacred ritual of visiting Mount Auburn has successfully passed from mother to daughter to granddaughter. To share that observance together was the greatest gift of all.

Thank you, Lord, for family tradition that keeps a mother alive through the thoughtfulness of a daughter. Thank you for the special, ongoing love of family.

To Ponder: What steps can you take to keep family traditions alive?

SUSAN BAILEY

APRIL 13

God's in Charge

The greatest blessing of prayer is not receiving the answer, but being the kind of person God can trust with his answer.

Anonymous

When my husband was diagnosed with leukemia, our youngest child was only seven months old and no one was prepared for what the next four years would entail. But even from the first day, my husband's level of acceptance was astonishing. His words to the doctor were, "God's in charge." His implicit faith that God would take care of everything did a great deal to calm my worried soul as we journeyed through months of chemotherapy, a year of recovery, the eventual relapse, a bone-marrow transplant, rejection, and the horror of watching his body deteriorate. No matter what, John would tell people, "I am doing great." For him, as long as God was "in charge," he was doing great.

It took me time to see it his way. On the night before he died, John accidentally spilled his medicine all over the floor. Usually when I tried to help, he would refuse because he wanted to "do things for himself." But this night, he just smiled and shook his head. We picked the pills up off the floor together. At that moment I remember thinking, "God, you've made him a saint. His humility is awesome."

Now as I think back to all that we suffered, and all the laughs we managed to have in the midst of it all, I realize that John was right. God is always in charge if we let him be.

God, help me be humble enough to accept that you are in charge.

To Ponder: Do you trust God with the answer to your prayers—especially if they aren't the answers you want?

A. K. FRAILEY

APRIL 14

Perseverance Changes Me

No matter how long the winter, spring is sure to follow.

Proverb

Sitting in the quiet chapel, I felt tired and discouraged. "This is not how I want things to be, Lord," I prayed silently. "What am I doing wrong?"

This had been my prayer for so long. It felt like a never-ending winter with no sign of spring.

What am I doing wrong? Why do I feel so dry, stuck, and hopeless?

I opened my bible to Luke 18:1–8. The parable is about a widow who pleas to a judge to be cleared of her difficulties. The judge grants her request, so she stops bothering him. Otherwise, he is afraid she will wear him out.

As I meditated on this parable, God responded to my own begging plea of "What am I doing wrong?"

In this parable, Jesus teaches about persevering in prayer. When we pray like the widow—with faith, confidence, and perseverance—God hears us and acts swiftly. It might not feel like God acts swiftly. But the message of perseverance is a hopeful one: to persevere means to continue, and to continue means to have already started. Thus, when God asks us to persevere, it means that we are already on the right track.

I wasn't doing anything wrong. God was just asking me to persevere. And so I did.

While my life wasn't magically transformed, I noticed things differently. I began to see little green buds on once barren trees. Perseverance doesn't change our surroundings; it changes us and brings hope. And hope changes everything.

Thank you, Lord, for answering my prayers, maybe not in the way I expected but in the way that was best for me.

To Ponder: Recall a time when you felt stuck. How did God help you through it?

SARAH DAMM

The Super Glue of Renewal

Forgiveness says you are given another chance to
make a new beginning.

Desmond Tutu

Renew: to make new or as if new again. To restore.

I know a woman who could renew or restore anything.
She was my grandmother. In her pocket was a tube of Super
Glue just in case she found anything broken in her house: a
china cup with a broken handle, the bead off a piece of jew-
elry, or a crack in the frame of a picture. But she was a fixer
of people as well as things. She was a healer of hearts. How
did she do it? Well, for people, it wasn't with Super Glue. It
was with forgiveness.

Each of us has something to forgive because people hurt
us, even those who profess to love us. We must let go of our
hurts, from an act of infidelity, prejudice, loss of a job, or just
plain meanness of another person. But we also have something to be forgiven for. So we must first look at ourselves,
at the ways we have hurt others, too. Until this is done, our
renewal is not really possible. Forgiveness works both ways.

*Jesus, help me to see that I must forgive others before I can expect
to receive forgiveness myself.*

To Ponder: Will you commit to forgive someone who's hurt you
in order to bring about your own new beginning and renewal?

KAYE PARK HINCKLEY

Embracing Limitations

My job is only to inform, not to convince.

Saint Bernadette Soubirous

It's difficult to imagine a saint who had more activity swirling all around her than Saint Bernadette Soubirous. French authorities, both religious and civil, were so gobsmacked that God would use such a small, sickly, and uneducated girl to both validate the dogma of the Immaculate Conception and open a healing spring that they questioned her repeatedly, trying to discern any changes to her testimony. Through it all, and while enduring gawking crowds and people intruding upon her personal life for a word or a blessing, Bernadette managed to keep both her serenity and her sense of humor. When a postulant within the convent asked to be shown its most famous daughter only to look upon the diminutive, slightly hunched Bernadette, the postulant gasped in revulsion and asked, "What, *that*?" At which Bernadette laughed and agreed, "Yes, *only* this!" Asked to explain a tricky point of dogmatic theology to investigators, Bernadette showcased both her humility and her dignity by not trying to jump through their hoops or to do more than she reasonably could. "My job is only to inform, not to convince," she said.

By understanding her limitations and refusing to judge herself for not meeting everyone's expectations, Bernadette sustained her own peace, and also protected herself from taking on the stress or demands of others.

Dearest Bernadette, please be with me when I am overwhelmed by demands and trying too hard to please everyone but God.

To Ponder: How often do you take on more than you know you can handle, as people jockey for your time? Can you allow yourself to admit to having realistic limitations without feeling like that means you have failed?

ELIZABETH SCALIA

APRIL 17

Prayer Time at the Family Zoo

It is not particularly difficult to find thousands who will spend two or three hours a day in exercising, but if you ask them to bend their knees to God in five minutes of prayer, they protest that it is too long.

Venerable Fulton J. Sheen

Paint yourself a mental picture: my spouse arrives home an hour after he promised because of a work "emergency." The dinner bomb that detonated in the kitchen is almost cleaned but impeded by little kids doing laps. The two oldest children are supposed to be finishing their homework but so far all they've done is regale me with tales of Why Their Lives Are *Awful*. The baby is screeching for his bottle and his bed.

I want to go hide in the bathroom (sometimes, I actually choose this route), but tonight, I've committed to the Rosary.

I sling Baby Grouchy Pants over my hip, grab our candle and the Rosaries, and hand out the beads. I quell the rising argument between the four- and six-year-olds over the pink versus purple Rosaries. Then I sit between the two older siblings elbowing each other for space on the couch.

Once we have Rosaries, I wait for them.

Just because we are praying doesn't mean the bickering stops. But as the children's voices begin to repeat the words to the Hail Mary and the candlelight flickers against the darkness, the small gathering in my living room reminds me of the larger family I find in the Catholic Church: a big, broken family, who despite individual personalities, hurts, and flaws, is united together in him, the wounded Body of Christ.

Mother Mary, help me to persevere during family prayer time and to refrain from discouragement. Help me remember the Catholic Church is a reflection of my own family: an imperfect group of people who desire to follow your Son.

To Ponder: What discourages you the most when you think about family prayer? How can you adjust your expectations? Have you been hurt in the Catholic Church? How?

COLLEEN MURPHY DUGGAN

APRIL 18

Unforeseen Grace

By the grace of God, I am what I am.

1 Corinthians 15:10

God has blessed me with three sons. The first spring they were all old enough to play baseball I took all three schedules, laid them out on the floor, and melted down. Short of bilocation, how in the world were we going to be present at all these games and practices? Thankfully, my husband, calm and confident, assured me it would all work out. It was a lesson in trust, and in the knowledge that I can't "do it all" by myself. We realized we would not make every game, and that was going to be okay. We would be present to as many as we could and then rejoice in the unforeseen grace that our sons would be growing in independence as well. Our family finished the season renewed.

In nature, God gives us spring as a time of great renewal. New growth bursts forth from the dead of winter. Animals rise from hibernation and birds return in joyful song. God is calling our humanity to be in a constant state of renewal as well. The graces received as a result of our salvation have just been renewed at Easter. Jesus is alive and renewing daily life. Even when we are facing challenges as big as stones rolled in front of tombs, his power, grace, and love bring the fragrance of a virtuous life. We cannot do it on our own. We must rely on the power he has that has conquered death. United with him on the cross, we experience the glory of the Resurrection.

Jesus, Lord of life, transform life's challenges into renewed life through your grace.

To Ponder: What life challenge are you facing? How can you see this as unforeseen grace and an invitation to the power of the Resurrection?

CINDY COSTELLO

I Am Me

You formed my inmost being; you knit me in my
mother's womb. I praise you, so wonderfully you
made me; wonderful are your works!

Psalm 139:13–14

My three-year-old loves to wear fancy dresses, and she used
to be happy when she got herself all dressed up and I told
her she looked like a beautiful princess. Until she learned
that queens outrank princesses. Then she only wanted to
be called a queen. But old habits die hard, and sometimes
I still inadvertently call her a "princess" in an occasional
slip of the tongue. So it was one morning when Her Maj-
esty donned her Easter dress in July and sashayed into the
living room, spinning grandly and admiring the twirl of her
pleated skirts. "You look like a beautiful princess!" I told her.
"No," she replied with disdain, "I don't." "Oh, I'm sorry," I
corrected myself, "a beautiful queen!" "No!" she answered,
"I'm more beautiful than either!" Then, after a pause, she
added: "I'm me!"

Mind you, this is at three years old. Sixteen should be
interesting. But she is right. And if she can keep that attitude,
remembering to be "me" instead of someone else, all will be
well—even at sixteen. After all, each of us is one of a kind,
handmade specially by God, unique and irreplaceable, never
before known in the universe and never to be seen again. If
we won't be ourselves, then who will? Who even could? But
allowing ourselves to flourish as the person God created us
to be? Now *that* is truly beautiful.

Let me appreciate your handiwork, Lord, in myself and in those around me today.

To Ponder: Have you been comparing yourself to others, trying to be someone else? What can you do to more fully embrace who you are, perhaps by using your unique gifts and interests to do something for your family or others?

JAKE FROST

APRIL 20

The Poisonous Stew of Resentment

I really only love God as much as I love the person I love the least.

Dorothy Day

"Where is she?"

It was Saturday morning, and I was waiting for my sitter, a college student, to show up so I could leave for work.

"She must be at a friend's house," I grumbled, "sleeping in after a night of fun."

Hours passed, but there was no sign of her. On the outside I was mostly collected and philosophic about my unexpected change of plans, but in my mind the courtroom was in session. *Perhaps* she was hurt or otherwise incapacitated—Rhonda the Judge could *admit* the possibility—but it was so much more satisfying to review, again and again, the brilliant scolding speeches I'd unleash when she finally showed up, tail between her legs.

Around six p.m. she phoned. She had been in the hospital.

And clear as day, I saw the utter futility of stewing in resentment. Our Lord's words came to mind: *judge not, lest ye be judged.*

The Lord has shown me, again and again, that resentment is the heart's poison, but I cannot purge this poison on my own. The Holy Spirit himself is its antidote. He bestows charity and generosity if we're humble and willing to be changed.

Lord, help me to live your command to love my neighbor as myself. Grant me a charitable heart that wills the best for others.

To Ponder: Is there a person against whom you hold a grudge? What practical steps can you take toward forgiving him or her?

RHONDA ORTIZ

APRIL 21

The Prayer before Our Eyes

I am deeply convinced that the necessity to pray, and to pray unceasingly, is not so much based on our desire for God, as on God's desire for us. It is God's passionate pursuit of us that calls us to prayer.

Henri Nouwen, The Only Necessary Thing

My two oldest boys are in the sweet stage of childhood where they love to climb into bed with us and cuddle every morning. I know this is a fast and fleeting phase, so I try to savor it (even as the very cells of my body scream out for *five more minutes of sleep, please!*).

But beyond longing for more rest, I've also had to shift my expectations for morning prayer. Once they started snuggling under my comforter, I couldn't curl up with my favorite psalms or the day's Gospel uninterrupted. No longer do I have five minutes of peace to pray alone when I first awake.

So now I am relearning to pray with my kids beside me, as I did when they were babies in my arms at dawn. I invite them to pray with me—"Good morning, dear Jesus, this day is for you. And I ask you to bless all I think, say, and do." Or I pray silently for all of us: "This is the day the Lord has made. Let us rejoice and be glad in it."

My morning visitors remind me not to mistake my plans for prayer with God's plan unfolding right before my eyes.

God of the new day, let me greet this morning with love. Help me see your invitation to prayer in each moment offered to me today.

To Ponder: How can you start your day in prayer, even if peace and quiet are hard to find?

LAURA KELLY FANUCCI

Reverence for God's Creation

Nature is full of divinity.

Henry David Thoreau

Long before Lady Gaga came on the scene, I was cared for by a remarkable woman whom my siblings nicknamed Gaga. Born almost a hundred years ago in rural China, Gaga left the tiny patch of land that was her family's livelihood and worked as a servant girl at the age of nine when her father passed away from tuberculosis. Every morning as her first act of the day, she would face the open window of our kitchen, kneel to offer a deep bow, and present two sticks of incense, the equivalent of lighting a candle today. She did so to thank the heaven and the earth.

Deep reverence and boundless gratitude overflowed from this simple and humble act. Despite not being rich in material ways, Gaga felt the shelter of the heaven and the earth, the Creator and the creation, inseparable and both part of her life and sustenance.

Where does reverence come from? It emanates when we behold something noble, something good, something holy. Even though Gaga did not know the book of Genesis, she intuitively knew Genesis: God's gift of creation for us, his breath that animates it, his indwelling, all this to sustain us, body and soul. In our culture, reverence has to be cultivated and find its way back to our routines, the way we think, and the way we act. All faiths point to the union of the Creator and creation; we know this but we do not live it. When we honor God's gift, we honor God.

Lord, in the words of Pope Francis, help us "be protectors of creation, protectors of God's plan inscribed in nature, protectors of one another and of the environment."

To Ponder: How can you honor God today? What act of reverence might you perform or begin?

DR. CAROLYN Y. WOO

APRIL 23
SAINT GEORGE

Courage to Face Dragons

The Fairy Queen has sent you to do brave deeds in this world. That High City that you see is in another world. Before you climb the path to it and hang your shield on its wall, go down into the valley and fight the dragon that you were sent to fight.

Margaret Hodges, Saint George and the Dragon

Today's the feast day of Saint George, a soldier in the Roman Emperor Diocletian's army. During Diocletian's persecution of Christians, Saint George presented himself to the emperor as a Christian and refused the emperor's bribes to sacrifice to pagan gods. He was tortured and martyred, and his courageous witness to the faith won over many souls. Saint George eventually became the patron saint of England, and Margaret Hodges's *Saint George and the Dragon*, handed down from medieval times, tells the legend of how Saint George slew a fiery dragon that had taken a village captive.

With the graces of Lent and Easter, warmer weather, and blooming flora, spring is a time of renewal of strength and courage to take on the challenges in our lives. Many of those challenges might be ones that we share with our spouse. Difficulties with money, children, and intimacy are common stressors in a marriage. Turn to Saint George and slay these dragons with the firm foundation of God's Word and faith.

Saint George, please pray for my courage in discussing with my spouse any contentious issue in our marriage.

To Ponder: What dragon in your life are you being called to slay? How can you ask your spouse for help so that you can battle the problem together instead of battling each other?

MEG MATENAER

APRIL 24

Taking Refuge in the Lord

Whoever requires bodily rest should take a breathing space in her room. And when no outer rest whatever is attainable, when there is no place in which to retreat . . . she must for a moment seal off herself inwardly against all other things and take refuge in the Lord. He is indeed there and can give us in a single moment what we need.

Saint Teresa Benedicta of the Cross

When my children were very young even Mass seemed to offer no reprieve. At an evening service one year I brought my two little ones to the staffed church nursery, certain I'd carved out space to commune with God at last. But when I heard the familiar squeal and looked back to see my rambunctious three-year-old freshly escaped from confinement running toward me, feelings of utter defeat and quiet tears came. Why did seeking God when I felt so desperate for him seem so insurmountable? If only I'd had Saint Teresa's words at my disposal then. Even now, I welcome them as water to one parched. To realize that I can, at any point in my day, "seal off myself" for a moment to be with the only One who can provide true refreshment brings such glad relief.

Dear Lord, you are everywhere, and you long to give me rest even more than I yearn for it. You alone quench my deepest thirst. Thank you for your endless provisions that have such power to revive my weary body and soul.

To Ponder: Imagine yourself turning now to the Lord for a need. What is it you thirst for this moment? What is it that he wants to give you this day? Allow him to replenish you.

ROXANE B. SALONEN

Mark's Mom

> When my kids become wild and unruly, I use a nice
> safe playpen. When they're finished, I climb out.

Erma Bombeck

Parenthood is less a ride on a carousel and more a ride on
a roller coaster; it is predictably unpredictable, exhilarat-
ing yet exhausting. The harder you clean, the more clutter
appears. As your energy decreases, theirs increases. It's not
until you're on the phone that anyone ever "really needs
yoooooooouuuuuuuu."

Still, amid the moments of chaos and insanity, you do
your best to introduce those souls most precious to you to
the only One who perfectly loves you.

Today we celebrate Saint Mark: evangelist, martyr, and
traveling companion to both Saints Peter and Paul. Though
not one of the original twelve apostles, it was actually at Saint
Mark's mother's house where the apostles would meet in
Jerusalem (Acts 12:12) and where they may have gathered
for the Last Supper and Pentecost.

About Mark's mother we know very little, yet had she
not been such a loyal and zealous follower of Christ, do you
think we'd be talking about Mark today? Would he have
written a gospel? Would he have followed Jesus to his death?
Most likely not.

Saint Mark's mother hosted God for a dinner party, har-
bored his closest followers during their persecution (Acts
12), and raised her own son to seek the Lord. She could never

have predicted how things would turn out, so she turned in and focused on loving the Lord with her whole heart; that made all the difference. Without this holy mother, we might only have three gospels. Thank God for mothers.

Lord, help me to trust that my own example of seeking you will, over time, translate to my children as well.

To Ponder: When everything is going well, what impetus is there to change or grow or improve? Do you spend more time "teaching" your children the faith or embodying it? Spend extra time hugging your kids today.

MARK HART

APRIL 26

Fasting in the Desert

And remember, I am with you always, to the end of the age.

Matthew 28:20b

I did not seem to have any kind of Lenten plan. My prayer was dry. I could not decide on any kind of fasting other than fasting from meat on Fridays. Even almsgiving seemed to be an issue.

I don't know what it was. I don't know if it had to do with depression and continued grief over the loss of my sister or if it had to do with the stress of being so busy at work and having no energy. I was just feeling blah about everything. I even had trouble writing. There was just no inspiration.

There was no music, no song in my heart. Everything dried up. I was in the desert.

But then, slowly, as Easter came closer, I could sense that things were changing. Slowly. Quietly. God was working in me, calling to me, nudging me, reminding me of his everlasting presence.

I found myself praying more. I sat in silence more. I listened more. I again sensed the nearness of God, the love of God.

Then one day the waiting was over. I heard the music again. I sensed new life. The tomb opened.

Resurrection.

Dear Lord, help me to trust that you are with me always, that I am never alone. Help me to know that no matter what I am going through, Easter is coming.

To Ponder: How do you get through those "tomb" times? Do you trust God is with you even when you do not sense his presence? In what ways do you see God in your everyday life?

COLLEEN SPIRO

APRIL 27
SAINT ZITA

No Good Deed Goes Unfinished

Angels can fly because they can take themselves lightly.

G. K. Chesterton, Orthodoxy

Chesterton says angels can fly because they are unburdened by pride and selfishness. Their self-forgetfulness defies gravity, allowing them to soar.

Thinking of others is good for us. Helping someone who needs us can lighten the heaviness of our thoughts and obligations. We may not be as light as angels, but at least we're watching our weight.

Today's saint is Saint Zita, a medieval Italian woman who worked as a servant in a wealthy household. Despite her poverty and servitude, Zita was constantly mindful of the needy. One story suggests Zita neglected her baking duties one day in order to visit someone in need. Her fellow servants ratted Zita out, but when the family came to the kitchen to punish the wayward girl, they saw delicious loaves being baked—by angels.

It's difficult to tell how factual that story is, but here's the truth of it: God's angels assist us every day. They "take themselves lightly," concerned only with serving God by serving us.

A friend of mine passed on a prayer tradition that I eagerly adopted: when people ask her for prayers, she stops what she's doing to pray immediately for that person; then she asks her angel *to keep* praying. Ask the angels to pray Psalm 104 with you.

Bless the Lord, O you his angels,
you mighty ones who do his bidding,
obedient to his spoken word. . . .
Bless the Lord, O my soul.

To Ponder: The Bible is full of references to angels, yet we often forget their powerful attentiveness. Wouldn't it be fascinating to start some conversations about angels? How many friends or strangers are waiting to tell us about God's mighty messengers?

GRACE MAZZA URBANSKI

APRIL 28

Making Good Memories of the Everyday

Sometimes I stop to think, now, that every day we are making memories. And I wonder whether I make happy memories enough for my own child. I feel sure that if families would be conscious of the fact that everything they do or say may one day be a memory, there would be less quarreling, fewer harsh words spoken. It is nice to be right, but better to be remembered pleasantly.

Gladys Taber, The Book of Stillmeadow

Recently, I had an epiphany. I realized that if you were to make a pie chart of everything I say to my kids in the course of a day, there would be a hefty percentage of "don'ts," a huge wedge of "why did yous," and a significant chunk of nagging reminders.

Comments like these are inevitable when you're a parent. All the same, I realized that other kinds of comments—words of praise when the boys do something sweet, thoughtful questions about their day at school, invitations to notice the beauty of the morning sky or to smell the cinnamon jar I've just opened—deserve to be a much larger piece of the pie.

My kids won't be young forever. Years from now, this day—this regular, plain old day—will be a memory for them. I want to make it a good one.

Loving God, remind me that kind words cost nothing but give so much.

To Ponder: How many positive statements did you make to your kids today? Take some time to review the day and reflect. If you want to do better, write yourself a little note and leave it in a place where you'll see it tomorrow.

GINNY KUBITZ MOYER

APRIL 29
SAINT CATHERINE OF SIENA

Discerning God

Be who God meant you to be and you will set the world on fire.

Saint Catherine of Siena

Have you ever seen a horse with blinders attached to his harness? Those are the little flaps of leather that keep a horse from seeing what is behind him. You frequently see them on race horses or other horses that are easily distracted. When the blinders are in place, the horse is better able to focus on what he is supposed to be doing.

Some mental blinders would be great, wouldn't they? God has made you (and your family) unique. There has not and will not be anyone exactly like you. Yet we are all made in God's image, and God has put you on earth to love him and serve him.

How are we supposed to know how to serve him? We have to put on blinders of our own, in some ways, continuing to look forward to what you're supposed to be doing and not to the past, to what you've done (wrong or otherwise). Talk to God. *Listen* for a response. Pray that you do his will. Finally, check the fruits of your decision—are your words, deeds, and actions having a good response?

Dear Lord, thank you for the blessings you have provided in my life. Please reveal your will for my life and give me the courage to follow your calling. Show your divine will to all those who seek it and help those who do not know your name but heed your call anyway.

To Ponder: Do you feel stressed, harried, or out of sorts with life? The yoke is easy and the burden is light when you are doing God's will. If you are not finding joy in your life, perhaps it is time for some change. Look up some resources or articles on Ignatian spirituality and discernment to guide you.

JEN STEED

APRIL 30

By Your Grace

God is not accustomed to refusing a good gift to those who ask for one.

Saint Ambrose

Right after we adopted our first baby I would take her with me to my weekly holy hour. She was only about two weeks old when I knelt down right in front of the monstrance and lifted her up directly in front of Jesus in the Blessed Sacrament and asked him to heal everything that might be in need of healing in her. I continued to take Maria with me to the chapel each week. An older fellow by the name of Joe had the hour right after mine, and he would come in and coo at Maria and rejoice with me that she had entered our lives. One week we had a conversation about her name. He told me it was a wonderful name and that his niece was also named Maria.

The following week, I had Maria with me again, and I said this prayer: "Lord, please keep her always in your light. Never let her stray from you." Suddenly I realized the immensity of what I was asking and said, "By your grace, Lord. I know it can only happen by your grace."

Just then Joe came in, and said, "Awww, how is little Grace today? Oh, wait a minute. Her name's not Grace. It's Maria. Little Maria Grace."

Now, Grace is not her middle name, but I hang on tight to that promise as a priceless gift to a mother's heart.

Dear Lord, may we always remember that you never forget your promises.

To Ponder: Are there times in your life when you have doubted God's faithfulness? What is at the root of that doubt?

SHERRY BOAS

May

THEME: CALM IN THE CHAOS

SAINT JOSEPH THE WORKER

Joseph's Example

Joseph of Nazareth is a "just man" because he
totally "lives by faith." He is holy because his faith is
truly heroic.

Saint John Paul II

We know so little about Saint Joseph, yet without his presence, undoubtedly Jesus's life would not have been the same. Scriptures paint the portrait of a foster-father who protected his loved ones at all costs and with very little fanfare.

Today, we recognize Joseph as the patron of our labors. When I ponder the life and spiritual legacy of Saint Joseph, my thoughts turn to my husband, Greg. While I often grow frenzied and frazzled as my to-do list grows, my husband is a calming presence and a consistent provider for our family. I'm quick to boastfully share my projects; Greg—like Jesus's earthly father—toils through a consistently long project list with no thought of sharing it on Instagram for a quick pat on the back. While I have a tendency to forget to offer my labors as prayer, Greg is not only reliable in the work he does but also modest and sincere.

My relationship with the "worker" in my own home makes it easy for me to understand and appreciate the huge role that Saint Joseph played as a spiritual anchor in the lives of the Holy Family.

Saint Joseph, patron of workers, help me to cope with the busyness of my days. May I offer the fruits of my labor as you did, faithfully and out of love for Our Lord.

To Ponder: How can you change your attitude toward some of your more routine housework to turn your labors into prayer?

LISA M. HENDEY

MAY 2

Keeping Focus on What's Important

Therefore be attentive to yourself, that you may be attentive to God.

Saint Basil

Walking me home from school one day, Mom paused at a street corner to scrutinize her shopping list. Satisfied that all items had been purchased, she dropped the list into the corner sewer. Mom started to walk away and then realized that the shopping list she thought she'd discarded was still in her hand. What wasn't in her hand was the twenty-dollar bill that she'd also been holding, and which, in a case of mistaken identity, she had dropped into the sewer.

Mom's crescendo of panic began. "What are we going to do?" she raved, wringing her hands.

I knew what *I* was going to do. I was going to die. What other option was there for an adolescent girl whose mother was creating a public scene?

Then my tall, charming classmate Freddie sauntered around the corner. If I was going to die, I had to do it fast.

"Hi, Mrs. L.! Hi, Celeste!"

Drat. I hadn't been fast enough.

"Oh, Freddie!" wailed Mom. "My twenty-dollar bill fell in the sewer!"

Good Catholic boy that he was, Freddie dropped to his parochial-school-uniformed knees, put his hand into the mouth of the sewer, and fumbled around on a slimy, dark underground ledge until he'd managed to grasp the bill. Freddie handed it to my mom, who rewarded him with a dollar: enough to cover the dry-cleaning charge for his uniform pants.

Jesus, help me to avoid confusion by being purposeful in my actions.

To Ponder: In the daily frenzy, we moms can lose focus even while we reprimand our children for "not paying attention." Practicing mindfulness fosters serenity and nurtures the spirit. Is a small, inner voice telling you to "pay attention"? Are you listening?

CELESTE BEHE

MAY 3

Hearing God's Voice

In the silence of the heart, God speaks. If you face God in prayer and silence, God will speak to you.

Saint Teresa of Calcutta, In the Heart of the World

Today is my youngest child's birthday. This handsome young man might not have been conceived, let alone born. In 1993, when our third son was ten months old, I nearly died from complications of an ectopic (tubal) pregnancy. We were ordered by the doctors to cease having children. In fact, they insisted that I get my remaining fallopian tube tied. I refused, explaining that my husband and I use (and teach) natural family planning.

We initially took the doctor's advice and agreed to limit our family to three boys. As time went on, however, my husband and I both felt God calling us to have more children. We prayed, discerned, spoke to our spiritual director, and then finally listened to the quiet voice of God urging us to seek another pregnancy. Two years later, we joyfully welcomed our fourth son; three years later, our fifth son (whose birthday is today) was born.

Sometimes amid the chaos, challenges, difficulties, and busyness of life, we might remember to pray, but perhaps we forget to listen. My husband and I are grateful that we listened to God's quiet voice and welcomed two more sons into our family.

God, help me to hear your voice in the busyness of my life.

To Ponder: What can you do to hear God's quiet voice in the day-to-day chaos and busyness of your life?

ELLEN GABLE HRKACH

Birthdays and Messes, Oh My

The life of a family is filled with beautiful moments.
. . . But if love is missing, joy is missing, nothing is
fun. Jesus always gives us that love: he is its
endless source.

Pope Francis

As the month of May approaches on our family calendar, my soul starts to inwardly tremble. Three family birthdays, Mother's Day, end-of-the-year school activities, and a ramped-up workload for my husband means those dates fill up faster than my nightly spoonful of Nutella. In the midst of planning for birthday parties that each year seem to get larger and larger, I often find myself needlessly stressed out about the details that just don't matter: *Should I get the bigger ice cream sundae cups? Should I invite so-and-so? Will my daughter feel like this present is "good enough"? Will anyone notice if I don't do goody bags?*

Bogged down in the details, I get frustrated and annoyed. On one hand, I want to celebrate the moments, both big and small, in our lives, and on the other, does any of it really even matter? There are earthquakes happening and children suffering and I'm agonizing over what color tablecloths to get?

But on a sunny May afternoon, when the food got burned and I forgot to give out the favors and my mother-in-law thought the table centerpiece I had painstakingly crafted was a garbage bin and tossed her leftover cake in it, I looked around and saw the details that really mattered: the smiles on my daughters' faces, the family and friends who loved them fiercely, and the love that enveloped us all through good and bad.

Lord, help me to see the celebrations in life for what they really are—celebrations of you and your love.

To Ponder: When planning for the celebrations and special events in your family's life, how are you honoring God in their midst? How can you celebrate the joys that God gives you in life without getting caught up in the sometimes-stressful details?

CHAUNIE MARIE BRUSIE

MAY 5
CONVERSION OF SAINT AUGUSTINE

In Angels' Care

God bids his angels to bear us away from dangers.

Psalm 91

The details worried me: scheduling, buying tickets online, shuffling paperwork for hosting an overseas friend for a month. What if I made an error?

Instead of "letting go and letting God" late one evening, my mind played out worst-case scenarios of all that could ground my family's guest on his side of the ocean. I reached for a fresh pillowcase. Out of an obscure corner of our linen closet emerged an old one belonging to my now seventeen-year-old son. The image of Saint Michael the Archangel flanked a prayer for protection to this saint.

"Okay, I want this one tonight," I called to my husband, holding up the case. I chuckled when my husband flipped over *his* pillow, revealing an image of a guardian angel with the classic "Angel of God, my guardian dear," prayer—an old treasure belonging to my other son. Angels pillowed our sleep that night. That little happening helped reset my heart onto a more peaceful, confident track.

Feeling that the trip's success depended on my efficiency and doubting God's guidance was prideful. Humbly pleading for heaven's aid and trusting that this aid would be given made me like an angel, according to Saint Augustine. This fourth-century saint said, "It was pride that changed angels into devils; it is humility that makes men as angels."

Dear Lord, thank you for giving us into the care of angels. Help us be as humble and trusting as angels.

To Ponder: Mothers are designed to multitask and fix life's problems large and small. Do you bear burdens alone, or do you give your worries to God and the care of his angels, especially your guardian angel?

MARIANNA BARTHOLOMEW

MAY 6

Be Still

All men desire peace, but few desire the things that make for peace.

Thomas á Kempis

Evenings in my home can get crazy. One child needs to be picked up from drama club, another has dance class, and two have choir practice. There are baseball practices, field hockey games, gymnastics, horseback riding lessons, 4-H meetings, home-school gym classes, and youth group activities. Yep, it gets crazy!

Is all this busyness necessary? My children love all these activities, but are they all truly beneficial? Do we really have to keep them so busy? Isn't God speaking to them, too, when he says, "Be still, and know that I am God" (Ps 46:10)? I think he is.

Our responsibility is to help our children learn to hear God: to stop at times, be quiet, and pray. We have to encourage them to turn off the television, iPods, and cell phones for a while and spend some quiet time with Our Lord.

Occasionally saying no to our children actually benefits them and the family. First of all, it is important to be able to accept no as an answer. After all, God sometimes says no, too. In addition, cutting down on some of the extracurricular activities provides more family time—time to eat a meal together, pray together, and play and converse with one another.

It may be difficult to choose what to cut out of our schedules; however, with prayerful discernment, God will help your family realize what activities are making life hectic.

Come Holy Spirit, grant us right judgment and the courage to say no to the things that make life unnecessarily busy. Help us to be still sometimes and relax in your love and peace.

To Ponder: Is it time to look at your family's schedule and re-prioritize?

KELLY GUEST

MAY 7
NATIONAL DAY OF PRAYER[4]

Be Transformed by the Renewal of Your Mind

Be transformed by the renewal of your mind.

Romans 12:2

If there is one thing that I need every day it is time set aside for personal prayer. I need to spend quiet time with God every day. That is how my spiritual and emotional batteries are recharged. It is how peace and calm enter into my heart and mind.

The content of the prayer isn't so important. It can be the Rosary, going to Mass, reading the Bible, or praying the Liturgy of the Hours. Or it can simply be resting in the presence of God. The important thing is for me to really make contact with God—to make the connection, to make it personal—no matter the content. In essence, I just need to be with God for a while every day.

When I don't spend time in prayer daily, life gets hard. Not right away. It might take a few days or even a week. But I start to notice little quirks and attitudes in my spouse that grate my nerves. My kids push my patience over the edge with what seems like little effort. People in line at the grocery store bug me, and I become appalled at all the bad drivers on the road. It's only by grace that I come back to my senses and realize that I'm the common denominator. All those people aren't making me miserable. I'm making me miserable.

And when I turn back to God, I find him right there waiting for me.

God, thank you for being so patient and loving with me. Your gentleness captivates me. Please renew my mind and my heart today.

To Ponder: What helps you to most easily come into God's presence? Can you get more of that in your life?

JEFF YOUNG

MAY 8

Discerning Balance

It is not enough to be busy; so are the ants. The question is: what are we busy about?

Henry David Thoreau

There is no question that motherhood is one of the busiest of vocations. After all, mothers are on call to their families twenty-four seven. We cannot predict when an immediate urgent need will arise: a sudden fever, a bad dream, an injury, an argument between siblings, bullying from the neighborhood children, and so much more, as we well know. Mothers jump right in as referees, peacemakers, nurses, protectors, soothers, and a myriad of other roles all wrapped up into the amazing mother repertoire.

In addition to a mother's natural busyness, since her heart is big and generous, she might also acquire some extra tasks along the way. Some duties she might get stuck with, other roles she might agree to, albeit halfheartedly, while others she desires to take on.

One hopes we mothers can pause and ponder our many roles and strive to not get involved in too many committees and duties that we stretch ourselves awfully thin and experience exhaustion or burnout. Let's not be like the ants.

Dear Lord, Jesus, please help me to strike a balance in my vocation of love. Blessed Mother Mary, please guide me in my mothering.

To Ponder: Do you strive to keep the children's activities and your own to a manageable limit? As tempting as it might be to stay up later at night than you should to make up for "lost" time, can you be sure to get the right amount of sleep to ensure sufficient rest and good health?

DONNA-MARIE COOPER O'BOYLE

MAY 9

Jesus the Nurturer

Now when Jesus heard this, he withdrew from there in a boat to a deserted place by himself. But when the crowds heard it, they followed him on foot from the towns.

Matthew 14:13

Young kids rarely leave you alone. They cling to you, quite literally, even when you desperately need space. They pepper you with questions and commentary. They have urgent needs, as well: a sippy-cup refill, a hug, a Band-Aid, and a kiss after a fall.

It's relentless. This lack of personal space is one of the hardest parts of being a mom.

It hit me one day that if anyone can understand this, Jesus can. He moved throughout his world surrounded by crowds. People were constantly in his space, grabbing his clothes, touching him, asking him questions. They had urgent needs: to be fed, to be comforted, to be healed.

I love Mary because she intimately understands the challenges of parenthood, but I'm starting to realize that Jesus does, too. He knows firsthand how it feels to be surrounded by clingy people and to feel that you don't have a moment's peace. When you feel you can't take it anymore, try this: imagine yourself going up to Jesus in a crowd and taking hold of his robe. See him turn to you and smile, encouraging you in the relentless but beautiful work of being a mom.

Jesus, it's not just women who understand what it means to nurture others. Help us to see you as a powerful support in our role as parents.

To Ponder: Is it easy for you to see Jesus as a nurturer? Take some time to imagine him patiently responding to your most urgent needs.

GINNY KUBITZ MOYER

Square Peg, Round Hole

My heart is restless until it finds its rest in thee.

Saint Augustine

When my kids were little they had a toy that both entertained and frustrated them. It was a red plastic ball with openings of different shapes and sizes. The object was to insert the correct shape into its corresponding opening. My toddlers couldn't always see the difference between a circle and an oval or a square and a rectangle so there were many attempts to jam the wrong shape into the wrong hole. Just like my kids, we, too, sometimes try to make things fit where they don't quite belong.

We were created in the image and likeness of the God who loves us; our hearts were meant to fit perfectly in his, but we often forget that and try to pack ourselves into roles where we don't fit. When the toy pieces didn't fit together the kids would bang, push, and get frustrated until they slowed down and looked things over carefully and attempted to put the pieces in gently and purposefully. During those times in life when we struggle to make things fit according to our plan, we experience that same chaos and frustration. God has the perfect antidote: rest in him. Only he knows how our life should fit together, and he simply asks us to love and serve him while we wait for him to put all the pieces in the perfect spot.

Lord, calm me in the midst of chaos and help me rest in you while you put my pieces together as you desire.

To Ponder: Are there pieces in your life that don't seem to fit together? Are you the wife and mother God is asking you to be? Rest a while in his presence and ask him.

SHERI WOHLFERT

MAY 11

Finding Jesus in a Full Calendar

Half an hour's meditation each day is essential, except when you are busy. Then a full hour is needed.

Saint Francis de Sales

About this time every year, I start feeling extreme stress. Our children take dance and play soccer. Both finish for the year the same week in May, which also happens to be the week our home-school co-op finishes up. So by mid-May, we're in the final throes of a crazy schedule that keeps me running *at least* five nights a week, and often makes me wish I could bilocate.

I also have a Holy Hour every Wednesday, and no matter how busy I am, I don't miss it. In fact, the busier I am, *the more I know I need it*. Morning and evening prayers are not enough in my busy season; I long for the quiet time I spend in adoration each week. I call it my weekly date with Jesus. Adoration is my opportunity to slow down and just *be* for an hour, to know that Jesus is God and to gaze on him in the monstrance. Even if I sit in adoration and study or read about the faith, I know it's a time that is set aside for quiet reflection. I can depend on this one time to have nothing else to do but to be with the Lord.

Lord, help me to carve out time in my busy schedule to be still, no matter how hectic my life seems to be.

To Ponder: What can you do to make prayer a priority in your schedule? Can you purposely schedule time to just be still and know that he is God?

CHRISTINE JOHNSON

MAY 12

Where Peace Begins

I dream of giving birth to a child who will ask,
"Mother, what was war?"

Eve Merriam

In this month of May, as we remember and celebrate our mothers, today's quotation is a jarring reminder that one of the best gifts we can leave the next generation is a more peaceful world. Given the current conditions, this seems like a daunting task, but if it doesn't begin with us, then who will undertake this most important mission in life?

The road to peace needs to begin in our own families first, for so many are at odds with one another. We all know someone who has fallen away from the faith or who practices a lifestyle not in agreement with the teachings of the Church. How quickly do we pass judgment on these individuals? In many households, families are torn apart over issues of money, drug and alcohol addiction, acts of unfaithfulness, or divorce. With all of these hurts, how are we ever to restore peace within our families?

The answer is prayer. Instead of condemning someone, pray for that individual; offer mercy and not judgment. Be a vessel of God's love. Offer to the Lord in prayer those people who cause you pain and suffering. Pray for the courage to let go of anger and jealousy. Jesus, the divine healer, can restore peace to our families; we just need to seek his help. Today, let us pray to be peacemakers in this world.

Lord, make me an instrument of your peace.

To Ponder: Whose actions are causing you pain? Seek the Lord's peace, mercy, and healing to come upon you and all those who hurt you.

DR. MARY AMORE

MAY 13
OUR LADY OF FATIMA

A Bullet in Mary's Crown

In her motherly concern, the Blessed Virgin came here to Fátima. . . . It is a mother's sorrow that compels her to speak; the destiny of her children is at stake. For this reason she asks the little shepherds: "Pray, pray much and make sacrifices for sinners."

Saint John Paul II

Honoring Our Lady of Fatima in Portugal in 2010, Pope Benedict XVI offered a prayerful context for what seems a strange gift offered to Mary. A would-be assassin's bullet permanently adorns the crown that sits atop Our Lady's statue there. The bullet came from Saint John Paul II after the assassination attempt on his life in Saint Peter's Square. "It is a profound consolation to know that you are crowned not only with the silver and gold of our joys and hopes, but also with the 'bullet' of our anxieties and sufferings," the pope said.

Ever devoted to the Blessed Mother, John Paul II attributed his survival of the attack on her feast day—May 13, 1981—to her direct intervention. He described that incident as one hand pulling the trigger and another hand guiding the bullet. He later presented the bullet to the bishop of Leira-Fátima. The bishop, in turn, enshrined it in Mary's crown, transforming a lethal image into a symbol of faithful maternal protection and a humble son's deep gratitude.

This feast commemorates the 1917 Church-approved apparitions of Mary as "the Lady of the Rosary." Appearing to three shepherd children between May 13 and October 13, Mary called for conversions through prayer—especially the Rosary—penance, and reparation.

Jesus, help me entrust myself to your Mother's maternal protection.

To Ponder: Why not pray the Rosary today or this week? Offer Mary your joys, hopes, anxieties, and sufferings.

PAT GOHN

Ascension

The Spirit creates joy, and joy is effusive.

Pope Paul VI

The Ascension of Our Lord might cause our minds to meditate on that scene at Bethany. Perhaps Jesus is on a rock or mound, elevated some from those invited to that special place. Jesus speaks to them with love, and yet there is an uncertain something about it all. His words finished, no more directives or wishes. He raises his right hand and blesses them as they had seen him do so many times before. And then he is slowly "lifted"—going up, up, and then entering a cloud. They keep looking. What does it mean? Where is he? It has been said that there would only be one other worldly "vision" of Christ, and that was when he appeared to Paul on the road to Damascus to make him an apostle.

Jesus returned to his Father having established his kingdom by his resurrection. And yet, what did he mean when he said, "Behold, I am with you always"?

Luke's gospel tells us that the disciples did him homage and returned with great joy. Again, how could they have great joy in the visual loss of their friend, mentor, and Savior?

One of Jesus's final gifts must have been the gift of belief and acceptance: total surrender that he could be with the Father and he could be here as well. They were alone. But they weren't. Paraphrasing Dr. Martin Luther King, Jr.: "Through his eyes, I've seen the vision of the Promised Land. And I will get there with him and with you. He is with us now. And we are never, never alone."

This day, Lord, give me a vision of you ascending and waiting for me and mine.

To Ponder: Do you ever feel alone, like God has forgotten or forsaken you? Spend some time today seeking out the lonely and offering them the blessing of your presence.

DEACON TOM FOX

MAY 15

Plan to Play

You can discover more about a person in an hour of play than in a year of conversation.

Plato

May is usually a crazy month in my house; my husband is a teacher and both our children are in school now, so our lives revolve around the school year. While our children might see May as the light at the end of the tunnel, as a mom, I only see the gifts for teachers yet to be bought, the last-minute projects, and the fear that I forgot to order yearbooks.

May brings with it a mixed emotion of excitement for the achievements of this school year and the anticipation of what's to come in the next. As moms, I think May can also bring with it a panic as we decide what our summers will be like and how we'll plan to keep the kids (and ourselves) from being bored and whiny. Last summer, my friend decided to put together a play-date group. It was made up of my son's pre-school friends and their families. She came up with some ideas on her own and planned events. She created a Google calendar and then she sent us all a link and invited us to host play dates, too. Every other week, there was a planned event. It gave the kids a chance to play, the adults a chance to socialize, and all of us a chance to explore our local town.

Dear Jesus, help us to find ways to make this summer a time of relaxation and restoration for our families.

To Ponder: In anticipation of summer, can you think of a few families whom you would like to invite to set up a schedule of summer play dates with you?

COURTNEY VALLEJO

MAY 16
SAINT BRENDAN THE NAVIGATOR

Journeying through Life's Unknowns

Help me to journey beyond the familiar and into the unknown. Give me the faith to leave old ways and break fresh ground with you.

Prayer to Saint Brendan the Navigator

Saint Brendan the Navigator (ca. 484–577) was an Irish monk who established numerous abbeys and monasteries in Ireland, Scotland, Wales, and France. For decades, he traveled the high seas from island to island, spreading the Gospel and establishing religious houses.

Of his many adventures, the most famous was his legendary seven-year voyage with a dozen or so other monks to find paradise. Colorful depictions written over the centuries have Saint Brendan encountering sea monsters, visiting exotic locations, and seeing visions. Some even have him discovering the New World. One thing, however, is certain: Saint Brendan was a tireless missionary who devoted his entire life to sharing the Good News. His story is an invitation for all of us to look at our own current voyage as disciples of Christ.

Saint Brendan's story makes me think about the ways I typically navigate the "high seas" of my life. How often I let a busy schedule take my focus off of those riding in the boat with me! How easily I allow fear to keep me from venturing into the unknown! One little crisis, a hurt feeling or disappointment, and I can end up feeling lost and without a map.

Saint Brendan, help me navigate the sometimes tumultuous waters of family living. Together with Christ, calm the storms that can so easily rise within me. Keep my little boat—and the loved ones riding in it with me—safe from fear and harm.

To Ponder: What is one small way you can help create smoother sailing for your family today?

ELIZABETH FICOCELLI

MAY 17
NATIONAL PACK RAT DAY

Cleaning Life's Clutter

A detached man should always be looking to see
what he can do without.

Blessed Henry Suso

I was in the last trimester of my third pregnancy, and I wanted to make room in our home for another human. In a hormonal moment, I decided to have a garage sale. I had no rhyme or reason as to what items went up for sale; I just wanted to see my floor.

The garage sale was a success, at least in terms of moving merchandise. One buyer, surprised at my willingness to accept her lowball offer, asked, "You just want to get rid of this stuff, don't you?" Precisely. Am I really that transparent? Unfortunately, my approach backfired. Turns out one item I sold was given to my family on loan, and I hadn't received the memo we were borrowing it. When the lender called a few months later asking for it back, I wanted to crawl into a hole. I ended up buying that family a brand-new replacement, probably spending ten times what I made selling the item in the garage sale.

I have since learned about a different strategy for de-cluttering. Set aside time to systemically go through your belongings. Pick up each object. Touch it. Handle it. Does it speak to your heart? Does it spark joy? If yes, then keep it. If no, dispose of it—or return it to its original owner. You may question whether this approach really works, but try it. You may be surprised at its effectiveness.

Lord Jesus, help me detach from worldly things.

To Ponder: Is there an area of your home you feel called to de-clutter? Today is a good day to "touch and handle" each item in that space.

LISA A. SCHMIDT

NATIONAL VISIT YOUR RELATIVES DAY

Know Your Roots

Happiness is being rooted in love.

Saint John Paul II

How do we know if we are truly "rooted in love"? Saint John Paul II tells us that it is "consistent giving which . . . bears witness to rootedness in love." How often I feel too busy to be a consistent giver! *This was a crazy day (again) so I'll just pick up a pizza for dinner. I have to get caught up on the laundry so I'll play a game with my son tomorrow. I'm exhausted so my husband will just have to understand that I'm too drained to spend some quality time with him tonight.* We all have days that don't go as planned and that fill up with tasks that have to get done. But this should be the exception rather than the rule.

How often does our day fill up with distractions rather than the work God wants us to do? How often does dinner prep get neglected because too much time was spent on Facebook? How often does laundry pile up because priorities weren't in order? How often does a refreshing nap go by the wayside in favor of reading one too many blogs?

There is good busyness and bad busyness. Good busyness gives to our family, to our relationship with God, and to our neighbor or friend in need. Bad busyness takes. It takes from our relationships, it takes our time, it takes our peace, and it takes our happiness.

Dear God, please help me to be a consistent giver today. Please let every action I take work toward the happiness of my family.

To Ponder: Is your daily routine "rooted in love"? What changes do you need to make to get rid of the "bad busyness" in your life?

CHARISSE TIERNEY

MAY 19

Trust in Life

I have the strength for everything through him who empowers me.

Philippians 4:13

A few years ago I went on retreat with the great spiritual writer Jacques Philippe, and when I asked him how we can concretely trust in God, he said something that forever changed me: "Trust in life."

So many times life goes "wrong" according to our view. Things do not unfold as we wish, or out of sync with our timeline. We look around us, and in the midst of great poverty and heartache, we wonder if God is even there.

So many problems need fixing, and we spin our wheels to find solutions. Countless times amidst a trial in my own life I thought my job was to figure it out and get it under control.

But as so many of our modern saints like Thérèse and Faustina remind us, the thing God wants most from us is simply our *trust*, not our control. Again and again in my times of hardship I would feel God telling me, "I am not calling you to a figuring out but a *letting go*."

It is precisely when the storm rages around us that we (though it be against our human instincts) are called to trust even more radically, walk even more blindly, and have a faith that is even more childlike. If we have said yes to God then we can trust that he is letting his will be done in our lives and he is working all things for our good. We can trust in him by simply trusting what unfolds right before our eyes. We can trust in life.

Lord, help me to be at peace with my life as it unfolds before me, trusting that you are letting your will be done.

To Ponder: Do I believe that God can and will work through every circumstance in my life for my good?

KARA KLEIN

MAY 20
SAINT BERNARDINE OF SIENA

The Heaven on Earth of Mercy

Jesus . . . you are the medicine of souls.

Saint Bernardine of Siena

Being a mom is about coming to peace with personal failure. Our responses to our children's needs and misbehavior frequently fail the patient, unconditional love standard. Today we can take a bit of solace on the feast of a very complicated man.

As a young man, Saint Bernardine volunteered in a hospital during a terrible plague. He spent months faithfully caring for an aging aunt, unrecognized and unimportant. Much of his relationship with God developed quietly. Trumpets did not announce his sainthood. He developed into a gifted preacher but he began with a voice that was hoarse and weak.

Other parts of him weren't very saint-like at all. His ideas about how to respond to homosexual people were hateful and cruel. His expressed prejudice against Jewish people caused harm to people within that community. Bernardine was known for his devotion to the holy name of Jesus and his preaching about the mercy of Jesus. He himself suffered on account of the unjust accusations of others, yet he had a blind spot toward homosexual and Jewish people. Saint Bernardine's sin makes us wince. So does our own.

Which is why there is hope for us: mothers with blind spots; mothers who are too harsh, impatient, inconsistent, selfish, and unmerciful; mothers who love their children and love Jesus but are downright miserable to be around sometimes.

Saint Bernardine, with the ugliness of your sins now washed away, pray for us to the holy name of Jesus that we, too, may be cleansed from our sins. Dear Jesus, fill us with the constancy of your love and mercy until it overflows in us.

To Ponder: Where are you missing the mercy God has for you? For those around you?

MICHELLE JONES

Finding Calm in the Chaos

When one does one's own duty, one must not be concerned, because God's help will not be lacking.

Saint Gianna Beretta Molla

When I was a young mother, all I wanted to do was sit in my rocker and hold my babies close to my heart.

I know that wasn't practical. My husband and other children needed my attention. Household chores called. As our family grew, so did the demands on my time, and I often felt torn between duty and desire.

There were times when I was so busy I felt like my life had devolved into a pit of chaos: dishes in the sink, clothes wrinkling in the dryer, babies crying. If I dared to look in the mirror, I wouldn't recognize the woman with the frizzy hair and the bags under her eyes looking back at me.

My dear husband would come home to this chaos and happily grab the youngest or neediest to let me finish dinner or put the oldest to bed.

I thought things would improve when the children got older and I returned to teaching. It didn't. The things that kept me busy changed, but I was still just a broken dish away from chaos. I had to come to terms with the fact that I could only do one thing at a time. Each task, when completed, brought order, and with order, came calm.

Dear Jesus, let every task I complete today be a blessing to my family and a reflection of your love.

To Ponder: Our duties and responsibilities are important and deserve our attention. However, sometimes we let them rule us, instead of us managing our tasks. What task can you turn over to Jesus? Ask him for his help in completing it, and then trust in him.

MARIA JOHNSON

MAY 22
SAINT RITA OF CASCIA

Holy Enough to Ask for Help

All that [Saint Rita of Cascia] said and did was prompted primarily by her fervent love of God, the ruling passion of her life.

Butler's Lives of the Saints

God answers prayers, including prayers for healing and provision. Knowing that, we sometimes wonder if the problems in our life might be because we aren't holy enough or haven't prayed enough. Saint Rita of Cascia is the counterexample: she was a woman of tremendous reverence and devotion, but whose life was a series of tribulations. Holiness isn't measured by how easy or "successful" our lives are, but by how we respond to the trials we must endure.

For many of us, the biggest enemy we face is ourselves. We constantly get sucked into the same awful sins. What makes us sin? Those "ruling passions." We feel a powerful urge for this comfort or that pleasure, an urge so strong we have a hard time resisting.

Saint Rita is the patron of desperate causes. Overcoming deeply entrenched habits and weaknesses certainly qualifies: how desperate we are to be free of the habit of hurting ourselves; how desperately we are unable to get free! In fighting that fight, one thing we can do is to ask God, with the intercession of Saint Rita, to make our love for him stronger than our love of the sin that's always pulling us down.

Dear Lord, help me to love you more than I love _____.

To Ponder: What is the "ruling passion" in your life? What need do you sometimes try to fill in unholy ways? Are there ways you can fill that need by a prayer, action, or habit that isn't sinful?

JENNIFER FITZ

MAY 23

Love When It Encounters Suffering

Goodness always tends to spread. Every authentic experience of truth and goodness seeks by its very nature to grow within us, and any person who has experienced a profound liberation becomes more sensitive to the needs of others.

Pope Francis

I always joke that someday I'm going to give a talk called "Suffering Is Like Being Pregnant." Now, that may hit home for many; pregnancy sometimes comes with discomfort, nausea, and morning sickness, but there's another connection here.

The moment you find out you're pregnant, everything changes. For example, the first time you go to the grocery store after learning you are pregnant, what do you see? Pregnant women *everywhere.* Why is that? Is it because all of a sudden everyone decided this was the right time to have a baby? No. It's because when you're pregnant, you notice all the pregnant women around you. When you are carrying life within you, you have a heightened awareness of others carrying life within them.

The same happens with suffering. When we are suffering, we are naturally more in tune to the suffering of others. So, too, when someone has shown compassion to us in our time of need, we are more apt to be compassionate to another. That's mercy.

Mercy is love when it encounters suffering, and there seems to be something to the fact that we are more merciful when we ourselves are aware that we have been the recipients of mercy.

Lord, in my pain help me be open and compassionate to the suffering of others.

To Ponder: We are the recipients of perfect love when it encounters suffering. We are the recipients of God's divine mercy. How does knowing this change how you will react to others when you see them suffering?

KELLY M. WAHLQUIST

Who's Got Your Back?

Do whatever he tells you.

John 2:5

My to-do list is a notebook, literally. Oh how I wish I were kidding, but I am not. Every day I am super busy. Each morning I wake, coffee up, and hit the ground running, tackling a project or task, errand or objective, subscribing to that old adage that "a mother's work is never done." Some days I relish my efficiency, and other days I rue that there are so many items left on my list.

However, at the end of every day, I know that whatever happened, I was in the palm of God's hand. I begin each day with a prayer. It sounds something like this: "Thank you, God, for this day, all I think, do, and say." This is more than just a catchy rhyme to kick-start my day: it is the desire of my heart. It is my way of following Mother Mary's instruction from the wedding at Cana: "Do whatever he tells you."

The needs of my family and household are often beyond the time I have to give, and I could get easily discouraged as I assess what I accomplish each day. When I start my day with that prayer, I know Jesus has my back and that what I could do was all he asked me to. In addition, I always call upon Mary for assistance. She cared for a home, a husband, and a child all while maintaining a close relationship with God.

Mary, Help of Christians, pray for me to hear your Son in my heart, scripture, and the sacraments so that I'm best prepared to tackle the busyness of life.

To Ponder: What is Jesus asking you to do today, and how can Mary be your help?

ALLISON GINGRAS

MAY 25

Light for the Darkness of Busyness

Most high, glorious God,
Bring light to the darkness of my heart.
Give me right faith, firm hope, and perfect charity,
With wisdom and insight, O Lord, that I might
    always discern Your holy and true will.

Saint Francis of Assisi, Prayer Before the Cross

This is my favorite prayer from Saint Francis of Assisi, and I think it's the perfect prayer for people who are overwhelmed by chaos or busyness.

When there's too much on my plate, I find that things start to slip through the cracks. Being in a hurry to get it all done can mean that it all gets done, but none of it is done well and precious little is done cheerfully. My strategy for getting through those times of chaos?

* I spend some time writing down what has to be done. *All of it*. Even—especially—the little things I'm sure I'll

remember to do, but which can be easily neglected or forgotten when I'm overly busy.

- I bake because there's nothing like getting your hands into some cookie batter or bread dough to force you to slow down.

- I lean on that prayer, asking for guidance in prioritizing my tasks, establishing routines, and getting things done.

Lord, I am overwhelmed and worried about many things. Please give me the grace to let go of anxiety and free my hands and heart.

To Ponder: What's your go-to prayer? Why does that particular prayer bring you comfort?

BARB SZYSZKIEWICZ, O.F.S.

MAY 26
SAINT PHILIP NERI

Let the Whirling Dervishes Whirl

We must always remember that God does everything well although we may not see the reason of what he does.

Saint Philip Neri

There is a story about an old Bedouin, sitting in the desert, surrounded by whirling dervishes, who howled and carried on in religious ecstasy. "Don't they distract you?" he was asked.

"Sometimes," the Bedouin said.

"Well, what do you do about them?" asked his perplexed interviewer.

"I let 'em whirl."

Saint Philip Neri had a philosophy similar to the Bedouin's. As founder of the Oratory—a community of lay and clerical Catholics that would first worship together and then engage in debate, a musical performance, the reading of plays, or even in a picnic-procession to another church—Philip was comfortable with the idea of letting the sometimes chaotic creative and religious energies about him spin out and wind down. Like a parent who understands that sometimes a toddler (or a teen) simply has to burn off excessive energy before he can settle down and read or talk (or listen), Philip knew that upon the winds of seeming chaos the Holy Spirit often flies. And so, while by no means passive, he dared to trust the not-always-easy-to-understand processes of God and be peaceful as the world before him whirled.

Dear Philip Neri, God's ways are not ours; help me dare to trust his purposes.

To Ponder: When your world seems to be going awry before your eyes, why is it so much easier to freak out and join the chaos than to sit back and see what emerges? Take a breath. Realize that no difficulty lasts forever. Can you live through five more minutes of it? Take another breath. And another five minutes.

ELIZABETH SCALIA

Fitting in Fitness and Prayer

Lack of prayer is the cause of lack of time.

Peter Kreeft

If you are a busy mother, it's tempting to dismiss the call to meditation. I have struggled with it my entire life, as I have a Type A personality. Each morning as the coffee kicks in, I want to get busy with the tasks of motherhood. Many times the children's demands cannot be put aside, and I leave prayer until the last moments I am awake and skip exercise altogether. My spiritual and physical health suffers, and I waste time during the day feeding my soul with spiritual junk (TV) and my body with junk food.

Eileen Benthal, a friend of mine whose daughter endured over eighty brain surgeries, wrote in her book *Breathing Underwater: A Caregiver's Journey of Hope* that she gives the first three hours of her day to exercise and prayer. A combination of scripture and meditation, running with the Rosary, daily Mass, and prayer journaling give her body and soul the nourishment necessary to care and advocate for her daughter at home, in the health-care system, and in the media.

Lord, help me to turn to you today, even in the midst of the busyness and chaos.

To Ponder: Do you make your prayer life a priority? What time that you now waste are you willing to give up in order to spend time at Our Lord's feet?

MAY 28

Love and Marriage

Never must they lose their sense of the wonderful mystery that the other person whom they love loves them, too, that the other lives for them, and that they own something far above all other earthly possessions.

Dietrich von Hildebrand

After moving our family two thousand miles, my husband and I found ourselves caring for six very needy children while adapting to new jobs, house hunting, and commuting several hours a week. These new demands did not include more hours in the day. Something had to give, and our marriage was put on the back burner.

We were giving to others all the time but not to each other. It is easy to be loving and giving with a partner who is loving and giving to you, but it is difficult otherwise. We became selfish and resentful. The children started to suffer. They could sense that our marriage, the basis of the family, was weakening.

We had to focus on us. We had no time for date nights, but we lost a little sleep so we could talk it out. We both made an effort to regularly express love and appreciation. We e-mailed each other throughout the day, and we prayed for each other. The children became more secure and less needy, giving us a little time for romance.

Even if time is limited, in our hearts our spouse must remain our priority. Get creative to communicate, support each other, and love each other generously.

Lord, you love us as a husband loves his bride. Bless our marriage with your grace through life's busy times.

To Ponder: Are you struggling with too much on your plate at this busy time of year? Where can you and your husband find a little time for communication, prayer, and romance?

KATE DANELUK

MAY 29

Honor Your Mother

The Holy Family is the beginning of countless other holy families.

Saint John Paul II, Letter to Families

In this wonderful month of May, dedicated to Mary, Our Blessed Mother comes to our aid to find calm in the chaos. To bring us closer to Mary, my father-in-law, José Antonio, leads the family every May on a *romería* or pilgrimage. We all drive to a nearby retreat house with an outdoor Rosary walk. Every several yards we find a dark wooden post decorated with Roman numerals in gold lettering and a bas-relief plaque depicting scenes in the life of the Holy Family.

The path passes through sunlight and shadow (or *sol y sombra*, as it's said in Spanish). The paved road changes to gravel and then hard-packed dirt overlaid with pine needles, dried to brown but still smelling of evergreen forests.

Every family member picks an intention to pray for as we murmur the well-worn words, half in English and half in Spanish. At the end, we gather near a statue of Mary to pray a litany in Latin. *Ora pro nobis, ora pro nobis*, we ask again and again. The kids, untouched by suffering and unaware of the need for divine comfort, play contentedly on the grassy hillside.

In contemplating the life of Jesus, Mary, and Joseph, we learn how much they have to teach us. In gifting our Blessed Mother with our prayers, we in turn receive the much-needed gift of peace.

Jesus, Mary, and Joseph, Holy Family of Nazareth, pray for us!

To Ponder: How close do you feel to the Holy Family? Invite them into your heart and ask them to make your family a happier and holier one.

KAREE SANTOS

MAY 30
SAINT JOAN OF ARC

Breaking for the Better Part

Never be in a hurry; do everything quietly and in a calm spirit. Do not lose your inner peace for

anything whatsoever, even if your whole world
seems upset.

Saint Francis de Sales

Though we consider chaos as lacking of any order and general confusion, *chaos* stems from the root word *chasm*. In this sense, chaos is an emptiness waiting to be filled. We can fill it with peace.

Jesus reminds us that, though we are busy about many things, we can choose the "better part" by pausing to hear God, who waits to say, "I love you for who you are. I am with you." Interior silence is discovered through the practice of quiet stillness. Venerable Mother Thecla Merlo contemplated the silence of Jesus in the tabernacle: "He governs the world and remains silent."

When busyness and chaos seem to be obstacles to getting things done, take a "better part" break with God, who has all of your needs covered (Lk 10:42). Isaiah 30:15 reminds us to rest in God and to be safe in him, for our strength is in quietness and calm. Remember, God "will rejoice over you with gladness, he will renew you in his love, he will exult over you with loud singing" (Zep 3:17).

Lord, you calm the chaos and busyness of my moments. You live to love and listen, and you love to understand me.

To Ponder: What stories do you tell yourself when your plans don't seem to come together? How do you fill the chaos? What prayer can you lift up to God, who waits silently for your presence?

MARGARET KERRY, F.S.P.

It's Not Over Yet

I am wild with impatience to move, move, move.

Mark Twain

At last! The end of this crazy month! May always seems to be bursting with sports practices, allergies, celebrations, spring planting, family events, and squirrelly children. Flip that calendar page over already!

Just a wee bit on the Type A side of things, I tend to want to skip to the end, tie up loose ends, and dream of a fresh day "with no mistakes in it yet," as Anne of Green Gables says.

But I once got my wish, and it changed my life. My brother's family had invited our five children over for a "cousinpalooza" sleepover. My husband and I had the whole house to ourselves for the weekend. We spent all day Saturday cleaning, scrubbing, and organizing until the house gleamed. I had always longed for the house to be Pottery-Barn perfect and to stay that way for an hour or two.

I got my wish, and then, totally unexpectedly, I began to cry. I realized how achingly *empty* my gorgeous house was. I realized that purging my daughter's "crap piles" also scrubbed away a little of her artistic personality. Shoes and books and toys *everywhere* might be evidence of five children's carelessness, but they're also the artifacts of the people I love most in the world.

God alone will end all things. God alone cleanses and saves us. My desire to be a little like God and order things properly is a gift, but I must always remember I am God's beloved creature and that even my messes are loved by God, because they show I am here.

Save me, God. Show me how to love like you.

To Ponder: How can tidying something today remind me of God's creative order? How can leaving something be help me live in the moment?

GRACE MAZZA URBANSKI

June

THEME: FAMILY FUN

NATIONAL SAY SOMETHING NICE DAY

Censoring Yourself for Your Household

If you can't say something nice, don't say nothing at all.

Thumper, Bambi

How many times have I quickly clapped a hand over a young son's mouth when my motherly "spidey senses" tingled enough to warn me that something negative was coming? Enough that I should have learned for myself that old adage that if I can't say something nice, I'm better off keeping my mouth closed.

This month, as we celebrate the arrival of summer's leisure, it's time to cultivate a little niceness in our homes. Say Something Nice Day started in Charleston, South Carolina, as a movement to combat bullying and to promote common courtesy. Today, I'm reminded that we're often less "nice" to those who live under our own roofs.

The unconditional love of family sometimes leaves us feeling at liberty to use less discretion in our communication. With my husband, I might say something out of anger I'd never say to a friend or neighbor. Losing patience with my children, I sometimes let my temper get the better of me and speak without kindness. While I'm not suggesting that we moms have to always have smiles on our faces, I do believe that the words we choose—especially the loving ones—set the tone for our domestic Churches.

Today, without any announcement or fanfare, intentionally go out of your way to say one nice thing to every member of your household. Then watch and see what happens.

Mother Mary, you treasured your spouse and Son. Help me to follow your example as I affirm and cherish my own loved ones today.

To Ponder: What causes you to be negative in your thinking or speech? How can you turn that frown upside down?

LISA M. HENDEY

JUNE 2
NATIONAL LEAVE THE OFFICE EARLY DAY

Choosing Fun

You'll never be happy if you continue to search for what happiness consists of. You'll never live if you are looking for the meaning of life.

Cardinal Luis Antonio Tagle

Today we're all supposed to leave the office early and enjoy some summer fun. Sounds great, huh? Well, what about the people who *live* at work? Yes, I'm talking about us, moms. When do *we* get to clock out? What about *our* overtime pay? At this point, I'd be happy for a coffee break or even a cigarette break, and *I don't smoke*.

I guess the point isn't that we have to change our physical location. It's more about changing our focus. Fun is important, but it's hard for us to set aside our incomplete to-do lists and be carefree when the work that we need to do is weighing on our minds. Sometimes fun seems like a luxury we can't afford. The ironic thing is, the more you work, the more you really *need* some fun.

I remember picking up my oldest son from elementary school. He would always run to the car with a big smile on his face, all his worries behind him. He was great at changing gears from work to fun in a matter of minutes. Worry about unfinished assignments or upcoming homework didn't get in the way of his joy. I've always admired that in him. Instead of letting the events of the day bog him down, he leaves them behind and moves forward. Walking out of the school door is his signal to let loose and relax.

Lord, help me to be more like a child at the end of the school day and not let the worries of work keep me from having fun.

To Ponder: What are some things that you can put aside to make room for more fun with your friends and family? Are there things you need to give up or postpone? Standards that you need to lower temporarily?

LAURA B. NELSON

JUNE 3

High Tides

Who shut in the sea with doors when it burst forth and issued from the womb . . . [when I] said "this far you may come but no further, and here your proud waves must stop"?

Job 38:8, 11

I moved away from home when I married, so our annual family vacation at the coast with my parents is a special gift that I guard jealously. Some of our loveliest memories with my parents were made there, but they're all deceptively simple.

The kids squeal and thrash in the surf under the twinkling eyes of the grown-ups, who sip from Bubba Kegs and move the umbrella with the sun all day. We cook dinner, wash up, and relax in rockers on the porch each night under a fingernail moon.

My traditional excursion to the antique shops in town and lunch at the main street bistro with my mom, the playful competition between the kids to see who gets to pile up on the recliner with my dad, their giddy anticipation of a whole week of cable cooking shows, the customary hand signal for "we have to pull off the highway to pee"—it's all so ordinary, but gosh, it brings tears to my eyes writing about it.

I relish the fragile thing that this love with my parents is because the tide of our time with them is ebbing. Standing still is not time's way. Its waves crash and soothe and buffet and cradle, but even the sea has its limits.

Lord, I cherish the currents of love I enjoy through those you have given me. May I remain aware that lifetimes are fleeting and the opportunities numbered.

To Ponder: How can you create family traditions with those you have been given? How can you preserve the memories of those traditions?

SONJA CORBITT

CORPUS CHRISTI[6]

Scripture and
Sacraments

The Holy Eucharist is the greatest treasure that the
Church has on earth: It is Christ himself.

Cardinal Francis Arinze

A woman in my Bible-study group told us she had been
raised Catholic but changed to the Presbyterian church when
she married. She missed the Eucharist in the Church of her
birth, but she also loved the focus that her husband's church
placed on reading scripture. She lamented, "Why can't the
Christian churches have both?" and went to eucharistic adoration in quiet Catholic chapels.

While Catholics are perhaps more known for the love
and devotion we have for "the sacraments," Protestants are
better known for their focus on "the word." Catholic teaching, however, asks us to hold both word and sacrament in
equal weight.

The feast of Corpus Christi has been celebrated in the
Church since the thirteenth century. Julianna of Liège was
a Norbertine canoness and the first promoter of the feast. It
reminds us that the living, breathing, glorified Lord is near
and seeks our friendship. He seeks to heal us and share the
details of our struggles, joys, and hopes. At the same time,
Christ reveals himself to us as knowable through scripture.
He encourages us to set aside our trepidation and read scripture as a love letter from the Lord. As Augustine heard on

the day of his conversion, *tolle, lege*—pick up and read—we should pick up the Bible and read it so we can better know the Lord and seek his will for ourselves and our families. It is not a "text" for "the experts," but our sacred writ and inspiration for our daily lives.

Lord, help me know you as I am known by you. Show me how to live in the joy of friendship with you.

To Ponder: Read Psalm 139 and find a time near the feast of Corpus Christi to pray before the tabernacle.

JULIE L. PAAVOLA

JUNE 5

Come Close to Me

Once you have surrendered yourself, you make yourself receptive. In receiving from God, you are perfected and completed.

Venerable Fulton J. Sheen

Sometimes it's very difficult to pray. Life is hectic; the day begins and all you want to do is retreat under your blankets and hide from everything, including God. But that little voice inside of you (you know, the one that pokes you in the ribs and reminds you to thank God for another day) is the desire that God placed inside you through grace. This gift of grace rains down on us all the time. All we have to do is cup our outstretched hands to catch the deluge.

My pastor told me once that every prayer is a reflection of our desire for closeness to God. In fact, because this desire for closeness is at the root of every prayer, every time we pray—even if it's just "Help me!"—God answers that prayer immediately by coming close to us. The smallest of prayers is a cry from our very souls for union with our Creator. So even in that moment when we're praying that the car starts or the milk lasts through breakfast, he comes to us and fulfills our deepest, unconscious need, the desire we didn't even know we had, the desire for union with him.

Dear Father, help me to desire greater closeness with you. Call me to seek you out in all things, everywhere. Just by this prayer, in faith, I know that you will come to fill the empty places in my heart giving me everything I need. Let me be open to that desire and love you as passionately as you love me.

To Ponder: How do you show your desire for closeness with God?

KATIE O'KEEFE

JUNE 6
NATIONAL GARDENING EXERCISE DAY

Adapting to Forced Change

Hope, which most of all guides the changeful mind of mortals.

Pindar

Today is National Gardening Exercise Day. It's a day set aside for time away from sedentary jobs and to spend some time working in your garden.

As I've aged, my ability to work in a garden has diminished. Gardening was my identity, livelihood, and love. But as the saying goes, hope springs eternal, and I wanted to adapt.

For whatever reason, we all may face limited mobility issues in ourselves or a loved one. A friend's daughter, under ten, lost use of her legs. A mother of eight recovered from a stroke and regained only partial use of her right side. A neighbor's husband, whose vegetable gardens provided food for the family, neighborhood, and soup kitchen, will for the rest of his life have difficulty standing since his accident. It may not be trauma that limits us; we may have bodies worn out and aged in the cycle of life.

The nice thing about gardening is the gentleness of learning to do things a different way. We still need exercise and must adapt to our changing bodies. Gardens provide not only emotional and physical therapy; they also bolster us spiritually. We draw closer to God when touching his creation, and while among the plants, we persevere in our infirmities.

Thank you, Father, for using the gifts that remain and teaching us how to change in a way that allows us to continue to bloom.

To Ponder: Impairments can be discouraging and challenge us to persevere. What are some of the ways you can adapt to still do the things you love? Is there someone you know who loves his or her gardens and is falling behind in caring for them? Why not offer to help pull weeds, deadhead flowers, prune, or fertilize?

MARGARET ROSE REALY, OBL. O.S.B.

JUNE 7
NATIONAL CANCER SURVIVORS DAY[7]

Letting Jesus Organize Your Agenda

The underlying cause of burnout, say psychologists,
is the repeated failure to achieve "unrealistic goals."

Anonymous

As a new marriage and family therapist, I would purchase book after book—books that were often left unread—in subject areas where I lacked expertise. It was my way to calm my anxieties about perceived areas of incompetence.

I approached my schedule similarly. I packed in all the good things every Catholic girl should do: time with God, family, friends, and fulfilling my responsibilities. My illusion was that if I *intended* to do something, it meant I actually would.

Repeatedly, I fell short on achieving my great aspirations to attend to all areas in my life. Not that every day was a disaster. However, in most cases, the schedule didn't work. I missed doing those important, non-urgent things and often attended to whatever was most urgent. My schedule was doomed from the beginning because it was unrealistic.

Feeling harried, rushed, and late just created more stress rather than satisfaction. On particularly bad days, it squelched family fun and spontaneity. And as any cancer survivor knows, stress poorly managed compromises your immune system.

God wants us to be well and whole. He doesn't give us more to do each day than what we can accomplish in twenty-four hours. But we must loosen the grip of control on our daily agenda and let the Holy Spirit clearly speak to us about what to put and not put on our calendars.

Lord, help me detach from my desire to control my schedule. Show me your wisdom on how to fulfill my vocation and the unique mission you have for me in a spiritually, emotionally, and physically healthy way.

To Ponder: What can you do today to surrender your schedule to God and trust that everything he wants you to accomplish will get done?

CHRISTINA M. WEBER

JUNE 8
NATIONAL BEST FRIENDS DAY

Friends

Friendship is unnecessary, like philosophy, like art.
. . . It has no survival value; rather it is one of those
things which give value to survival.

C. S. Lewis, The Four Loves

As mothers, we spend a lot of time focused on family. God loves family. He reveals himself to us as a family in the Blessed Trinity. The Son came to earth in the Incarnation as a member of the Holy Family. He taught us to call God our Father and him our Brother. But he also called us friends.

Some of us have one best friend, but I'm one of those women who does not. So today, I have time to remember and pray for special friends throughout my life: friends from various times and places who were very special; friends whom I am excited to see whether it has been a week or a decade since we last met; friends whom I can connect with in the same way as we used to even though we have both grown and changed.

Truly, my sisters top the list, topped again by my husband, topped ultimately by the friend who loves me most, to the point of death: Christ. Friendship is a love that crosses into family, marriage, and faith. Friendship is something that takes us beyond being simply social creatures like wolves or monkeys. It is what makes us human and reflects that we are made in God's image.

Lord, bless my friends and my friendships. May your precious blood sanctify the love between us.

To Ponder: Who are the friends who have enriched your life? What can you do to be Christ to others through friendship? How is God calling you to grow as a friend?

KATE DANELUK

Remaining Connected

Marital love is a reflection of how God loves. It is
free, total, faithful, and fruitful.

Christopher West

June is a wedding month and a time to celebrate marriage. I
reminisce about the days of innocence and youthful stupidity,
but I long for the days when old age sets in. I yearn for what
my grandparents have: high-school sweethearts who are still
in love and never go to bed angry. The latter was their advice
at my own wedding. But I have realized I can either go to
bed angry, stay awake and stew, or make the choice to keep
my vows to my spouse.

Considering how we spent our first seven months living
out of motel rooms due to work, we really couldn't escape
from one another. There was always the bathroom as an
option, but who really wants to sleep in the tub? Needless
to say, we had to make up. And we did it the way any new-
lywed couple would.

The giving and physical connection during those early
months cements the love that God wants us to have for our
mate. When it was only the two of us, life was less of an
obstacle. Right now, we have a child who often needs and
wants our attention. This fruit of our love makes spending
time alone harder, but he is an ever-present reminder of the
love we vowed to share.

God, please help me to put my marriage first and stay true to the vows I made on my wedding day. Remind me that children need to know that their parents love and respect each other.

To Ponder: Whom do you put first: your husband or children? Why?

TANYA WEITZEL

JUNE 10
NATIONAL HERBS AND SPICES DAY

Grow Where You Are Planted

Although the life of a person is in a land full of thorns and weeds, there is always a space in which the good seed can grow. You have to trust God.

Pope Francis

Every day, Salvador, the custodian at the Catholic school where I work, has a lunch that looks like he picked it up at Chipotle. He assures me that it's just leftovers from his wife's cooking. I asked him what her secret is to great Mexican cooking, and he says, "It's the cilantro." Oh yes, we all know what fresh cilantro can do to ordinary salsa. Salvador grows it, literally, in his yard. I have clover in my yard; he has cilantro. "Yeah," he says, "it grows wherever I plant it."

Come to think of it, I have a rosemary bush in my garden that grows out of control, despite how many times kids have trampled over it. Grilled rosemary chicken is delicious.

Can we be like those herbs? We know that God has put us in this precise place and moment. We may not be the star herb at the center of a beautiful garden, but we can grow where we are planted and make a difference in the lives of those around us. We can do this despite being "stuck" in an ordinary, weedy yard or, worse, worn down by those around us.

Jesus, help me to live fully in my present situation and grow and flourish there.

To Ponder: Sometimes as mothers we feel trapped. We love our kids but want to do "more important things." Diapers, dishes, and endless errands are tedious and mindless. What are some ways you can be reminded that the little things *are* the important things? Ask God for help in seeing this.

TAMI KISER

JUNE 11
SAINT BARNABAS

Remain Faithful

When he came and saw the grace of God, he rejoiced, and he exhorted them all to remain faithful to the Lord with steadfast devotion; for he was a good man, full of the Holy Spirit and of faith. And a great many people were brought to the Lord.

Acts 11:23–24

Do you know who Saint Barnabas was? He was that other guy who worked with the great apostle Saint Paul. For many, names of saints like Barnabas are akin to forgotten vice presidents. Americans can generally name many past presidents of the United States, yet only a tiny fraction of the population can name even a few vice presidents by comparison.

And that's the problem right there: comparison. Becoming a saint is never about winning a popularity contest. It's about faithfulness. And perhaps, in Barnabas's case—as it often is for us—it's about learning to be free enough to rejoice in the good at all times, no matter who gets the credit. Barnabas was sent by the Church at Jerusalem to see what was brewing in Antioch. Turns out there were many good things being done for the Lord.

That's a heavenly perspective for us to keep. When we see the grace of God, rejoice! When we see something good, say so! Affirm it! Encourage it! Support it!

And one more thing: it's okay if we become a little or unknown saint. As long as we're that "other gal" or "other guy" who loves Jesus. In heaven all will be known. Meanwhile, Barnabas offers advice to live by: remain faithful to the Lord with steadfast devotion.

Jesus, make me an affirming and encouraging saint.

To Ponder: In whom can you spot the good today? Rejoice by offering a prayer of thanks. Then affirm it in some way by a word or deed.

PAT GOHN

All in the Family

> I want you to be concerned about your next-door
> neighbor. Do you know your next-door neighbor?
>
> *Saint Teresa of Calcutta*

When we bought our house, Tony lived next door. A widower in his nineties, he loved telling stories about his family and the neighborhood he'd lived in for decades.

After Tony passed away, the house stayed in the family. His granddaughter Joyce and her daughter lived there for a while, followed by Joyce's sister Julie and her husband and kids. Our daughter has grown up with the family Tony loved talking about—playing outside, celebrating birthdays, and talking late into summer evenings.

Still, Julie and I joke about how rarely we see each other, even living next door. Work, kids' schedules, and other obligations sweep aside the best intentions along with the best-laid plans.

As I write this, it's almost April, and the winter has been cold. Julie's fifteen-year-old daughter was diagnosed with cancer in February and is waging a brave battle, determined to beat "Mortimer Dorkus," her name for the cancer. Thankfully, the odds are in her favor. The first time I saw this child, she was a toddler in her father's arms at Tony's funeral, and now she is facing this.

What are my other neighbors facing? I'm embarrassed to say that I get most of my news about them from their Facebook pages. Fortunately, I know that as the weather gets warmer and we're outside more, we'll be more tuned into one another's lives. But for now, our knowledge of what anyone is going through is somewhat pitiful.

Lord, Mother Teresa traveled across the world to help her neighbors. Help me step out of my own world to connect with those around me.

To Ponder: What keeps you from connecting with your neighbors?

LISA LAWMASTER HESS

JUNE 13
SAINT ANTHONY OF PADUA

Laughing at Ourselves

Tony, Tony, look around, something's lost that must be found.

Prayer to Saint Anthony of Padua

He's a Doctor of the Church; he was referred to as "wonderworker" for the miracles God performed through him. Anthony of Padua was also a Franciscan, though, and they tend to have fairly jolly senses of humor, so perhaps from heaven—with his legendary humility—he finds it amusing that more often than not his patronage and assistance is sought when car keys and eyeglasses have been misplaced.

The holy men and women of heaven who intercede for us are due much reverence, of course, but sometimes the simple stories and early rhymes with which we first learn about them help us develop a fondness that turns into intimacy, through which they help us learn to laugh at ourselves. I once made a mess of a project I was sure I could ace. When I failed

I turned to my dear friend, Saint Philip Neri, who used to start his day praying, "Lord, don't trust Philip to get it right." As I whine to Philip about my asinine pride, I can imagine his gentle voice saying, "Yes, God can't trust *you*, either." It makes me laugh; it also makes me realize that as a saint, I would be the patron of lowering expectations.

Saint Anthony, help us to grow in love for each other through the gentle jibes of humor, born of humility.

To Ponder: If you were a saint, what would you be the patron of? How might your kids answer that, though? Make a game of that question in your family, and let everyone suggest answers. You will learn what gifts you see in each other.

ELIZABETH SCALIA

JUNE 14

My Perfectly Imperfect Kitchen Table

If you wait until the wind and the weather are just right, you will never plant anything and never harvest anything.

Ecclesiastes 11:4

My kitchen table is about thirty-five years old. It was originally my mother-in-law's table, but I wouldn't call it charming and treasured in an antique sort of way. I'd say it's sturdy and sufficient and not worth replacing despite its outdated appearance and stained seat cushions. It's one of the many furnishings in my home that I don't particularly love.

When we moved into our house nearly twenty years ago, I told my husband I wanted to wait until everything was perfectly decorated before I invited people over. I wanted custom-made window treatments and paintings hanging on every wall. But eventually I realized that it was futile to wait. I began hosting book club meetings, baby showers, and Fourth of July parties. And I tried not to notice the flaws and imperfections as I welcomed guests into my home.

Decades later, I still have empty walls and hand-me-down furniture. But I also have friendships and memories formed over long conversations at my less-than-perfect kitchen table. My home will always be a work in progress—just like I am.

Lord, please help me to let go of perfectionism and keep my eyes focused on the things that truly matter. Give me the courage to invest in other people even when the timing doesn't seem ideal.

To Ponder: Are you waiting for perfect conditions before you move forward on something important? Is there an area of your life in which you need to release perfectionism and trust in the Lord?

THERESA CENICCOLA

A Small Day's Work

We shall never know all the good that a simple smile
can do.

Saint Teresa of Calcutta

Do you smile at people? I do now, but I didn't always. I grew up in New York and learned from a young age to not make eye contact with strangers, especially on the subway. Then I moved to Florida, where everyone was always nodding hello and smiling. So I started responding by smiling back. And no one has ever been offended by my smile. A smile costs you nothing to give and you may get one in return, which is lovely.

What would happen if instead of scowling we smiled at the person who cuts us off on the road, or takes the close parking spot, or has twenty items in the ten-items-or-fewer lane? Not a sarcastic smile, but a genuine smile that reaches up to your eyes and says, "You seem to be in a hurry or stressed or annoyed, so here, let me share my smile and hope your day gets better."

Make this your day's work, to share a smile with everyone. Depending on the situation and your comfort level, add a "God bless you" or "have a nice day" or whatever is appropriate. If you go out with your family, have them do the same. You could even have your children keep a log as to people's reactions when they smile at them.

Lord, help me to share my smile with all those I see today; let them see you in me.

To Ponder: How did your day go when you consciously decided to smile at others? Do you think you made a difference today?

DEANNA BARTALINI

JUNE 16
The Day in Focus

As the family goes, so goes the nation and so goes the whole world in which we live.

Saint John Paul II

Our family's tradition of morning prayer started out of sheer desperation. We had a five-minute drive to my daughter's preschool, and she was in a hysterical three-year-old fit in the back seat.

As we were driving toward her school, I quickly prayed to refocus both of us. It sounded something like this: "Dear Lord, please let my daughter know how much you and her mommy love her. Thank you for the wonderful blessing of her kind teacher and wonderful friends." It was simple, and yet, her tears stopped. This prayer opened the door for calm, loving communication, even amid a tantrum.

As the years have progressed, her two young brothers were added to our morning routine in the car while we call Daddy, who will pray with us, on our way to school and work. While we do not need to calm tantrums anymore (well, not usually), we all know the power of prayer and the importance of praying as a family. We pray for each other, extended family, or the occasional stuffed animal as well as people in need of prayer from around the world whom we hear about in the news.

I had no idea when we started this practice how my family would benefit. We never drive to school without a prayer. Our family has grown accustomed to praying before we leave each other for the day. It puts our day in proper focus no matter what challenge any of us is facing that particular morning.

Dear Lord, help my family to always turn to you, together.

To Ponder: What might be an age-appropriate manner to pray with your family today?

MEG BUCARO

JUNE 17

Through the Eyes of a Father

The devil will try to upset you by accusing you of being unworthy of the blessings that you have received. Simply remain cheerful and do your best to ignore the devil's nagging. If need be even laugh at the absurdity of the situation. Satan, the epitome of sin itself, accuses you of unworthiness! When the devil reminds you of your past, remind him of his future.

Saint Teresa of Avila

She emerged from the tree row and took in the view. Her children were perched on top of the sharply rising hill, creating a silhouette of youth and vigor against the azure sky. Her heart expanded, and her conscience awoke at the unfamiliar feeling. A heart this full seemed to verge on the brink of gluttony as she drank in the beauty of her family. She couldn't think what she had done to deserve this—an entire day spent in the wonder of God's creation with her husband and children. But her Creator never focused on the forgiven and forgotten mistakes of her past. He only saw her future through the eyes of a doting Father. He saw a soul filled with the same possibility as the day he created it and a heart worthy of his gifts because he willed it to be so.

Dear Jesus, please help me to ignore Satan's lies and instead see my soul the way you do: full of possibility and worthy of your love.

To Ponder: Do you ever find yourself thinking "I don't deserve this" when an unexpected blessing comes your way? Quiet your thoughts and instead gratefully accept God's gifts with a humble spirit and a joyful heart.

CHARISSE TIERNEY

JUNE 18

Making Time for Wonder

For it is owing to their wonder that men both now begin and at first began to philosophize.

Aristotle, Metaphysics

Every parent has been there: Why is peanut butter sticky? Why does God make it rain? Why does Daddy have to snore so loud? What does this word mean? Why are they laughing? At a certain age the questions come thick and fast, until finally we resort to the question-ending parental "because." (The even more quelling "because I say so" is reserved for veiled protests like, "Why do I have to brush my teeth?")

The "because" works for a while, and then, of course, they learn to ask, "Because why?"

Kids ask these questions because they wonder about things and want to know the answers; we see that wondering as the beginning of knowledge. Without wondering, we don't ask the questions.

It can be hard for parents of young children to take time for their questions, let alone time for God, and perhaps one way back to him is to spend time wondering. Who is God? Why did he die for me? What does he want of me? Wonder leads to knowing, and wonder about God leads to prayer.

It's a surprisingly easy thing to make time for. It requires no materials, and you can do it while doing many other things: while driving to and from school, while doing chores, while waiting for the school bus. And if you share your questions with the kids, you can enlist their sense of wonder in keeping it going.

Lord, please remind me to think of you in wonder as I go about my day. Bring to mind those questions you'd like me to ask, that I may come to know you better.

To Ponder: What keeps you from praying?

WILL DUQUETTE

Inspiring Blooms

I have only to come down the verandah steps into
the garden to be at once restored to quiet, and
serenity, and my real and natural self.

Elizabeth von Arnim, The Solitary Summer

Last year, on a day when the kids were in school and I was
not at work, I spent my free time visiting a beautiful estate
and garden a short drive away. The hundred-year-old house
is gorgeous and worthy of a tour, but the vast gardens are
the real star. All around me were camellias, dogwood, lilacs,
tulips, and roses getting ready to bloom. I wandered happily
down the paths, smelling flowers and snapping pictures and
soaking in the loveliness all around me. It was the perfect
way to spend my day alone. I've managed to make a few
more return visits since then.

Gardens have a certain kind of magic. When I take a
solo stroll through the flowers, I find my stress dissipates
and my sense of wonder increases. The beauty and variety
of the blooms is inspiring, a testament to the endless creativity of God, and I always feel my own imagination unfurl in
response. These garden visits do more for me than a visit
to the mall; they help my soul settle into proper alignment,
reminding me that the world is beautiful and good and that
there is something sacred about making other things grow.

*God, you fill the world with inspiring things. Thank you for your
creative abundance.*

To Ponder: When was the last time you spent a few hours in a garden? Do a little looking and find one you can visit, then set a date to go. Wander the paths, ponder the beauty, and let your soul blossom.

GINNY KUBITZ MOYER

JUNE 20
WORLD REFUGEE DAY

People, Not Labels

These young people, who have come to learn how to strive against the propagation of stereotypes, from people who only see in immigration a source of illegality, social conflict, and violence . . . can contribute much to show the world a Church, without borders, as mother of all; a Church that extends to the world the culture of solidarity and care for the people and families that are affected many times by heart-rending circumstances.

Pope Francis

Today there are more than fifty million refugees in the world, the largest number since World War II. Extreme violence and extreme poverty breed extreme misery that erupts in death, destruction, extremism, or extraordinary courage. Of these four options, why would we not choose extraordinary courage telegraphed in the people who bet all their savings, put their lives in the hands of crooks, take on life-defying journeys, and leave behind everything and everyone they know to start not just from the bottom but from the shadows, only that they can work, be safe, and offer a better future for their children?

As a connected world, none of us can be sheltered from the consequences. As a global community, such misery assaults our conscience and humanity. As faith communities, we recognize this suffering as Jesus's cross. It is up to us to choose the part we will play in this modern story of the Passion. Will we be like the crowd, Pontus Pilate, the Pharisees, the soldiers, Judas, the other disciples, or Simon, the Cyrenian? Let us look to the Resurrection to bring about new life and healing, to look at refugees differently, and to claim Christ by claiming them.

Please help us see immigrants as people first, with inherent dignity and rights, before we get lost in the economic, legal, and political wrangles that leave no place for the face of God.

To Ponder: Who are the refugees and immigrants in your life? How can you pray for them and support them?

DR. CAROLYN Y. WOO

JUNE 21

Vacation

Come away by yourselves to a deserted place and rest awhile.

Mark 6:31

Like a retreat, a vacation is bound up with the idea of getting away from normal, everyday life. It is all about a change of scenery and routine. The point is to reconnect—with family, with friends, with God, with nature. New places, new people, new experiences bring renewal, recreation, and restoration of a proper perspective. A vacation can generate new insights, new ideas, or even new solutions for problems. When we continuously spin our wheels in the normal routine of life, we often dig deep ruts that bog us down and block our view. Plodding along, we stagnate in a stressful and unproductive monotony. Vacation has the potential to reignite both creativity and productivity, and getting away from it all can often lead to renewed appreciation of "it all"—family, hometown, and work.

But vacation never means time off from prayer and Christian morality. "What happens in Vegas stays in Vegas" stands for an approach to vacation that we frankly have to reject. The Christian celebrates and enjoys the blessings of God's creation on vacation, but all is sanctified by prayer and thanksgiving. While it is not exactly the same thing as a retreat, vacation for a Christian should always mean not only rest and relaxation but also a renewal of our relationship with God and a restored sense of vocation.

Some would protest that going away on vacation is a luxury. It is a want, they say, not a need. While vacation may not be necessary to survive, I maintain that it *is* necessary to *thrive*.

Thanks for the gift of my family, Lord. Help us find a way to relax together in a way that honors your will for us.

To Ponder: Given your budget and schedule, what can be done to get your family away this summer in a way that would re-create and refresh you?

DR. MARCELLINO D'AMBROSIO

Rediscover Your Spouse

Friendship, as has been said, consists in a full
commitment of the will to another person with a
view to that person's good.

Saint John Paul II

When was the last time you really looked at your spouse or
spent real quality time together? Think back to when you
first met and began dating. If you were to meet him today for
the first time, what would catch your attention? How would
you describe him to another person? What are some of his
greatest strengths and character traits?

Perhaps it's time to rediscover your spouse and reignite
your relationship. Here are a few suggestions:

- Pray together and pray for your spouse throughout the
  day. Ask God to give you eyes to see your spouse as God
  sees him and to love your spouse as God loves him.

- If this is a time in your life when babies never sleep and
  always want to eat, sit with your spouse while you feed
  your baby, talk to each other about your days, and share
  your ideas and thoughts.

- Have fun together with your spouse and as a family. Try
  mini-golf, board games, riddles during dinner, water
  games at home, playing in the yard, or a family trivia
  night.

- Do something for your spouse that is out of your comfort
  zone but meaningful.

- Thank God for your spouse every day. Keep a list of all the things you love and appreciate about your spouse. Thank him for his love and all he does for you and the family.

Dear Mary, pray for me and help me love my spouse as you loved yours, with gentle humility and charity.

To Ponder: How can you show your spouse you love and appreciate him today?

ERIKA MARIE

JUNE 23

The Playfulness of Holiness

God cannot give us a happiness and peace apart from himself, because it is not there. There is no such thing.

C. S. Lewis

Did you ever imagine what life was like for the Holy Family? Were they serious all the time? Always praying and studying the Torah? If Joseph, Mary, and Jesus are our model for family life, what does that mean? Clearly the gospels reveal a family that was obedient to the laws and teachings of their faith as well as a family that actively participated in the feasts, festivals, and celebrations of their community.

But what about the other days when Joseph worked at his craft and Mary made a home for her family and Jesus lived under the roof growing in wisdom and stature? I do not think the Holy Family spent all their time in stern-faced prayer and penance.

I imagine their days probably passed by like most families' days, full of the work and joy and suffering of life. And, like most of us, I imagine there was also a healthy dose of laughter and fun. Because holiness breeds lightness, breeds joy, breeds laughter.

As we reach for holiness and virtue in our families, let us also remember that fun and laughter are gifts of a holy life. Life with Christ is full of as much bustle and joy and adventure as it is of serious work and hard suffering.

Lord, help us remember the importance of play as we journey toward holiness as a family.

To Ponder: Take time to grab your family and play. Make some simple fun together. Laugh wildly at the silliness of things. And remember as you laugh and play to let yourself be re-created by the love of a God who sat at the feet of his own earthly mother and father and played, too.

COLLEEN CONNELL MITCHELL

JUNE 24

Big-Time Family Fun

Give me neither poverty nor riches; feed me with the food that I need.

Proverbs 30:8

Having grown up on a lake and living near the ocean for fourteen years, my best memories and therefore my biggest dreams for family fun include time on the water. Unfortunately, we no longer live on a lake or near the ocean and vacation rentals big enough for our large family are often beyond our financial reach. Sometimes I am tempted to despair of dreaming of "big-time" family fun.

Not long ago, however, my husband and I attended a marriage retreat where we were encouraged to not only dream big dreams, but to also come up with ways to approximate our big dreams: mini dreams.

To be honest, I was a bit skeptical about this way of contentment. "Could mini dreams be satisfying?" I doubted it. But I decided to give it a try, so last summer we purchased a membership to a private lake near our house. We spent more time on the water that summer than if we had rented a lakeside cottage for a week and for a fraction of the cost. Most of all, it more than satisfied my dreams of big-time family fun.

Jesus tells us to ask Our Father God to "give us this day our daily bread," and this prayer of trust and contentment is appropriate not just for our physical nourishment but for all areas of life, including creating family time that is fun and fulfilling.

Father, thank you for giving me big dreams for my family and helping me to fulfill them.

To Ponder: What are your dreams for family fun? How might you approximate even your biggest dreams in mini ways?

HEIDI BRATTON

Coming to Terms with Mother Mary

From Mary we learn to surrender to God's will in all things. From Mary we learn to trust when all hope is gone. From Mary we learn to trust her Son.

Saint John Paul II

I am a little envious of others with a strong devotion to Mary. In truth, I've been a little intimidated by Mother Mary. Being a mother is one of my things. I identify myself as a mom; my kids have been a part of my life for close to half of it. My role and responsibilities as a mom guide many of the things I do each day. The faults and failings I bring to confession usually have something to do with my glaring failure to mother with grace, patience, and virtue.

Mother Mary was born without sin and unhesitatingly embraced God's life-changing will for her life. She raised the sinless Son of God with a saint, Joseph. I sound a little defensive, don't I? I sound like I'm trying to justify my impatience, my weakness, my failings, my struggle to tackle my to-do list with love and grace and joy.

I feel intimidated and I sometimes assume that Mother Mary might be shaking her head, judging me as I try and fail to raise not-so-perfect kids. Burdened with my own insecurities, I assume that their struggles reflect my mothering: what I have done or failed to do. I forget to call out to my Mother to guide me through.

But Mother Mary is without sin, without pride. She reaches out not to judge us or reprimand us but to gently steer us toward her Son. She loves us as our Mother.

Mother Mary, I love you. Guide me as I practice trusting in your Son. Help me to connect with you, learn from you, emulate you and draw closer to your Son through your love and your direction.

To Ponder: What will you ask Mother Mary to help you with today?

MONICA MCCONKEY

JUNE 26

Being Childlike

I cannot dance, O Lord, unless you lead me.

Saint Mechtild of Magdeburg, The Flowing
Light of the Godhead

I always wanted to be the perfect parent. I wanted to give my children cherished memories of Martha Stewart birthday parties, perfectly decorated Christmas trees, and unconditional love. However, in my attempts to instill picture-perfect moments in my children, I had managed to completely remove the spontaneous joy that should have come from the love I had for them. Thankfully, this painful reality hit me a few years ago and I vowed to change my ways.

I still am hopelessly boring when it comes to pretend play with my son, and I can never make those noises that only boys can make. And while princess parties are easier for me than destructive Lego scenarios, there is always a part of me that feels a little awkward as I twirl in a swirl of pink tulle with my three-year-old. But I try. Because it is in these spontaneous moments of childlike love and laughter where the bonds of family are truly strengthened.

No, I will never master the art of being the fun parent. But I am learning to awaken my inner child and respond to the moment just as Our Lord would want.

Remind me, Lord, what it was like to be a child, and give me the grace to become more childlike in your eyes.

To Ponder: Sometimes we forget that strong family bonds are often fostered through fun. If you grabbed a blanket and ate lunch on the floor with your children, would they be surprised? How can a childlike heart bring more love and joy into your home?

CASSANDRA POPPE

JUNE 27
OUR LADY OF PERPETUAL HELP

The Insanity of Some Days

Yes, indeed, many of us have lost touch with our identity as children of God. But it is precisely this childhood that Mary wants us to claim. With the same heart that she loved Jesus, she wants to love us.

Henri J. M. Nouwen

It's the dead of summer. Have hot and humid days forced the kids inside? Did the recent vacation leave everyone feeling a little too close for comfort? Even the best outings can play havoc with the most patient souls. Throw in some sugar here, some hormones there, and, before you know it, you're praying to "Our Lady of Perpetual Help Me!"

We returned home from a summer trip to a flooded house. A fifty-cent plastic piece had broken on our water softener, leaving thousands of dollars of damage and hundreds of hours of work. Eden had just turned to Gethsemane.

My stress began to erupt. The baby was crying, the kids were arguing, and the house lay in ruin. All I could see was dollar signs. It was in that moment that my wife leaned in and whispered, "Look at how blessed we are. We still have God and all these beauties . . . and that bottle of wine in the cabinet."

What a gift a holy woman is to her family. What perspective she offers. My lady was reminding us all that Our Lady was right beside us praying and inviting us to remember we are God's children and have nothing to fear.

Lord, help me to enjoy the unexpected and to embrace the insanity of the day; give me the grace to say yes to all you entrust to me.

To Ponder: What area of your life causes you the most stress? Is the Lord inviting you to let it go? That which takes our attention off God quickly becomes our god. Ask Mary to help you to surrender all today.

MARK HART

Our Bodies Are Gifts

The glory of God is man fully alive.

Saint Irenaeus

Have you ever thought of your body as a gift? Primarily, it is a gift you have received. Secondarily, it is a gift that you give.

Our Creator has given us our bodies as gifts to be cherished, protected, guarded, and loved. Whenever our bodies are used, objectified, or disregarded, we fail to recognize our supreme dignity. In a culture wrought with body issues, it is good to be reminded of the truth: love itself created us in his image, body and soul. Thanking him for the gift of our bodies is the beginning of giving God glory. Henri Nouwen said, "You are a divine choice." God willed every one of us into existence and rejoices in giving us a body fully alive.

Such an understanding of ourselves leads us to be gifts to others. In our vocations, God calls us to offer our bodies as a "living sacrifice, holy and pleasing to God" (Rom 12:1). In all things we can ask, "What is the next loving act?" As people of prayer, we get up for morning Mass, imitate Mary, and kneel in adoration of the Blessed Sacrament. As mothers, we give our bodies when our child is sick with fever—kisses, caring words, and a cloth for his head. As teachers, we give ourselves over to answering constant questions. As wives, we give our presence to our husbands through attentive listening.

Love has created you. Loving others gives God glory and makes you fully alive.

God, my Creator, I thank you for giving me this body. Show me the joy of ever new ways to love.

To Ponder: How do you show the world the love of God through your body?

CINDY COSTELLO

JUNE 29
SAINTS PETER AND PAUL, APOSTLES

Everything
Used for Good

Lord, you know everything; you know that I love you.

John 21:17

Saint Peter famously denied Christ three times; after the Resurrection, Our Lord accepted his repentance. At the end of his life, Peter was again given the chance to choose martyrdom or cowardice, and by the grace of God, his faith did not fail. In the same way, Saint Paul, who was a fierce persecutor of Christians until his conversion, was given the chance to shed his blood for Jesus, and he did.

So many times life is like that: we fail today, and God gives us another chance at the same test. Meanwhile, the sin we committed yesterday allows us to be an instrument of God's healing in the future. We think, for example, of how so many mothers who have chosen abortion later become persons who can help other mothers in crisis pregnancies or who can help fellow post-abortive mothers know that there is healing and grace for all of us, no matter our past.

This is the beauty of life with God: nothing need ever be wasted. Not one sin, not one fault, not one ounce of suffering need be meaningless. Everything we do can be turned by God for good.

Dear Lord, I have done things I am so ashamed of I can't even talk about them. I ask for your forgiveness, and I thank you that even these darkest moments of mine can be turned into a source of light for someone else.

To Ponder: Whom are the people you are able to help because you know what it is like to be in their position? Can you see how God is using your weaknesses to make you a vessel of his divine mercy?

JENNIFER FITZ

JUNE 30
NATIONAL METEOR WATCH DAY

Finding God in Creation

I read my eyes out and can't read half enough. . . . The more one reads the more one sees we have to read.

John Adams

There is nothing more appealing to me than something new to learn. Every new book or idea leads to dozens more, and my list is longer than I will ever get to in my lifetime. In winter, I learn about every subject from quantum mechanics to how to get kids to help with chores around the home. In the summer, though, I like to explore God's marvelous creation firsthand: how a flower opens during the day and closes at night; what our favorite pine tree looks like before it releases its pollen; or why the wasps choose to build their nest in the kids' tree house every single year.

Go outside with your children and observe the world that God created. Admire the order. Wonder at the colors and variety. Since today is National Meteor Watch Day, talk about what meteors are and find out the date of the next big meteor shower. Make a plan to go to a dark spot to watch the sky and listen to the night sounds, marveling in the oldest fireworks show around.

Dear Lord, thank you for your beautiful creation. Help me to learn about you through your creation and spark the fire of learning in my heart. Let the fire you start point others to you.

To Ponder: What area of faith interests you? Biblical history? Marian apparitions? Saints? Angels? Commit to spending at least fifteen minutes a day reading a good Catholic book about a spiritual area that you'd like to learn more about. Bonus points if you include your children or friends.

JEN STEED

July

THEME: SLOWING DOWN

Finding Mission Territory

God made time, but man made haste.

Irish Proverb

In my home state of California, a long-standing tradition exists among students in our Catholic elementary schools. Our fourth-graders undertake the California Mission Project. Students select one of the twenty-one missions founded by Saint Junípero Serra and his fellow Franciscans, visit their mission in person, and fashion an architectural rendering of their selected landmark.

I often wonder what Saint Junípero Serra might think of parents statewide scurrying at the last minute to help their children finish these projects. In our home, our son Adam's Mission San Buenaventura project became a father-son partnership that spanned weeks. My wonderful husband, never one to take the easy way out, helped Adam spot tiny details in the church's construction that were both religiously significant and artistically beautiful. They took their time.

Unlike others who threw together last-minute concoctions built of Popsicle sticks and tape, Adam and Greg savored the project, studying both the details of their mission and the historical events of that important era. They even went so far as to sculpt and fire a tiny fountain whose small pump actually allowed for running water in the center of the mission's courtyard. As they built, they learned together about the life of Saint Junípero Serra, whose thousands and thousands of miles traversed on foot up and down our state left an imprint of Christianity for the generations to come. Padre Serra's travels were slow and steady, but his legacy was lasting.

Saint Junípero Serra, help us to emulate your passion for the Gospel in our own mission fields and homes.

To Ponder: What is your "mission territory"? How can you slow life down enough to spot opportunities to share the good news?

LISA M. HENDEY

JULY 2

The Fruitfulness of Receiving

God is writing an original script with each of our lives. He's not writing a remake or adaptation of someone else's life but something never before written. Through each of us, God wants to open up countless possibilities of saying yes for all who come after us. Never underestimate the power and fruitfulness of your yes to God!

Katrina Zeno

What's the most important thing you can do in the spiritual life? Oddly, the answer is nothing.

Well, not exactly nothing. You're doing something, but that something is letting something else happen. Receptivity is standing open before God in prayer, receiving what he gives you, and responding to his call. Receptivity is simple. All you have to do is give consent and allow him to work. It's anything but easy. I want to be in control of my life. Giving that completely to God is scary. What will he ask me to do? The greatest example of receptivity in history is the Blessed Virgin. At the Annunciation, Mary consented to be the Mother of God. Essentially, God asked her to give up everything and follow him, and she did . . . more fully, in fact, than anyone ever did. The result of her receptivity? Action. She left immediately and ministered to Elizabeth and then became the mother of all humanity.

Receptivity is not inactivity; it is full openness to God's activity in you, which is more fruitful than anything you could possiby do on your own.

Lord, give me the grace to listen, the humility to be receptive, and the strength to respond generously to your call.

To Ponder: What amazing thing does God want to do through you if only you would give up control and allow it? Do you offer resistance to this instead of openness and receptivity?

MARC CARDARONELLA

In Order to Believe, I Need . . .

Doubt isn't the opposite of faith; it is an element of faith.

Paul Tillich

Saint Thomas the Apostle was one of Christ's chosen twelve. He was a great evangelizer, a wonderworker, and a martyr for the faith. Despite his impressive accomplishments, Thomas is best known for one thing: being a doubter. He earned this unshakable label when refusing to believe the stories of Jesus's resurrection. He needed to see Christ and his wounds for himself before he would believe.

Maybe it was Thomas's great doubt that would lead him to be such a great believer. Once he saw the proof of Jesus's resurrection, he was able to proclaim the words we echo in Mass today: "My Lord and my God!" And he never doubted again.

Still, we hold Thomas locked for eternity as the one who refused to believe until he had seen. Maybe we do that because, deep down, it resonates with us.

Like Thomas, I've had plenty of moments of weakness, fear, and lack of faith. I've questioned the whereabouts of God when my husband has been out of work for long stretches. Or when my teenagers make scary choices. Or when a really good person dies. I want to see the evidence that God is here and is in control and that everything will work out in the end. I, too, need to see the wounds in order to believe.

Saint Thomas, increase my trust and confidence to follow Jesus, especially when I am most weak and in need of signs and proof.

To Ponder: Whom may you have labeled unfairly because you chose only to look at one aspect of his or her life? What specific action can you take to make it up to that person for this injustice?

ELIZABETH FICOCELLI

JULY 4
INDEPENDENCE DAY (USA)

Happy Birthday, America

Patriotism is a love for everything to do with our native land: its history, its traditions, its language, its natural features. It is a love that extends also to the works of our compatriots and the fruits of their genius. Every danger that threatens the overall good of our native land becomes an occasion to demonstrate this love. . . . The native land is the common good of all citizens and as such it imposes a serious duty.

Saint John Paul II

In New England, colonial history is celebrated with vigor—even the smallest towns offer fireworks displays. The grandest of all are the fireworks in Boston. It's pure Americana, accompanied by the Boston Pops Orchestra playing the "1812 Overture" underneath the stars along the Charles River.

I've always loved fireworks. There's something wonderful about taking the family, putting out lawn chairs and blankets, gazing at the night sky, and conversing together.

I remember when my oldest was a toddler—he was excited all day, anticipating the fireworks. Sadly, when the first one fired, followed by cannon-like booms, an explosion of tears erupted from him for the rest of the show. As my son sobbed into my shoulder, I recalled that today's holiday is both joyous and bittersweet. We rejoice in our freedoms as Americans. Yet the fireworks and the "bombs bursting in air" remind us of the dangers that liberty faces daily.

Jesus, increase my love of country and its people, as you increase my longing for heaven.

To Ponder: Why not enjoy the fireworks outdoors or on television? Share with your family the goodness in our nation. Offer a prayer for the patriotic men and women who defend it today, and those from years gone by.

PAT GOHN

JULY 5

The Pity of Jesus

Compassion is preferable to cleanliness: with a little bit of soap I can clean my bed, but think of the flood of tears I would require to clean from my soul the

stain that harshness against this unfortunate
would leave.

Saint Martin de Porres

It occurred to me after a recent family gathering that my interaction with others often consists of smoke and mirrors. Like when I sensed my sister's depression and used all of my energy to avoid talking with her about it. Or when I intuited my daughter's discomfort about visiting home after my remarriage and then conversed with her about everything except the aching subject.

As I reflected upon how hard I can work to avoid addressing another's pain, I came upon a reading about the pity of Jesus: "At the sight of the crowds, his heart was moved with pity for them" (Mt 9:36). Closing my eyes, I tried to imagine Jesus's interaction with the pain of others. I envisioned him encountering the blind, the deaf, the hemorrhaging, and then I visualized him using a lot of nervous energy to make small talk with them instead of confronting their anguish directly. It seemed ridiculous.

Jesus went from place to place, person to person, talking with the wounded, touching the sick—straightforwardly addressing their suffering. Instead of avoiding human agony, he entered it, speaking pity into pain and mercy into misery.

I can become blind and mute in one split second when I stumble on a hemorrhaging heart. Afraid that I can't stop the bleeding, I bind up my fear instead. Yet all that may be needed are the simple words: I see your hurt, I see you. To truly see the sufferer is the medicine of mercy, applied right to the human heart.

Piety, which stems from the word pity, does not mean "holier than thou." It means holy *with* thou, *wholly with thou.*

It means being willing to acknowledge another's pain and let it break open my heart.

Jesus, grant me a courageous heart to enter into the suffering of others.

To Ponder: Do you avoid others' pain? If so, of what are you afraid?

JUDY LANDRIEU KLEIN, M.T.S.

JULY 6
SAINT MARIA GORETTI

The Beauty of Waiting

He loves, He hopes, He waits. Our Lord prefers to wait himself for the sinner for years rather than keep us waiting an instant.

Saint Maria Goretti

We all love conversion stories, but the best ones are always the dramatic tales about men or women who took their sweet time coming to Jesus, because they teach us again and again about the patience of Christ Jesus, the second person of the Trinity, the God who does not tell humanity to perform for him and hop to it.

We live in a world that demands us to "hop to it" all the time. In fact, we help to create that world. How often do we express impatience with our phones if they do not load a site as quickly as we have come to expect? We're so spoiled by the instant-everything delivery that defines our lives that we're no longer even cognizant of how very nearly miraculous our communications have become. We don't even think about how a click of a button brings a message from one continent to another, or from earth to a satellite. Computers in Houston, Texas, talk to a rover on planet Mars in the time an angel can deliver a message from God.

But Jesus waits, and he does so willingly, for our answer and for our turning toward him. We could take a hugely important fundamental lesson from that.

Saint Maria Goretti, please intercede for our busy society at the throne of the eternal. We will wait, thank you.

To Ponder: How many times in a day do you urge your kids, your spouse, the traffic—and even yourself—to "get moving, hurry up"? Would slowing down really be so bad?

ELIZABETH SCALIA

JULY 7
FATHER-DAUGHTER TAKE
A WALK TOGETHER DAY

Seeing the World Anew

Look Mommy, there's no plane up in the sky!

Pink Floyd, "Goodbye Blue Sky"

From my daughter's earliest years she was an outdoor adventurer and the big sky only increased her sense of wonder. We began to play a game of spotting airplanes during our outdoor trips. She had this uncanny Radar O'Reilly–like ability to find a plane that I could scarcely see or hear until she would say her famous words, "Airplane! Ha! Ha!" And there it would be.

Over the years, she has collected rocks that she found interesting from just about every hike in every different city and state. She also used to stop and pick up any litter she found on the trail and then go in search of a trash can—which is both admirable (great respect for creation) and unnerving (if you are trying to get a jog in as well).

I led my daughter to the outdoors because it is what I remember and love best about being a child. It was outside that I first felt God's presence so that I could recognize God in the smallest of places inside. This is how I spent my days before the more predictable life of riding a school bus and wearing a uniform came to be. I so cherish more than anything else our communion with nature and the Creator.

And it all began with her seeing the sky and seeing more than I could see.

I give you thanks, O God, for revealing through my daughter what I did not see without her.

To Ponder: What gifts does your child enable you to see in the world? Where has your child taken you? How has your world and appreciation of God's presence grown?

JAY CUASAY

Retiring the To-Do List

Marriage is the most basic expression of the vocation
to love that all men and women have as persons
made in God's image.

Christopher West

Janet and Danny, the parents of eight grown children, came to visit us. We live right outside the city and they wanted see the sights. But once they arrived, they spent most of their time with us. They sat on my front porch swing, sipped lemonade, and watched my children splash around in the kiddie pool.

They didn't ask to watch television or use the computer, and I never saw them check their electronic devices. Instead, every morning after cereal bowls and coffee cups were cleared off the table, Janet braided my daughters' hair and offered impromptu art lessons. Danny took all the children strawberry picking.

Once, as I flew around the kitchen tackling daily chores, Danny rocked the baby and joked in a southern drawl that would make you weep because you were born north of the Mason-Dixon line: "I'm working so hard, I don't know what to do with myself."

During those few days, Janet and Danny taught me how important it is to slow down in order to cultivate the important relationships around you. Daily life often leaves me feeling frantic and stressed, but last summer my friends reminded me that the best things in life happen when we take time and pay attention.

Mother Mary, I'm addicted to hustle and bustle. Even though I know there is a better way, I don't make the effort to lighten our load. Help me to keep my priorities in check—to spend time developing relationships with your Son first, and then my husband and children.

To Ponder: What is one area of your life you know you need to simplify so that you can make time for the people around you? What can you do today to make that happen?

COLLEEN MURPHY DUGGAN

JULY 9

Be a "Queen of Peace"

From Mary we learn to surrender to God's will in all
things. From Mary we learn to trust when all hope
is gone. From Mary we learn to trust her Son, Christ
the Son of God.

Saint John Paul II

Along US Highway 101 in Santa Clara, California, a thirty-two-foot tall statue of Our Lady, Queen of Peace, gleams in the sun. Another flanks Holy Spirit Catholic Church in New Castle, Delaware. Visitors stroll in gardens, relaxing and praying in the shadows of these stainless-steel monuments.

Just as Our Lady adorns our landscapes and lives as Queen of Peace and of Heaven, we as daughters, sisters, wives, and mothers can also be queens of peace. When the stomach flu hits like some demonic domino game and we're scrambling through laundry and distributing flat pop and saltines, we may not feel queenly. When our teens oversleep on finals day or stockpile dishes under their beds, or when a dear friend forsakes us for another, we may forget our royal calling as a "queen of peace."

But how we respond to crises will shape our days along lines of prayer or chaos. At home, we can spread peace as quietly as a whispered prayer and a soothing hand on a brow. In our jobs or as we volunteer in our communities, we can be the team player who doesn't gossip—the one who offers uplifting words and smiles. If we ask, Mary, Queen of Peace, will lead the way.

Dear Lord, please help me respond to heaven's call to be prayerful and "queenly" so I can spread peace in my home and wherever I go.

To Ponder: When your day is hurtling down its track like a runaway train, do you take a moment to pray and remember your noble calling as a daughter of God, friend, wife, and mother? How might you live as a "queen of peace" today?

MARIANNA BARTHOLOMEW

JULY 10

Self-Care

To make good choices, I must develop a mature and prudent understanding of myself that will reveal to me my real motives and intentions.

Thomas Merton

When I was in graduate school studying counseling, the focus of nearly every course resulted in the same topic: self-care. This term meant little to me at the time because I was in my twenties, unmarried, and without children or other major responsibilities. Fifteen years later, I know well the importance of self-care because I am a full-time caregiver to two children with unique, special needs.

Slowing down and caring for our own needs often appears selfish and trite. I have found that slowing down is an aspect of self-care that requires intense discipline—to eat healthy and nourishing foods, to nap if I'm given the opportunity, to carve specific time each day for solitude and prayer, and to continually evaluate my priorities.

I have found no better way to deepen my self-awareness than by deliberately slowing down and listening to God's voice speak to my heart. In that silence—often forced and always intentional—he guides me, grants me strength and peace, offers clarity, and gently reminds me to refocus when I become distracted from his will for me as a wife, mother, and friend.

Heavenly Father, you nurture me in the silence of my heart. Teach me to slow down and care for my mind, body, and soul today.

To Ponder: How can you be more intentional in slowing down, caring for your needs, and setting aside time today to hear God's voice and bask in his peace?

JEANNIE EWING

Poustinia of the Heart

Slow down. Everything you are chasing will alight
on you like a firefly at dusk.

Anonymous

Our culture and society encourage speed and productivity, emphasizing doing instead of being. Attending to laundry, cleaning, shopping, and all the small doings of the day don't feel like being an apostle. It is easy to be impatient waiting for God's invitation for us to do more.

Saint Augustine explains, "By making us wait, God increases our desire, enlarging the capacity of our soul and making it able to receive what is to be given us." Though it seems contradictory, slowing down is the answer to our longing to do more.

Catherine Doherty, founder of Madonna House, wrote, "What you do matters, but not much. What you are matters tremendously." She promoted the practice of *poustinia* (desert time), to help people slow down and find God in daily life. Catherine expanded the idea to a "*poustinia* of the heart," where we find communion with God by cultivating a silent, still space within.

Taking the time to slow down is how we find our call to highlight God's kingdom. Catherine Doherty's favorite image of the Christian life is a person standing with arms outstretched, "one hand, in faith and prayer, touches God; the other hand is extended in service to the neighbor."

Saint Benedict, whose feast we celebrate today, reminds his communities that their spiritual and personal growth is a call to be a blessing to others.

Lord, in choosing the "better part" (Lk 10:42), I let you highlight your kingdom. Help me to "prefer nothing, absolutely nothing, to the love of Christ" (Saint Benedict).

To Ponder: How might you live Saint Benedict's encouragement to "listen and attend with the ear of your heart"? What is your balance between work and prayer?

MARGARET KERRY, F.S.P.

JULY 12
SAINTS LOUIS AND MARIE-AZÉLIE MARTIN

Finding Silence in a Hectic Life

Wouldn't you feel you had a rich reward if God, so well pleased with you, gave you a child who would become that great saint you have so longed for?

Visitation Sister Marie-Dosithée, Zélie Martin's sister

It is very difficult in our fast-paced culture to slow down and just listen for the gentle voice of our God. Life was hectic for Louis and Zélie Martin, too. With businesses to run, children to raise, and an active life of charitable work, the parents of Saint Thérèse of Lisieux could have made excuses. Yet, they were determined to live according to the call of God in their souls rather than according to the culture of materialism that continuously bombarded them with distractions and temptations.

Louis and Zélie were meticulous in their adherence to the laws of God and the Church, but they were cheerful and generous of heart, encouraging their children to enjoy the simple pleasures of their lives. Sundays were particularly special, with long walks after morning Mass, lovely conversations, simple games, and time for prayer.

Even through periods of intense suffering—the deaths of four of their nine children and Zélie's terminal breast cancer—their sanctity, combined with the delight they took in each other's company, presented a beautiful example to others.

Jesus, teach me to delight in your laws and bring joy to my family so that our lives will shine with your radiance.

To Ponder: In what ways do your family routines support the joy of your shared life of faith and help you to listen more closely to the voice of the Holy Spirit?

⸳LISA MLADINICH

JULY 13

Slow Down and Look Up

Our spiritual life is God's affair because whatever
we may think to the contrary,
it is really produced by God's steady attraction

and our humble and self-forgetful
     response to it.
It consists in being drawn, at God's pace and in
     God's way,
to the place where God wants us to be.

Evelyn Underhill, The Soul's Delight

Slow down and look up. I heard these words over and over in my heart that busy summer, while washing dishes or folding laundry or frantically working on six projects at once.

Slow down and look up. Every time I paused to pray for peace or plead for help, this was the quiet response I received. Finally, I started to listen.

I slowed down my actions during simple tasks—cooking, cleaning, or caring for children. I stopped to look up at the sky outside my window as I rushed around my days.

Gradually I felt the tight coil of stress release. Slowly my life returned to God's pace. In the flurry of that busy season, I had forgotten the calm center: God's love beckoning me back to the place he wanted me to be.

Slow down and look up. This is still the gentle reminder I need each day: to let God lead and to keep my eyes lifted above.

God of the Sabbath, help us to hear your call to slow down and seek you. Lift our eyes and hearts toward your love, and let us re-center our lives in you.

To Ponder: Where in your life do you need to slow down? When might you need to look up and remember God?

LAURA KELLY FANUCCI

Getting to Acceptance

God teaches the soul by pains and obstacles, not
by ideas.

Jean-Pierre de Caussade

"Settle down," Mama said. She used to say that a lot when
I was a toddler and a little boy. Even as a teenager, with the
accompanying fury of emotions, I recall Mama telling me on
many occasions, "Settle down."

As a small child, it was next to impossible for me to really
settle down. I was so full of energy and so empty of any
understanding as to why I should want to settle down. *Settle
down? For what? And miss all this fun?*

As a teenager, however, I began to see the importance—
even the necessity at times—of settling down. Rash decisions
and rash actions often backfired, and practical wisdom forced
my teenage self to admit that Mama was right.

I'm an adult now, and I confess that I still find it difficult
to settle down. The pressures of earning a living and raising
a family weigh on my peace of mind and soul. So many little
things happen in my daily life that I wish would have happened differently: a fender bender, a dead battery, running
late to a meeting, a sick child, a broken plate, spilled milk.
Things that I may or may not have been able to prevent.

But when I settle down and turn to God, I start to see that
the simple acceptance of every daily happening as God's will
for me is the key to peace and joy-filled living.

Mama Mary, please help me today to settle down so that I can better see God's hand at work in my life.

To Ponder: What steps can I take to carve out time every day to settle down and become aware of God's presence?

JEFF YOUNG

JULY 15

Inspired by My Marriage

Contented man, limited and bound by circumstances, makes those very limits the cure of his restlessness.

Venerable Fulton J. Sheen

Every weeknight around 5:30 p.m., my six young children are gathered around the table (or, more likely, I am begging for cooperation to get them there). I am at my wit's end. I am feeling restless and dying to run out of the door.

I long for and listen closely for the garage door to open, knowing that my long day alone with the children will soon be a shared day and that I will no longer feel trapped and lonely (despite my company) in my kitchen. I adore my children, but I am giddy for an extra set of hands and to hear a voice that may actually respond with kindness and appreciation.

When I hear Daddy returning to us, I (a little too excitedly, say the kids) exclaim, "Oh, thank God!" It is a prayer of thanksgiving for my husband's safe return and a renewed hope that I may actually make it until bedtime.

"Are we *that* bad?" my eight-year-old daughter often asks. "Do you love Daddy more than us?" my seven-year-old son chimes in. The younger kids just giggle at a family joke that they don't really understand.

Joking aside, the prayer is heartfelt. And I dare hope that my children will remember how happy Mommy was when Daddy came home, rather than remembering how cranky Mommy could be when she was trying to oversee homework, calm overtired toddlers, and make an edible meal.

May our marriages be an example, an inspiration, and an influence for our children. May the limits that we often face as mothers be a source of joy.

To Ponder: What are ways that you show your children how much you love your spouse?

TRISH BOLSTER

JULY 16
OUR LADY OF MOUNT CARMEL

Creating a
Buffer Zone of Time

Be still, and know that I am God!

Psalm 46:10

I am in perpetual motion, and, honestly, I like it that way. It would probably be better for my family if I were to slow down a bit, to take a little more time to smell the roses and such, but it remains a fact that I like to be busy. If I do not give this tendency over to the Lord, however, I fear that instead of a pious scripture as the memorial on my tombstone, my kids will put something more like, "Mom said, 'Just do something. Sit, stand, or get outta the way.'"

One positive step I have taken toward slowing down is to establish more of a buffer zone of time around all my activities. It's amazing how just this one change in behavior has made life feel much less frantic.

Rather than waiting until closing time when the kids are exhausted at the zoo, we leave mid-to-late afternoon when they are still in good moods. We (at least try to) leave early for church instead of right on time. We come home from vacation on Saturday rather than on Sunday (something I used to think was an insane waste of precious vacation time), thereby having a day to ease back into the normal schedule rather than being slam-dunked into Monday morning.

I am not yet very good at being still, but I am at least moving in the right direction.

Father, I do want to know you. Help me to be still enough, for long enough, for that to happen.

To Ponder: Are you too busy? Even if you cannot reduce the number of activities in your life, could you at least put a little more breathing room between activities?

HEIDI BRATTON

Being Brave Enough to Not Be Fine

Trouble is a part of your life, and if you don't share it, you don't give the person who loves you a chance to love you enough.

Dinah Shore

How many times do we ask someone casually, "How are you?" and expect him or her to *really* tell us? Most of the time, I think we expect the usual responses: "Fine, thanks. And you?" or "I'm doing okay." We are so conditioned to hear these replies and move quickly on our way that most of the time when people ask how we are we don't bother to tell them. We smile, say, "Fine," and go on with our business.

God doesn't want us to be alone, though. That's why he made us in community. Adam needed a helper and companion, so God made Eve. Jesus even needed companions—he had twelve of them. We don't help ourselves or anyone else when we pretend to be "fine" all the time. Sometimes sharing trouble is giving someone else a chance to show us how much he or she cares.

"A friend loves at all times, and kinsfolk are born to share adversity" (Prv 17:17). The next time a friend or loved one asks how you are, instead of saying, "Fine, thanks," consider telling him how you *really* are. Maybe things aren't going so well. Maybe you could use some help. Maybe you just need a hug. Whatever it is, we were made to bear one another's burdens.

Let's give each other a chance to do just that.

Jesus, I want everyone to think I am doing okay on my own, but sometimes, I could use help. Please help me to be vulnerable with those I love rather than pretending to have it all together all the time.

To Ponder: With whom—and how—can you share a burden today?

ABBEY DUPUY

JULY 18

The Blessing of Extended Family

We meet no ordinary people in our lives.

C. S. Lewis

Family reunion: two words that translated into, "Long car ride for a long weekend to see strange people I only see once a year who seem to know me, but I don't know them, and they pinch my cheeks a lot." That's what I thought when I was seven or eight.

The trip was to my grandfather's old home, where I became reacquainted with all of my relatives, but especially my great aunts—four strong women who dominated the festivities with their wit, wisdom, musicality, and delicious home-baked pies.

They let me turn the crank to make ice cream and encouraged me to get out there with all the cousins to play volleyball. When I got older, I liked sitting and talking with them. They certainly seemed interested in me and what my life was like. We talked while refinishing a floor, picking rhubarb, playing croquet, or discussing the family genealogy.

But my favorite part came when the entire family got together to sing the blessing, "Praise God from Whom All Blessings Flow" in four-part harmony. Whenever I tried to find a harmony to sing, someone else had it covered. It sounded great.

The aunts have mostly passed now, but I still remember, think, and pray for them. Now I am the older aunt who brings the pie and talks to all of my nieces and nephews. And when my kids ask me why they have to take a long car ride for a long weekend to visit unfamiliar people they only see once a year, I smile.

Lord, bless and protect my extended family, the wise ones before and the eager ones coming up.

To Ponder: How can you make a real effort to value your extended family this summer?

ELENA LAVICTOIRE

JULY 19

Poppin' Prayers at . . . Mass?

The Holy Eucharist is our most powerful prayer.

Father John Hardon

It's the two-hundredth day of the year. If you have attended Mass at least once every weekend (plus a couple days of obligation), you have probably been to Mass close to forty times since the beginning of Advent; even more if you attend weekday Masses.

The Mass can feel pretty familiar, can't it? We show up, sit in the same pew, participate in the people's responses, listen to readings of scripture we have no doubt heard many times before, and watch and listen to the mysterious actions and words of the priest.

Have you ever studied the intertwined prayers spoken by the priest, recognizing how they change to reflect the readings of the day or the liturgical season?

Lately, I've been following along with my *Missal*, particularly the Opening Prayer, the Preface, and the Eucharistic Prayer. Each one is a beautifully worded articulation of our faith, summing up God's goodness and the key mysteries of our faith and giving God the praise and honor he is due. Some prayers are said at every Mass; others have been specifically chosen for this liturgical season or for the particular saint's day. These wisdom-packed, faith-filled words of the priest are the Holy Spirit-infused culmination of two thousand years of Church wisdom and tradition. It's exciting to be a part of it, isn't it?

Holy Spirit, stir up within me the beautiful words of the Mass, inspire me with the Word, and fill me with reverence and awe for the Eucharist and gratefulness for the sacrifice Jesus made for my sins.

To Ponder: Start reading these prayers during your private prayer time and marvel as they pop out at you at the next

Mass you attend. How can you share this "poppin'" experience with others in your family?

MONICA MCCONKEY

JULY 20

Listening to Little Voices

We need to be patient if we want to understand
people who are different from us.

Pope Francis

Patience is a virtue, but we aren't so good at practicing it because everything comes to us so quickly that we don't have to. We live in a drive-thru, on-demand culture, and we can get everything—from movies to prescriptions to dinner—in a flash. A big part of our mission to see Christ and be Christ is to look for him in everyone we meet, and that takes some patience and effort.

One Friday I was preparing my first-graders to go to eucharistic adoration for the first time, and it was clear that my lesson was not sinking in. I noticed a little girl who sat with her hand raised and I didn't really think she could contribute greatly to the lesson. But it was clear I wasn't getting the job done, so I called on her planning to use those seconds to regroup.

Something in her voice made me stop and patiently listen. She lovingly explained that we would be seeing Jesus and he was waiting on the altar to see us and listen to all the things we wanted to tell him about. One little boy asked if he could talk to us, and she said, "Maybe, but you have to sit very still, and if he speaks it will be like a small whisper in your ear that your heart can understand." We all learned that day.

Lord, please slow me down. Help me take time to see you in every person I meet this day.

To Ponder: Do you listen to others patiently and intently? Do you reach out to those who can offer you nothing in return? What is your plan for slowing down today?

SHERI WOHLFERT

JULY 21

Are You Reading Poison or Treasure?

A dose of poison can do its work but once. A bad book can go on poisoning minds for generations.

William Murray

There is something magical about books. As George R. R. Martin opined, "A reader lives a thousand lives before he dies. . . . The man who never reads lives only one." And oh, the lives to be lived!

You can walk alongside Job or Rahab in the Bible, on the shores of Perelandra, through the forests of Narnia, the pits of Mordor, or inside Hogwarts. If works of fiction can stir your soul, how much more can stories of great saints?

I was an early reader and have been an avid one for my whole life. In my quest for reading material, limited by my local library, I must admit that I have read more than my fair share of trash. Literal trash. Sometime after getting married, I realized that those books were poison for my mind. It has taken years for some of those "lives" to recede back to a part of my brain where they are rarely seen. Have you "seen" things in books that you wish you had not?

Dear Lord, guide my reading. Lead me to green pastures of books that will inspire my life as your child, that will show me your truths, and that will lead me to change. Protect my mind from the evils that may have entered through poisonous books. Give me a discerning heart.

To Ponder: Are you reading poison? Do your books leave you inspired or leave you wanting instead? Are your children reading good books? Do you know? Take a critical look at the books that are entering the minds in your home.

JEN STEED

JULY 22
SAINT MARY MAGDALENE

Holding on, Letting Go

Jesus said to her, "Do not hold on to me, because I have not yet ascended to the Father."

John 20:17

A friend said after hearing about a heartbreaking incident, "It makes me want to pull my baby into my arms and hold her there forever." Holding onto our loved ones, physically wrapping our arms around them, is a way of taking hold of heaven. Just for this moment, you are safe in my arms. For this moment, we are together. It is a way of saying with our bodies, "I want to be with you. I want to be close to you. I never want to lose you."

Mary Magdalene loved Jesus intensely, and she had already lost him twice: once at his crucifixion, and then again on Easter morning when she found his tomb empty and thought his body had been stolen. When she sees him in the garden the morning of the Resurrection, it is like the moment when the lost child suddenly reappears, the combat veteran somehow survives the deadly mission, the terminal illness is inexplicably cured. *I thought you were gone from me forever, and now I've got you safe in my arms again.*

Jesus tells her: Not so soon! We aren't home safe yet. There's still more to come. There's more work to be done.

Dear Jesus, sometimes I am so tired, so lost in this overwhelming life of mine, that I want nothing more than the security of your eternal embrace. Help me to accept the times when I feel so apart from you, when I am dying of loneliness for you. Give me the courage to keep fighting the good fight until I can finally rest in your arms forever.

To Ponder: Is there anything in your life right now that you are holding onto that Jesus is asking you to let go of?

JENNIFER FITZ

Seeds of Faith

Mary is the lily in God's garden.

Saint Bridget of Sweden

Every summer, we visited my grandma in Arkansas. I loved her house, with her Blessed Mother statue on the front lawn and a forest of trees in the backyard.

One reason for our trip was to drive Grandma to Minnesota, where the rest of the family resided. Looking on a map, the trip could have taken a day. But we took the scenic route, detouring to places from Grandma's past and sightseeing along the way. Sitting in the back seat of Grandma's station wagon, the trip took forever. But the extended travel time did not go to waste.

With each new leg of our journey, Grandma led us in the Rosary. As a child, praying the Rosary was not part of my life. But it was part of hers. And while I did not know how to pray it well, I hung onto every word of every prayer and tried to keep track of where we were on the beads.

Fast-forward thirty years. It is summer again. I sit on the front porch during my early morning prayer, and I picture the Blessed Mother sitting next to me. I recall how Mary gradually has become a significant part of my life. I wonder when it began. And then I remember praying the Rosary in the car with Grandma. It was her introduction to the Rosary that planted the seed that led me to my current devotion to Our Lady.

I smile at this memory, and I thank God for my grandma, whose name just happened to be Mary.

Lord, thank you for planting seeds of faith deep in my heart through my grandma's example.

To Ponder: Looking back, who helped shape your faith life? Thank God for that person today.

SARAH DAMM

JULY 24
NATIONAL COUSINS DAY

A Life of Riches

Children give life, joy, and hope. They also give
worries and sometimes problems, but that is better
than a society that is sad and gray because it has run
out of children.

Pope Francis

Growing up with the Lakota and Assiniboine on the Fort
Peck reservation in northeast Montana, I witnessed some of
our nation's most abject poverty. And yet I, a "white" girl,
the daughter of teachers, felt so much envy at times—not in
things, for lack was everywhere in that regard, but in people. I had one sibling; everyone else seemed to have at least
three. And everyone seemed to be related. There were cousins
aplenty. In fact, even those who came from different blood-
lines still recognized their common history and referred to
each other as "cousin." For many, value came most of all
in family. I looked on with longing, wishing for a piece of
that connectedness. Perhaps that's why the Church's teaching on remaining open to life seemed so right to me, and

why, in adulthood, I ended up with my own little clan of five children.

Welcoming a large family has meant inviting an intense, boisterous, complex life—a messy one at times—but what a gift I was given in childhood! What a sublime peek at a life of riches!

Dear Lord, thank you for opening my eyes to the beauty of life at a young age. Help me remember that in embracing the messiness of a life surrounded by many, I become better equipped to learn how to love you.

To Ponder: What precious memory do you hold of special times with an extended family member—an aunt, uncle, or cousin? How has that relationship added bounty to your life?
ROXANE B. SALONEN

JULY 25
SAINT JAMES, APOSTLE

Recharging Our Batteries

And in the morning, a great while before day, he rose and went out to a lonely place, and there he prayed.

Mark 1:35

On the Sabbath, when work and travel were forbidden, Jesus and his disciples went to Simon Peter's house, where Peter's mother-in-law was confined to bed with a fever. Jesus immediately healed her and lifted her to her feet. What did she do? Did she slump into a chair and wait for sympathy to be poured out on her? No, she immediately began to serve the needs of those in the house.

A priest in my parish told a funny story stemming from this gospel passage. After he'd given what he thought was a great homily on it, expecting some accolades, one of the elderly women of the church met him with a great sigh of displeasure. "Well, isn't that just like a man," she said, "expecting a sick woman to get up and serve him!"

The entire life of Jesus tells us that our lives are for service. But this gospel passage tells us something else, too. After serving, what does Jesus do? He goes off to a lonely place to pray. He has given away so much of himself that he now needs to be by himself, to recharge his batteries and, above all, to get in touch with his Father, the source of all his energy. Doesn't this speak about the second of the two greatest commandments? Love your neighbor as yourself.

Jesus, help me to love myself enough to rest, so that I may return, refreshed, to a life of service.

To Ponder: Are there times when you need to say no, without feeling guilty, as Jesus does?

KAYE PARK HINCKLEY

SAINTS JOACHIM AND ANNE

Waiting on an Answer to Prayer

The very meaning of life is found in the giving and
receiving of love.

Saint John Paul II, Evangelium Vitae

Today is the feast day of Our Lady's parents, Saints Joachim and Anne. Having been barren until old age, the Lord finally granted their request for a child and gave them Mary, a child unlike any other, who would become the mother of the Savior.

When God seems to turn a deaf ear to our prayers, the temptation to despair and anger can be overwhelming. The pain of this seeming rejection of God can lead us to abandon our prayer life and fill our days with endless activities to numb the sting.

We can look to Joachim and Anne, though, as models for what we can do when we feel as though our prayers aren't being answered. Instead of concluding that their difficult circumstances were the result of their being less loved by God than others, they persevered in faith, praying and fasting that God grant their prayer, which he did and in a way in which they never could have imagined.

Saints Joachim and Anne, please pray for me that I not lose hope in our Father's love and care for me.

To Ponder: Have you become discouraged in prayer? Is there a prayer that you've given up on?

MEG MATENAER

JULY 27

Silent with God

In prayer, more is accomplished by listening than by talking.

Saint Francis de Sales

I love going on private retreats. By the time summer rolls around, I sense that it is time to go on retreat again. It is as if the Lord is saying: *Slow down. Turn off the noise. Listen to me speak to your heart.*

I went on retreats by myself for several years and then my husband and I started going on retreats together. We attended the retreats in our diocese for deacons and their wives, but they were more social than prayerful. Then last year my husband and I heard about a Trappist monastery located out of state and we signed up for a four-day retreat. It was just what we needed. There was prayer and silence and inspiring talks. We even got up at four in the morning to pray with the monks. That prayer time included thirty minutes of silence.

In the dark.

In front of the Blessed Sacrament.

Before the retreat, I was concerned that my husband and I would talk to each other too much and lose that precious silence, but my fears were unfounded. We turned off the noise and we listened to the Lord. What a gift to experience the silence and the peace together!

We are going back this year.

Dear Lord, thank you for calling us to grow closer to each other and to you. Help us to take the time every day to sit in silence and listen.

To Ponder: How does God speak to your heart? Do you take time to slow down and retreat from your daily routine? Try scheduling daily prayer time with your family. Take time every day to listen to God.

COLLEEN SPIRO

JULY 28
The Grumpy Franciscan

The joy I admire in others restores my own inward
and outward joy.

Attributed to Saint Francis of Assisi

Saint Francis of Assisi was known for his joy: in God, in God's creation, and in God's people. As a secular Franciscan, I have promised to strive to live the Gospel according to Francis's example.

I fail daily.

You see, I am not a person who comes by joy naturally. A better description for me would be The Grumpy Franciscan. It takes effort for me to look on the bright side.

I don't see Saint Francis as someone who looked at his world through rose-colored glasses, though. He lived in an area where political warfare was a way of life, during a time when the Church faced quite a few crises and scandals. And he did not go around pretending that all of this was okay. Instead, Francis looked for ways to "rebuild the Church" through changing God's people, one heart at a time. And he found joy.

The grumpy heart has the potential to find joy. Even *my* grumpy heart.

Lord, I am grateful for the ability to share in the joys of those I love. Help me to spread joy for love of you.

To Ponder: When is it most difficult for you to find joy? What can you do to share the joy of the Gospel with others?

BARB SZYSZKIEWICZ, O.F.S.

JULY 29
SAINT MARTHA

The Faith of Martha

Jesus wants to be your friend, your brother, a teacher of the truth and life who reveals to you the route to follow in order to reach happiness.

Pope Francis

In the scripture story depicting Mary and Martha, it is Mary who appears to be the better friend to Jesus because she is sitting at his feet while her sister Martha is busy in the kitchen preparing dinner for everyone. The underlying message in the story of Mary and Martha is not about busyness versus prayerfulness, but rather about the importance of developing an authentic relationship with Jesus. This is our goal in life, and it can only be achieved by spending time with Jesus in prayer. Jesus seeks a relationship with each one of us, just like he had with Mary and Martha.

While it is Mary who is initially praised for her actions, ultimately it is Martha who truly discovers who Jesus is in her life. At the death of her brother, Lazarus, it is Martha, not Mary, who professes, "Lord, I have come to believe that you are the Christ." This declaration of faith made by Martha in the depths of her grief clearly demonstrates a spiritual progression from a life of busyness to one of an authentic relationship with Jesus. How did she achieve this? Scripture doesn't tell us, but somewhere along the way, Martha clearly chose to step away from the kitchen and to follow Jesus. Are you up to the challenge?

Lord Jesus, help me to deepen my relationship with you.

To Ponder: What daily tasks are preventing you from building your relationship with Jesus? How can you streamline your life in order to spend more time in prayer?

DR. MARY AMORE

JULY 30
Can I Have More?

He said to them, "Come away to a deserted place all by yourselves and rest awhile." For many were coming and going, and they had no leisure even to eat.

Mark 6:31

We've all been there. The harried dinner hour. Serving food, cleaning up a spill, sitting down with a sigh, and finally taking a bite only to hear, "Can I have more?" It's the time of day that I want to sit and rest before the evening rush and drown a rough afternoon in a bowl of ice cream. But, instead, I often find myself delaying my meal so I can serve more, forgoing the ice cream so I can give more, and hoisting my tired self out of my chair so I can love more.

In the above scripture passage, Jesus, too, is craving rest. He is grieving for his cousin and friend, John the Baptist. He and his apostles need a break from the demands of their ministry. But the crowds follow, saying, "Can I have more?" Jesus, moved with pity, shows us that our hearts find rest in the work God gives us to do. The miracle of the multiplication of the loaves and fish answers their plea for more with an abundance that reflects the infinite depth of God's love.

Dear God, please help me to demonstrate the depth of my love for my family through my physical actions, even when I feel I have nothing left to give.

To Ponder: How can you find rest in the work God gives you to do? Turn your act of service into a prayer. Savor the joy of doing God's will. Rejoice in your capable body. Sometimes it is the most exhausted bodies that house the most rested hearts.

CHARISSE TIERNEY

Hurry Up and Wait

Act as if everything depended on you. Trust as if
everything depended on God.

Saint Ignatius of Loyola

We moved out to the country not because we had a hankering for country living, but because we'd been priced out of the housing market in the city where my husband worked. I was isolated in a neighborhood where we "transplants" were hard-pressed to make meaningful connections with the locals.

I did everything I could think of to connect with the local community: I became active in our parish only to be turned away from activities; signed the kids up for sports and clubs only to have them fall through; joined a mothers club only to find myself excluded on a regular basis. To paraphrase Saint Ignatius, I acted as if it all depended on me. I was heartbroken when my isolation only grew.

Strangely, I am learning to trust. By experiencing repeated rejection, I learned firsthand a bit of how Jesus must feel to reach out to us and have his wounded hand slapped away or ignored. I've been strengthened with the knowledge that even our failures bring us closer to the crucified Christ. Our work for his glory is wider and lasts longer than any neighborhood.

Saint Ignatius, on this your feast day, intercede for us before the Lord. Ask him to help us see where we need to do more and where we need to trust more. We ask this in Jesus's holy name.

To Ponder: Where in your life is it easier to act like it all depends on you? With your children, your husband, your community? Where in your life is it easier to trust God? What might be preventing you from acting, trusting, or both?

ERIN MCCOLE CUPP

August

THEME: CHALLENGES

AUGUST 1
SAINT ALPHONSUS DE LIGUORI

Turning to God

He who trusts himself is lost. He who trusts in God
can do all things.

Saint Alphonsus Liguori

The night we moved my mother temporarily into a skilled-nursing facility I wept aloud. Mom had undergone extensive hip-replacement surgery. Struggling with Parkinson's disease, she needed extended time for recuperation before returning home. As visiting hours ended, I pitched a childlike sobbing fit and was permitted to spend the night in Mom's room. It wasn't one of my finest moments, but I was glad to be with her as she transitioned to her new environment.

For the next week, as Mom recovered, I spent many hours amid her fellow patients. She shared her section of the hospital with amputees, a quadriplegic, noncommunicative stroke victims, and a few patients suffering from dementia. I'm ashamed to share that initially I was frightened to even make eye contact with most of them. "Mom won't be here long," I reasoned to myself.

One morning, while Mom was in physical therapy, I sat working outside of the patients' activity room. Music began to ring out. "Jesus loves me, this I know," sang the patients from their wheelchairs. The chorus resounded loudly, "Yes, Jesus loves me!" Peeking through the door, I saw those who faced such great challenges to their health singing and smiling.

I prayed that morning for the strength to help Mom but also to trust in God's love in all things, especially the hard things, as these new friends did.

Saint Alphonsus, I desire to love God with all my heart as you did. Help me to follow your example of courage amid challenging circumstances.

To Ponder: How do you turn to God in moments of fear, trauma, or grief?

LISA M. HENDEY

AUGUST 2

Finding Joy

The Spirit creates joy, and joy is effusive.

Pope Paul VI

Whenever I'm faced with a decision, my favorite discernment question to ask is, "What will give me joy?"

For many years I was afraid of joy. I didn't see the difference between it and the hollow, fleeting titillation of sinful indulgence. If I was happy about something, I must be sinning somewhere, right?

But joy is a fruit of the Holy Spirit and is therefore a sign of God being at work. Joy is lasting, life-giving, and peaceful. And while we're most likely to feel joy when we're happy, joy can even be present in life's most challenging situations, for it is not based on the state of our emotions. We can suffer and have joy at the same time.

I've learned that the presence of joy can be an important sign when I'm discerning God's will. Is there joy in this choice or in the prospect of this choice? If so, then God's Spirit must be upon it.

I'm learning to trust that God wants me to have his joy and to make life decisions in light of this fact. Even the toughest decisions I have to make—the ones that call me to deny myself—can be joyful decisions. Doing the right thing brings peace.

Lord, Holy Spirit, grant me a generous share of your joy. Let joy be a lamp for my feet and a light on my path.

To Ponder: Name a joyful person in your life. What other qualities do you most admire about him or her? Take a moment to jot them down and offer God a prayer of thanksgiving for that person.

RHONDA ORTIZ

AUGUST 3

Overcoming Challenges

Joy is prayer; joy is strength; joy is love; joy is a net of love by which you can catch souls.

Saint Teresa of Calcutta

Several years ago my husband and I received a life-changing medical diagnosis for him. Although we often said we'd slow down and scale back our work to enjoy travel, we rarely acted on it. Now, we suddenly faced the unknown.

I feared I would never experience joy again. We felt that life stood still, but that was an illusion. We kept on. As our children went off to college, my husband and I spent more evenings at home alone. When our youngest left, we fell into a pattern of early dinners and evenings of television. We hit a slump, not just in our relationship, but in our social life and our general outlook. We became comfortable, and that led to complacency in our lives.

My prayer life fell into a cruise-control pattern, too. Then my husband did something fun. He placed a bird feeder in the front yard. Since we were still eating early, we started taking our coffee on the front porch. Soon, we were watching the birds until well past dusk, the television forgotten.

Those birds—hungry cardinals and territorial blue jays—brought moments of joy into our evenings. They brought us joy, and as Mother Teresa said, the joy was a prayer. It brought us strength, love, and a net that caught our souls.

Lord, thank you for the beauty of creation. Thank you for your love.

To Ponder: Do you ever find yourself in a funk, not stopping to smell the flowers or hear the birds chirp? Make a date with your husband, your children, or a dear friend, and discover a piece of God's beautiful world.

MARIA MORERA JOHNSON

Prayer for Priests

Be sure to say thank you!

Mom

As a high-school teacher, my hackles rise anytime someone says, "Oh, teachers have it so easy. They are done at three o'clock each day." That comment doesn't acknowledge the evenings writing lesson plans or the weekends spent grading stacks of essays. In some ways, when the school day ends, the work is just beginning.

My husband works in ministry at a large parish, and every now and then he encounters someone who believes that priests have an easy ride: "They only work on Sundays, right?" In reality, the priests' weeks are filled with meetings, ministering to the sick and dying, raising funds to replace crumbling brickwork, saying daily Mass, and answering the crises of faith of parishioners who desperately need a one-on-one meeting in a vulnerable moment.

On this feast day of Saint John Vianney, patron saint of priests, it's good to remember that the job of a priest is far more difficult than it may seem from the outside. Burnout can happen, and words of encouragement go a long way. And asking a priest if there are any intentions he'd like you to pray for is one of the most powerful ways to say thank you.

Lord, help me to recognize that priests are human, too. Help me to be aware of all they do and to remember to pray for and with them.

To Ponder: Who is a priest who has made a large impact on your life? If you are able to say thank you, take time to do so. If not, pray for him.

GINNY KUBITZ MOYER

AUGUST 5
OUR LADY OF THE SNOWS

Snowfall in August

Love feels no burden, regards no labor, attempts what is beyond its strength, pleads no excuse of impossibility, for it thinks it can and may do all things. Love, therefore, does many great things and achieves them where he who does not love faints and lies down.

Thomas à Kempis

Today as we reflect on Our Lady of the Snows, we are reminded that impossible things can be possible. On the balmy morning of August 5, 352, snow fell on one of the seven hills of Rome to mark the spot where a church was to be built in honor of Mary. There on that hill now stands the Basilica of Saint Mary Major, where Jesus's crib is housed and pilgrims go to pray to gain indulgences for a holy year. It is said that the snow is a beautiful symbol of the graces Mary sends down to us—as numerous and varied as the snowflakes.

Sometimes as moms, we feel like we are asking God for snowfall in August. We don't see how there could be any possible solutions to the problems we face. But what is a little snow for the almighty God? Do we forget how mighty God is or how merciful? Do we fail to remember how much he loves us? And our children?

For me, whenever I am faced with something impossible regarding one of my children, I give up sugar and pray. And sure enough, God transforms that white powdery substance that I have offered as a fast into snow in August.

Dear Lord, give me faith in the impossible and perseverance in prayer.

To Ponder: What is stopping you from believing God is powerful and generous enough to answer your impossible requests?

SHERRY BOAS

AUGUST 6
THE TRANSFIGURATION OF THE LORD

Elevated Viewpoints

Nothing, however little, that is suffered for God's
sake can pass without merit in God's sight.

Thomas à Kempis

I stared out of the plane window for an hour as we sat waiting to take off. When the Lord said, "My yoke is easy, and my burden is light" (Mt 11:30), he must not have been stuck on a tarmac. I longed to get home, and every raindrop that hit the window became a miniature cross I had to carry.

I was filled with lamentations. Everything was dreary and dark and there was no light in sight. Once we took off, however, and ascended through the clouds above the storm, God granted me a true gift: perspective. On the ground it was gray and overcast; I allowed my perspective to get stuck there. Above the clouds, God reminded me, "This is how I see things. Darkness can never overpower the light." God wasn't just elevating my plane, he was elevating my perspective and outlook.

It's fitting that the Transfiguration took place atop a mountain. Elevation alters our vision. Prior to a climb, small things appear large, but once we've scaled the summit that which is large appears notably smaller. Perhaps that is another reason the Eucharist is the "source and *summit*" of our faith (*Lumen Gentium,* 11; *Catechism of the Catholic Church,* 1324).

Dear Jesus, help me to see through the sufferings and the storms, through all the disfigured moments to behold you in the transfigured ones.

To Ponder: When your spirit gets depressed, do you seek God first or last? When your heart is heavy, do you dwell on it or do you ask the Lord for a new perspective? Ask the Blessed Mother to pray with you, replacing your wounded heart with her immaculate one.

MARK HART

Legacy of Love

In your parents' house, there is always someone
sitting at the table and there is always food.

*My daughter's memories of her grandparents'
home*

My parents were married on this date. We recently celebrated their golden anniversary. I still have memories of celebrating the fiftieth anniversaries of both sets of grandparents in my parents' home when I was younger. Those couples are gone now, but they left memories and marital bonds worth holding up.

The truism is that without your parents, you would not be here. Although we will always be "their child" to our parents, if we have a healthy and honest relationship there is much wisdom and understanding to share about married life, being spouses, and being parents across generations. In my case, I try to be less stressed and more peaceful.

Father Donald Jette, S.S.S., the priest who celebrated my parents' wedding, passed away a few years ago. He was the celebrant at my grandparents' golden anniversary and a frequent honored guest. The last time we gathered was around the enormous dining-room table at the Jersey Shore. My daughter, less than a year old, sat at the head of the table making an absolute mess of a spaghetti meal. The noodles fell onto an expensive Persian rug below and the sauce smeared the elegant table. But no one fussed. Father Jette, who had seen his share of our family stresses, watched me amused and said, "I can tell that she is a well-loved child."

O Lord! You prepared for us a heavenly banquet in your Father's mansion. I believe because I know such a house full of love.

To Ponder: How have the changes in your life from being a child, to a spouse, to a parent given you wisdom and peace with other generations?

JAY CUASAY

AUGUST 8
SAINT DOMINIC

The Spiritual Importance of a Pair of Good Shoes

Arm yourself with prayer rather than a sword; wear
humility rather than fine clothes.

Saint Dominic de Guzman

Today is a feast near and dear to my heart—the feast of Saint Dominic. Steeped in Dominican spirituality through school and parish life, I have learned to love Saint Dominic's practical style of evangelization. It is said that one of his directives to the friars as they went out to evangelize was to have a good pair of shoes and keep them in good repair. It's tough to walk a long, hard journey in a pair of ill-fitting shoes.

This story brings to mind one of the most profound things my daughter ever said to me. We were searching for shoes for her wedding day, and she wanted something beautiful but comfortable. She said, "You know, lots of brides want to go for these sky-high stilettos, but I think the steps you take down the aisle the day of your wedding are the first steps of your journey through life together. I want to be able to really walk that path. I can't do that in stilettos."

Far from being the "happily-ever-after" path of fairy tales, sometimes that path is full of rocks and potholes. God helps us meet those challenges and, through prayer, gives us the right shoes for the journey. Take time to pray with your spouse today, and, in honor of Saint Dominic, be sure to ask for a good pair of shoes for your journey together.

Dear Father, I trust you to equip me with the right tools for the journey. Help me remember that we are not alone, for you are always our help and our guide.

To Ponder: Have you asked God for the right "shoes" to do what needs to be done today?

KATIE O'KEEFE

AUGUST 9
SAINT EDITH STEIN

The Way to Forgiveness

Every single experience in life is grist for the grindstone of holiness.

Donald Nicholl

In one of my favorite *Dr. Who* episodes an evil "time lord" refuses to allow the Doctor to speak "the one word." The story recalls their ruptured relationship and challenges they both faced. The evil time lord does everything possible to stop Dr. Who from speaking the word:

Doctor: "I have one thing to say to you. You know what it is."

Evil Time Lord: "Oh, no you don't!" (Gets up and pushes the Doctor away until he hits a wall.)

Eventually the Doctor finds a way to the words, "I forgive you." As he does, the rift in time is healed.

While we may face the challenge to forgive someone or hear the words of forgiveness, it is primarily God's action and we participate in it. Today's saint, Edith Stein, models this way to face challenges: "When we entrust all the troubles of our early existence confidently to the divine heart, we are relieved of them . . . from God's point of view nothing is accidental, my entire life, even in the most minute details, was pre-designed in the plans of divine providence and is thus for the all-seeing eye of God a perfect coherence of meaning. Once I begin to realize this, my heart rejoices in anticipation of the light of glory in whose sheen this coherence of meaning will be fully unveiled to me."[8]

Jesus, help me let go of yesterday's hurts so I am able to face today's challenges and enjoy today's blessings.

To Ponder: What is most challenging you right now? Forgiveness will prevent this challenge from destroying your heart. Forgiveness opens your mind and heart to see other possibilities. Whom do you need to forgive so that your burden is lifted?

MARGARET KERRY, F.S.P.

Choosing Love over Fear

Christians the world over should be taught that
Christ's teaching to love their enemies is
not optional.

Father George Zebelka

Yesterday was the anniversary of dropping the atomic bomb on Nagasaki. In Hiroshima as well as Nagasaki, the largest casualties suffered were by civilians, including women and children. Father George Zebelka was the Catholic chaplain who blessed the bombs that fell on Hiroshima and Nagasaki.

Afterward his guilt in blessing objects of massacre weighed heavily. He traveled to Japan to beg forgiveness from the living and the dead. For the rest of his life, he was a tireless advocate for peace.

Life still does not feel stable. Reports of terrorism, conflict, and war dominate the news. In some parts of the world Christians are routinely persecuted and killed. It is difficult to bring our fear to the foot of the cross rather than give in to yet more fear and eventually hatred. Jesus preached our obligation to love, especially those who hate us.

Dear Jesus, the ugliness of what our hatred does is not something we are comfortable with, but you don't ask us to be comfortable, you ask us to love each other. Help us to remember Hiroshima and Nagasaki, and in the face of so much suffering may our hearts cry out: never again.

To Ponder: Does your fear drive you toward more fear and hatred or does it drive you to your knees to pray for peace? In the face of conflict and unrest, do you dare to pray for the love of Christ to change you? What would happen if you prayed until you loved your enemies?

MICHELLE JONES

AUGUST 11

Beautiful Obedience

I don't need a church to tell me I'm wrong where I already know I'm wrong; I need a church to tell me I'm wrong where I think I'm right.

G. K. Chesterton

As members of the Church militant, we should know from the examples of the saints that we need ongoing daily illustrations of holiness. I once saw such an illustration when, as a twenty-two-year-old feasting her way through Europe, I visited Assisi.

I saw behind a gate a single Poor Clare nun, draped in black, her face veiled. There stood a woman cloaked in silence, her whole life poured out for Christ in a way that I couldn't begin to fathom. But the image of that woman standing behind a gate remains burned in my memory. This woman offered the world a beautiful mystery, an image of a soul seeking to rest in Christ by stilling her own voice to better hear the voice of God.

When I am faced with a real challenge, be it personal, emotional, or physical, she remains an almost iconic image for me of an obedient will. We know that all things are possible with God; but her silence sings a living testimony: *It's possible to resist the world.* It's not that the business of the world does not matter; we all have things we must manage—even the Poor Clares do. Dust bunnies, bills, meals, and laundry still happen. But she, and those like her who have accepted the stillness of her life, are like a covered chalice after the Eucharist has been shared. They still need to be purified, polished, and wiped free of dust, but they will hold and pour out Christ to others—by their obedience, by their choice to leave behind everything else.

Lord, help me to seek you and to accept correction. Guide me to true obedience.

To Ponder: Is there an area of your life where you struggle with obedience to God's will? What small step can you take today to address that?

SHERRY ANTONETTI

AUGUST 12
MIDDLE CHILD DAY

Leave the Doing to God

Hold your eyes on God and leave the doing to him.
That is all the doing you have to worry about.

Saint Jane Frances de Chantal

It's Middle Child Day for every child who ever felt left out. All of us middle children were once the youngest and forced to give that up. I was the baby for seven years and welcomed my younger sister as my live doll-baby. My older sister smugly told me I couldn't be the spoiled baby anymore, but I didn't care because of my new role as big sister who took charge of the baby.

Here's me, the middle sister: one hand reaches out to catch up with my older sister while I look behind me and catch the hand of my younger sister and bring her along. I'm still that way with my goals in life—playing catch-up while bringing on another project. That's why I need Saint Jane Frances de Chantal's reminder to hold my eyes on God and not on what's ahead or behind me.

God lets me wait for the surprise ending as my sisters did. My older sister would make me wait, just like I did my little sister, for a surprise kiss or cookie until the big task was finished—cleaning the bathroom, cooking dinner, or decorating for a party.

When I work hard at my goals and wait on Jesus, I enjoy the ending more than the start because of the joy of looking in his eyes and anticipating a glorious ending.

Lord, help us to keep our eyes on you and leave the doing to you as we wait for a glorious surprise ending.

To Ponder: Today, how can you begin to hold your eyes on God and leave the doing to him?

NANCY H. C. WARD

OUR LADY, REFUGE OF SINNERS

Why We Need Her

Even if you are the worst sinner in the world; even
if you are already in despair, fly to Mary and invoke
her aid; she shows mercy to everyone who calls upon
her with a sincere desire to turn from sin!

Saint Alphonsus Liguori

A question many Protestants ask is, "Why do you Catholics
need Mary? We have Jesus, who forgives all of our sins if we
are repentant; so, why Mary?"

We need Mary in the same way that a child will sometimes go to his Mama and ask her to accompany him, because
he knows he did something bad and needs to tell Papa about
it, but it seems too hard.

We need her for such moral support and for the sway we
know she holds with her Son—the one she pulled away from
wedding revelry in order to save the shame of a prepared-
ness-challenged bride and groom. We need her because Jesus
pronounced her Mother to all from the cross. We need her
because whom Jesus calls "mother," we—seeking to follow
him in all things—are to do as well.

The first refuge for a sinner is with the most trustworthy
person ever born. Mary, entrusted to present the Incarnate
Word to an evil-challenged world, raise him into manhood,
and then watch him die, is that person.

O Mary, conceived without sin, pray for us who have recourse to you; in our sin and our failures, be our first and best champion as we seek forgiveness through your son, Christ, Our Lord.

To Ponder: The devil may not be able to make you deny Jesus, but he can certainly get you to misunderstand Jesus's mother.

ELIZABETH SCALIA

AUGUST 14
SAINT MAXIMILIAN KOLBE

Called to Martyrdom

Media, like food, is good. But if we let our need for it control us, it becomes not good. Fasting from media is a way to keep us, not media, in control.

Eugene Gan

Saint Maximilian Kolbe is remembered for his final heroic sacrifice: he freely gave his own life so that another man, a husband and father, might be spared. This act of self-denial didn't come out of nowhere. That final moment of martyrdom was the summit of a long slog up the hill of Christian discipleship.

The virtue of *fortitude* helps us to do what needs to be done. Whether it is dying for the faith or unloading the dishwasher, it is the same virtue that allows us to answer God's calling. We all have a calling to be saints just as heroic as Saint Maximilian Kolbe. What form that heroism will take remains to be seen.

For many of us, it will be a martyrdom to change diapers, change the oil, and change ourselves, by the grace of God, into half-decent people who mostly behave. But that workaday death to self is no less heroic if we take it on joyfully, one act of self-denial at a time.

Dear Lord, it is a very long way from where my soul is today and perfect union with your divine will. Please show me one thing I can do to be more like the person you created me to be.

To Ponder: What is one thing that consistently gets in the way of your ability to love and serve God? Pray for God to show you how to grow in self-control and generosity in that area of your life.

JENNIFER FITZ

AUGUST 15
THE ASSUMPTION OF
THE BLESSED VIRGIN MARY

Replenished by the Grace Trifecta

May the spirit of Mary be in each one of us to rejoice
in God!

Saint Louis de Montfort

Our Blessed Mother is an incredible example of the power of being full of grace. We see, through her example, how we can overcome many obstacles through God's grace. Grace is the undeserved yet freely given gift of God's Holy Spirit living within us. When my "grace well" is running dry, I replenish through the grace trifecta: prayer, scripture, and sacraments.

Prayer opens the channel of communication between me and the heavens so I may be open to receive grace. Spending time in the Word of God undeniably augments my prayer life. In the scriptures, I encounter God in an intimate way, opening the ears of my heart to hear his voice. In God's word, I am instructed, counseled, and encouraged. In the Eucharist, I am nourished by the Body and Blood of Christ. This is all grace.

When I feel overburdened and unable to see beyond my fear, stress, or the enormous obstacles before me, I know that with the grace of God I will overcome. Our Blessed Mother shows me that to be full of grace means to be open to God's will and ready to say yes to whatever that will is.

Dear heavenly Father, we thank you for the gift of grace—that amazing endowment of your Holy Spirit living within us that helps us to answer yes to whatever you will ask of us, to overcome our burdens, and to provide strength to help us live a holier life.

To Ponder: When was the last time you came to the well of God's grace for strength to overcome life's challenges? When was the last time you took advantage of the grace trifecta of prayer, scripture, and the sacraments?

ALLISON GINGRAS

AUGUST 16

Eye of the Needle

Almsgiving, according to the Gospel, is not mere philanthropy: rather it is a concrete expression of charity, a theological virtue that demands interior conversion to love of God and neighbor, in imitation of Jesus Christ, who, dying on the cross, gave his entire self for us.

Pope Benedict XVI

In Matthew 19:24 and also in Mark 10:25, Jesus tells those around him that it is harder to get through the "eye of the needle" with a camel than for a well-to-do person to get into heaven. The response even from his disciples: "Who, then can be saved?" In a way, Jesus sets the bar pretty high for those who live comfortably. But what's behind this teaching?

The "needle" was a small gate through which people passed at night when the main gates into Jerusalem were closed. They would have to bend over to come through the "needle" and enter the city. Everyone who heard the Teacher would understand that no one would try to take their biggest animal, the camel, through that gate, day or night.

The real message? Work hard. Salvation isn't guaranteed for anyone. And if you are a busy person who never finds the time to pray, or if you are well-off and distracted by success and have little concern for the poor, you may find the main gate locked, and it will be hard for you to enter through another gate.

Lord, help me to open my heart (and my wallet) according to your will and your teaching.

To Ponder: Meditate today on Jesus's teaching about Lazarus and the rich man (see Luke 16:19–31). Put yourself into that story. Would you be closer to Lazarus or the rich man?

DEACON TOM FOX

Being Brave and Budgeting

Nothing great is ever achieved without much
enduring.

Saint Catherine of Siena

Our family shops in secondhand stores all the time, though
we didn't always do this. When my husband and I were
first married, we didn't have any kind of budget. God had
blessed us with steady income, but we were often wasteful
with it. It took a huge financial scare and a lot of discipline
to work our way out of debt. It meant that we had to give up
some things we had as well as put off unnecessary things we
wanted. I had to let go of many of my possessions, selling
them on eBay. I even worked part time from home to earn
extra money. The whole experience was a lesson in perseverance as well as humility. It takes humility to tell your peers
that you're not going out on the town with them because you
don't have the money.

But going through that struggle has given me more sympathy for people who are struggling to make ends meet and
might need to rely on some kind of assistance to make it to
the end of the month with food in the fridge. Living within
my means forces me to battle my pride and covetousness—to
learn to be happy with the many blessings I already have
rather than to chase after the next thing I want to get.

Father in heaven, help me to be satisfied with the abundant blessings you've poured out on me and to not chase after material desire at the cost of my soul.

To Ponder: Do you own your possessions, or do they own you? How can you work on detaching yourself from your possessions and putting their importance into place?

CHRISTINE JOHNSON

AUGUST 18

August: Month of Meteor Showers

Listen to the sermon preached to you by the flowers, the trees, the shrubs, the sky. . . . They invite you to glorify the sublimity of that sovereign Artist who has given them being.

Saint Paul of the Cross

One summer night in 1965, my older brother Joe was standing on the fire escape outside the window of our Bronx apartment. Head tilted back and with my dad's binoculars pressed to his face, he was looking intently at the sky. High above the city, the stars were bright and a clear crescent moon was on the rise. It was indeed beautiful, and I think Joe might have stood there stargazing all night if my dad hadn't called him inside. But call him he did, and Joe reluctantly stepped in from the fire escape.

Aware of Joe's disappointment at having to come indoors, I had a surprise waiting for him. I'd taken a blackboard and drawn on it an array of lopsided stars and a sadly distorted crescent moon.

"Here, Joe," I said, showing him the blackboard. "You can be inside and still look at the moon and stars. See?" I demonstrated by propping up the blackboard and looking at it through the binoculars. Not surprisingly, Joe declined the invitation to "stargaze" at my chalky pictures.

Maker of all things, the whole of creation reflects your divine artistry. Every now and then, please remind me to lift my eyes from the cares of this world and behold your glory in the skies.

To Ponder: The greatest works of the most skilled artist are little more than chalky images compared with the splendor of the night sky. The psalms tell us that the heavens themselves declare God's glory. Isn't it time to throw a stargazing party?

CELESTE BEHE

AUGUST 19

The Sum of You

We are not the sum of our weakness and failures; we are the sum of our Father's love for us and our real capacity to become the image of his Son.

Saint John Paul II

We all have those days when way too much is happening and there is not enough of what we need to get through the day. Let's face it: coffee, chocolate, and wine can only take you so far. All of our shortcomings are so painfully obvious to ourselves that we may wonder how we have made it this far in life. Sometimes the challenges we face are because of poor decisions; other times tragedy strikes or problems creep up and we did nothing to cause it. It doesn't make a difference, though, if we remember that God knows we are suffering and is there to help us. The Holy Spirit lives inside of each of us and wants to help us and guide us toward seeing ourselves as the Father sees us. Life is not for the faint of heart; Christianity is not the easy road; the Christian life gives us hope to overcome whatever we face in life.

When we spend time praying with scripture or pouring our soul out to God, he strengthens us and reminds us he is with us. We have a Father who wants to love us beyond our wildest imaginings. If we can see past the trial and accept his love he will lift us up and give us the grace to face and overcome the challenges.

Father, you created us in your image. Teach us to see ourselves as you do.

To Ponder: Do you focus more on your weaknesses and failures or do you embrace what God wants for you?

DEANNA BARTALINI

AUGUST 20

How Did We Get So Lucky?

We come to love not by finding a perfect person, but by learning to see an imperfect person perfectly.

Sam Keen

The other night when my husband suggested we "go to bed," I had a revelation. Groaning inwardly yet again at the thought of making love, I heard a voice within saying, "Consider yourself lucky. He finds you desirable."

I have always hated my body. Now that I am nearing sixty I can barely look at myself in the mirror.

This perception of ugliness has made giving myself to my husband difficult over the course of our thirty-eight-year marriage. How can he possibly find me attractive? And yet, he does.

He never really "looks" at other women. He only sees me.

In our bedroom we have a painting of the Blessed Virgin Mary praying over the Blessed Sacrament. She watches over us. And the other night when I heard that message, I sensed it was her, wise and beautiful mother that she is, reminding me of the blessing I have in my husband. Rather than dread his affections, why not welcome them in gratitude?

I realized too that I still find him desirable despite his beer belly and graying hair. We are both lovely in our imperfections.

It's time for me to say "thank you" in my heart and through my actions to my husband every time he wants me. It's a reminder of how God wants us, with our lumpy bodies, broken lives, and stained souls.

Thank you, Father, for loving us as we are. May we always strive to be all you want us to be.

To Ponder: How can you show your spouse that he is a blessing to you?

SUSAN BAILEY

Are You My Mother?

For, since it is the will of Divine Providence that we should have the God-Man through Mary, there is no other way for us to receive Christ except from her hands.

Saint Pius X

Last night, after my husband had bathed the baby, I trailed him up the stairs to feed her and put her to bed. Reaching out my arms to take her from my husband, my nine-month-old daughter looked me over, then decidedly turned her back on me and hugged her father. Having been the "preferred" parent for oh, I don't know, the last seven years—a.k.a., all of our parental years—my mouth dropped open in shock. *After all I do?* I thought. *After all the nighttime nursing sessions and backbreaking `round-the-house-laps on my hip?*

Of course, my husband and I laughed about the incident and, eventually, she did come to me, but I couldn't help but feel a little prick in my mothering pride. The truth is, sometimes I struggle with feeling that because I have a vocation as a mother that I am supposed to be "everything" to my children. But I have been blessed with a wonderful spouse, and it's been a learning curve for me to not see his strengths as my own failures. Instead of beating myself up when the baby reaches for him or when he volunteers for bath duty (again), why can't I celebrate his strengths, too?

God, let me appreciate the gifts that my spouse brings to our marriage and learn to accept our unique abilities, strengths, and merits to each other and our family.

To Ponder: Have you ever felt guilty for not living up to what "you are supposed to" as a wife and mother? How can you recognize the true gift of partnership in a marriage and show your thanks and appreciation to your spouse? Just as Mary gives us the gift of Jesus, what special gifts do you give your family as a mother? And how can your husband's gift to the family be a blessing to you and not a source of guilt for you?

CHAUNIE MARIE BRUSIE

AUGUST 22
THE QUEENSHIP OF MARY

God Is with Us When We Suffer

One could say, in a sense, that [Saint Thérèse] sees her life as the story of a soul who went from suffering without God to suffering with God.

Father Jacques Philippe

I don't suffer well. The littlest pain or inconvenience can derail me for hours or days. I admire those amazing souls who seem to suffer with grace. You know the ones. Despite the pain they feel, despite any inconvenience, they have patience with themselves and others; they don't complain. Rather, they smile. They are even joyful.

We cannot escape the cross. Each of us is called to carry the cross daily. As a matter of fact, the original meaning of the word *Christian* was "little Christ," meaning one who is like Jesus Christ. And the principle act of Jesus's life was his passion (suffering), death, and resurrection. The older I get, the more clearly I see that no one can escape suffering. We all suffer. The difference is that some of us suffer with God while many suffer without. Suffering with God enables us to be like those amazing souls that I admire so much, those souls that suffer with grace, those souls who inspire us to become more and to love more.

But how to do we move from suffering without God to suffering with God? I think it starts with acceptance and faith: acceptance of our current circumstances and faith that God meets us right there in the midst of them.

Mama Mary, you know what it is like to suffer with God. Please help me to accept my life as it is and to trust that Jesus is right here with me.

To Ponder: When it comes to suffering, where are you in your life's journey? Do you suffer with God or without God? How can you grow closer to God in your suffering?

JEFF YOUNG

Backpacking on the Spiritual Journey

Without the burden of afflictions it is impossible to reach the height of grace. The gift of grace increases as the struggle increases.

Saint Rose of Lima

I live in area of the world where one encounters backpackers quite often. Sometimes, I look at them hefting their laden packs over their shoulders as they head off on a hiking adventure or other such journey and wonder if it wouldn't be easier to just leave the burden behind and head out light and easy, trusting they'll find what they need somewhere along the way.

But expert backpackers seem to know better. Experience has taught them that to bear the weight of the burden is necessary, good even, for their well-being rather than as an obstacle or detriment. They know that in the event of an emergency, a change of plans, or a real obstacle to their journey, the things they carry in that pack might very well be the difference between surviving and thriving and having things go very badly very quickly.

In the spiritual life, Saint Rose of Lima's quote above reminds us that our afflictions and spiritual struggles are much like those backpacks. What seem like burdens that are hindering us from making fast, light progress on our spiritual journey are actually the very tools that allow us to access grace at the moments when we most need it to carry on.

Let us remember today that the things we see as obstacles, burdens that wear us down, can be the very things that speed us to the heart of Christ, if only we will let them. Resist the temptation to leave your backpack behind in order to climb faster and lighter. Instead, remember as you feel the weight on your shoulders that, in the burden of your affliction and sufferings, there is an arsenal of tools that can get you to your final destination in heaven. The height of grace, the summit of your spiritual journey, is in reach. Climb with intention and use the tools God offers you in your afflictions to make it there.

God, let me cooperate with your help so I can grow stronger as I backpack on the path of holiness.

To Ponder: What affliction do you face? How can it be a way for you to thrive today?

COLLEEN CONNELL MITCHELL

AUGUST 24

No More Missing Shoes

I believe that if you show people the problems and you show them the solutions they will be moved to act.

Bill Gates

It's 7:34 a.m. and, in order to be at school on time, we have to leave by 7:40 a.m. It would seem like I still have six minutes, but that six minutes needs to include grabbing backpacks (possibly putting lunches in them), finding my keys, getting out of the house and into the car, and putting on seat belts. That might seem like an ordinary or even simple task, but as a mom with two young kids, some days I feel like it's nothing short of parting the Red Sea.

They're miracle minutes really; I find that even leaving two minutes late means more red lights and more traffic. So how can I make the most of those miracle minutes without feeling like a drill sergeant who is barking orders at my battalion? For me, it's being as organized as possible. My saving grace is a closet by the front door that holds the backpacks and my favorite thing: a shoe organizer.

The missing shoes no longer exist in my house. When we come home from school, the shoes are taken off and put in the container, and each morning the kids head to the closet to grab their shoes and backpacks. Seems simple enough to set up, and yes, I'm tempted to skip putting the shoes away after school every day, but avoiding the missing shoes the next morning is well worth the few minutes the day before.

God, help us to find the best ways to keep our families organized and peaceful.

To Ponder: What's one organizational tactic that you can put into place to ensure school mornings are peaceful?

COURTNEY VALLEJO

Healing the
Body of Christ

Love is stronger than the moment when there is
arguing. . . . A little gesture is sufficient, a caress, and
then let it be! Until tomorrow! And tomorrow
begin again.

Pope Francis

Since today is Kiss and Make Up Day, it's a great opportunity to focus on forgiveness. Forgiveness is an essential skill in marriage and family life because none of us is perfect. We hurt the ones we love in big ways and small ways. The challenge is to begin again every day, to remain vulnerable and not walled off from one another.

Refusing to forgive someone else is like refusing to heal a wound to the Body of Christ, since we are all together his body. Longtime grudges can turn against us, leaving us awash in bitterness and resentment. We have to ask ourselves what our lack of forgiveness will cost us.

In contemplating the marks of the nails in the hands and feet of Christ, we can realize that the offense against us is nothing in comparison. We can let go of our rancor and banish it from our mental landscape. But sometimes, in order to reach forgiveness, we have to confront the problem.

Ask Our Lord in prayer if you have any unforgivingness in your heart. Ask him to help you discern whether you should let your anger go or whether you need to confront the problem directly. Then, reach out to the person who hurt you, kiss, and make up!

God, please help me to forgive my friends and family and to realize that I need forgiveness, too.

To Ponder: Forgiveness is central to the sacrament of Reconciliation. Will receiving God's mercy and forgiveness through confession help you to extend forgiveness to someone else?

KAREE SANTOS

AUGUST 26

Hang On

When you get to the end of your rope, tie a knot and hang on.

Franklin Delano Roosevelt

When my eldest son came to me after a particularly challenging day at the nursing home (he was studying to be a CNA), I remember wondering how to best encourage him when he obviously wanted to quit the program. He was working with a severely disabled, almost comatose woman, and the situation nearly broke his heart even as he felt overwhelmed with helplessness.

After raising a prayer to heaven, I shared with him some of the times when God led me through painful experiences in order to train me for something in the future. It was hard for my son to go back to the nursing home the next day, but after he finished the program and got his degree, it was very clear that he was glad he had stuck with it. Neither of us know how God will use his knowledge in the future, but his skill in caring for the weakest members of society will never be wasted.

In helping my son face his challenges, I was encouraged once again to marvel at God's ability to hold me up when I would rather surrender to an easier path. God's wisdom is greater than mine.

There are plenty of times I want to quit, Lord, as you well know. Hold me up and help me see your will for my life.

To Ponder: When faced with a challenging situation, it sometimes helps to turn the question around and ask yourself, "What will I gain if I don't quit?" Rather than focusing on the benefits of giving up, focus on the wonderful possibilities if you hang on.

A. K. FRAILEY

AUGUST 27
SAINT MONICA

Praying in the Dark

The martyrdom of the heart is not less fruitful than the shedding of blood.

Saint Thérèse of Lisieux

Saint Monica was an amazing wife and mom. Through patience and prayer, she converted her abusive, unfaithful husband and his equally difficult mother and inspired the religious vocations of her daughter, Perpetua, and her son Navigius. But Monica had one incredibly stubborn problem: her son Augustine.

Enchanted by fashionable philosophies and ensnared in a heretical cult, the brilliant young man was lost in his pride, unable to see the beauty of the scriptures. They seemed hokey and homespun to his sophisticated sensibilities.

Though she was sometimes tempted to despair, his mother hung on in faith, encouraged by her bishop, who told her, "It is not possible that the son of so many tears should perish." The Lord honored her faithfulness, as well as her tears. Saint Augustine eventually became a bishop, a saint, and a Doctor of the Church.

Centuries later, when Monica's relics were discovered in Italy, many miracles were granted to those who carried them to Rome. To this day, her maternal heart is quick to respond to anyone in need, especially wives and mothers.

Jesus, when my heart is breaking, soothe me with Saint Monica's tears. Strengthen my faith and help me to treasure my vocation, especially when my crosses are heaviest.

To Ponder: Have you ever felt abandoned, waiting interminably for God to answer your prayers? In reality, he never leaves your side and loves you with tender devotion. Recall the darkest moments of your life and ask God to show you how much he loved you in those times of pain and isolation.

LISA MLADINICH

Tackling Problems at Their Root

For You formed my inward parts; You wove me in
my mother's womb.

Psalm 139:13

I have been working at a K-8 Catholic grammar school for two years now. I oversee the assistance given to students with learning differences and directly tutor those students with the greatest differences. Before I started this job, I honestly never thought about how diverse each of my students might be. I just assumed that all struggling students could be lumped together and helped by the same, basic kind of assistance such as slowing down the pace, reducing the amount of the material presented, or by simply providing a quieter learning environment. Boy, was I wrong. Every one of my students is unique and benefits from a different combination of assistance.

I think the same is true for the struggles we encounter as moms. Even the same struggles (postpartum depression, for example) will be uniquely manifested in different moms. The key I've found to helping my students as much as possible is the same key I've found for getting help with my mothering struggles; that is, to identify and tackle the root of the specific struggle. No lumping them together allowed. Sometimes this means taking my faith life more seriously. Sometimes it means being more open with my family and friends. Professional counseling, more exercise, better nutrition, or maybe even the right kind of medication may be just the right thing for me or you.

Father, thank you for knowing my very heart and soul and for loving me all the more because you do.

To Ponder: What are you struggling with today? Is this an ongoing struggle or a temporary stressor? Whom or what might you turn to in order to improve your situation? Will you seek that help today?

HEIDI BRATTON

AUGUST 29

When Little Things Become Huge

Do ordinary things with extraordinary love.

Saint Teresa of Calcutta

So often we feel we must accomplish extraordinary achievements to make any kind of a significant difference. The vocation of motherhood is comprised of millions of tiny, seemingly ordinary things such as little acts of love, usually performed while sleep deprived or a tad overwhelmed. But nonetheless, the extraordinary blessing in a mother's love comes straight away in that glass of water given in the night, that special kiss and hug that makes everything right again, and those transforming words, "I love you."

When we offer our whole lives to the Lord each and every day and ask him to love through us, our seemingly tiny acts of love and service to our family become huge. Everything matters. Each ordinary occurrence can become a beautiful opportunity for extraordinary grace and an abundance of love.

Dear Lord Jesus, I bow my heart before you even as my hands are busy with the care of my family. Thank you for the amazing vocation of motherhood, where everyone in my domestic Church can grow in holiness through every ordinary day.

To Ponder: Do you sometimes doubt the importance of your ordinary days at home with the family? Can you take some time soon (why not today?) to ponder how the Lord is working through your loving actions to your family? Are you allowing him to do so? Doing your acts of service with prayer and extraordinary love, rather than a mediocre attitude, can truly help transform human hearts—yours, too.

DONNA-MARIE COOPER O'BOYLE

AUGUST 30

What Challenges Us Makes Us Stronger

Nothing is more common than for men to think that because they are familiar with words they understand the ideas they stand for.

Cardinal John Henry Newman

My grandfather only had a third-grade education. He spent his life working for the city until a tractor ran over one side of his body; he then spent the last twenty years learning to live with a disability.

I remember someone saying how sad it was that he'd only had a third-grade education. With his sharpness of mind, he could have been so much more.

So much more? This man woke up every day of his life and went to work. He never begged, borrowed, or stole. His family did not go to sleep hungry. He loved and gave generously. He didn't neglect his wife and children.

My grandfather's lack of education became his means for an education. My grandfather learned and knew things about life that no term paper could identify and no professor could approve. Above all, this lack of education taught him never to take anything for granted. As far as the world knew, he was illiterate; but I saw so often how smart he was and that is the image I will forever have of him.

Some look at his life and say, "He could have been so much more." I look at my grandfather's life and say, "He was exactly who God wanted him to be."

Dear God, help me to remember that all my successes in life have to point back to you; otherwise, they are meaningless.

To Ponder: What makes you a success? Do you override people in order to look better than them? Do you bear your responsibilities joyfully?

CAY GIBSON

Locked-Up Words

If you are not in over your head, how do you know
how tall you are?

T. S. Eliot

Saint Raymond Nonnatus spent his life overcoming challenges. Born in Spain in 1204, his mother died while in labor. He was delivered by Caesarean. Because of the feat of his difficult birth, Saint Raymond is the patron of midwives and women in labor.

Next, the saint overcame the challenge of convincing his father that he had a religious vocation. His father, recognizing his son's piety, eventually consented. Through prayer and persistence, Raymond was able to join the Order of Mercy.

The Mercedarians were founded to ransom enslaved Christians. In Algeria, Father Raymond bought the freedom of over a hundred Christian slaves. When he ran out of money before the last twenty-three Christians' freedom was secured, he offered himself for their ransom. Knowing the priest could bring in a large sum from his order, the Mohammedans accepted the exchange.

While imprisoned, Saint Raymond was tortured and made to run the gauntlet. Still, he continued to evangelize. He so impressed his guards that they converted to Christianity. Angered, the governor ordered that the preacher's lips be pierced with a red-hot iron and sealed with a padlock. Still, he continued to praise God.

The Mercedarians paid for their illustrious brother's release—the governor all too happy to see Raymond head back to Spain. His treatment while in prison, however, had taken its toll. Not long after he returned to Spain, he passed on to heaven.

Lord, through the intercession of Saint Raymond Nonnatus, help me overcome the challenges in my life.

To Ponder: Do you need a spiritual padlock on your lips sometimes? What can you do to help ensure that your words build up the kingdom of God?

KELLY GUEST

September

THEME: LIFELONG LEARNING

Created for a Divine Purpose

I wanted a perfect ending. Now I've learned, the hard
way, that some poems don't rhyme and some stories
don't have a clear beginning, middle, and end.

Gilda Radner

The exact origins of National No Rhyme (Nor Reason) Day
are lost to obscurity. But I like to think that perhaps a mom
was behind today's celebration of words in the English language that don't rhyme. Perhaps that mom was a teacher or
maybe the parent of a child who didn't quite "fit" everyone
else's idea of how learning should look.

Who's to say that the word "purple" should be banned
from a poem simply because it lacks a rhyming mate? Then
again, who's to say that a child with ADHD should be seques-
tered or bullied because he is unique and special? And why
does education need to end with a degree? God created each
of us, matchless and precious, for a divine purpose. After half
a century of living, it's easier for me to see now that God's
classroom is often the playground, the walking path, the
kitchen table, or the pew.

When we place limits around poetry to only the words
that fit, we squelch creativity. When we try to live by others'
standards of success, happiness, or holiness, we limit the vast
and extraordinary potential our Creator has placed within
each of us.

Master, you made me unique and in your image. Help me to embrace the parts of myself that make me different. May I live fully to glorify you.

To Ponder: Do you struggle with the status quo? How can you venture beyond the confines you have set for your life to achieve the dreams that God has placed in your heart?

LISA M. HENDEY

SEPTEMBER 2
SAINT INGRID OF SWEDEN

Making Life a Prayer

The duty of the moment is what you should be doing at any given time, in whatever place God has put you. If you have a child, your duty of the moment may be to change a dirty diaper. . . . But you don't just change that diaper, you change it to the best of your ability, with great love for both God and that child.

Catherine Doherty

When I was a young mother, it bothered me that I was rarely able to pray a Rosary uninterrupted, attend daily Mass, or have quiet scripture reading time. Then I read Catherine Doherty's book *Dear Parents* and the light bulb finally went on. Our entire lives can be a prayer. For the young mom, this prayer could be her duty of the moment: changing a diaper, cooking, doing dishes. For a young father, it could be rocking a fussy child when Mom needs a rest. For a teen, the duty of the moment could be taking out the trash, tidying his or her room, or volunteering. For older couples, their duty might be babysitting their grandchildren or volunteering at a soup kitchen.

Thank you, Lord, for all my "duties of the moment."

To Ponder: What is your "duty of the moment" today?

ELLEN GABLE HRKACH

SEPTEMBER 3
SAINT GREGORY THE GREAT

Love Is an Action Word

The proof of love is in the works. Where love exists,
it works great things. But when it ceases to act, it
ceases to exist.

Saint Gregory the Great

We say we love many things: I love red lipstick; I love espresso; I love Europe. Love has become a very diluted, trivial word and notion in our society.

We have reduced love to a mere feeling and have come to believe in matters of love that if I feel it, I act upon it. And if I don't feel it, I can't do it. We let our feelings be our guide.

Feelings are important, but they're fickle and influenced by a multitude of factors. We can choose to love someone even if we don't feel it. And in our weak, fragile humanity there will in fact be *many* times we don't feel it. But if we are to love, we will act, and we will act rightly. And if we keep acting, oftentimes feelings will follow.

Feelings are not based on outward circumstances. Feelings ultimately come from *within*: the state of our own hearts.

Our joy doesn't come when we have found the perfect person or situation to make us feel all warm, fuzzy, and finally comfortable. It comes when we choose to love. When we choose to serve, to be kind, to reach out. When our love becomes real, visible, and concrete. When we put our love into action. For we were made to love and be loved. And it is in giving this love that we receive the fullness of life and joy for which we so long.

Lord Jesus, help me put my love into action through works of kindness and service today, even if I don't feel it.

To Ponder: Do you let your feelings determine how you choose to live, and how you choose to love?

KARA KLEIN

SEPTEMBER 4
NATIONAL WILDLIFE DAY

In Joy for Animals

Swiftly arose and spread around me the peace. . . .
And that a kelson of the creation is love.

Walt Whitman, "Song of Myself"

Listening to children make up names for their exotic animals made of Legos or clay makes me smile or sometimes burst out laughing.

All the creatures God created in Eden were named by Adam. Imagine the fun Our Father had parading each creature before Adam and asking him, "What shall we call this one?" Imagine the delight of Adam—or any child seeing an animal for the first time—as he walked around it, petted its nose, stroked its ribs, and proclaimed to God its name.

In gratitude for his creation, we can ask for a blessing on our pets and the animals that serve and feed us.

Blessing of Animals
Wonderful are all God's works. Blessed be the name of the Lord. The animals of God's creation inhabit the skies, the earth, and the sea. They share in the ways of human beings. They have a part in our lives. Francis of Assisi recognized this when he called the animals, wild and tame, his brothers and sisters. Remembering Francis's love for these brothers and sisters of ours, we invoke God's blessing on these animals, and we thank God for letting us share the earth with all the creatures. Thank you, Father, for the joy of animals—pets, birds, and the amazing creatures of seas and forests.

To Ponder: When was the last time you thanked God for his creatures? Today offer a prayer of gratitude for a favorite exotic, beautiful, or companion animal.

MARGARET ROSE REALY, OBL., O.S.B.

SEPTEMBER 5
SAINT TERESA OF CALCUTTA

Being the Sheepdog
(Instead of the Master)

Be faithful in small things because it is in them that your strength lies.

Saint Teresa of Calcutta

In 2009, I felt called to enter into Catholic ministry. I wondered how God would accomplish it and if I'd be able to balance family and a career. I admit I had delusions of grandeur, expecting that, since I was technically working for God, the doors would open wide and I would have an abundance of work. For many years opportunities came at a snail's pace. Despite marketing, prayer, and lots of hard work, I could measure the fruit of my work in strawberries instead of watermelons. I began to grow discouraged and brought my frustrations to Jesus in adoration.

In that moment, I saw myself as a sheepdog. The sheepdog does not add up the number of sheep and then decide to assist his master. He simply follows the shepherd's command and herds the flock. Whether God expands the ministry is no longer an issue. My strength, I have discovered, lies in being faithful in small matters.

Thank you, Lord, for the reminder that whether we are changing a diaper, vacuuming the floor, making a lunch, visiting the homebound, or praying with our kids, if we are faithful in those, we will be blessed. Forgive me for the times my vanity or pride has gotten in the way of the work you have for me to do. May I always see that every person and task placed in my life is important, and if I am only there to share your love with that one person or in that one way, I shall do it with all my heart.

To Ponder: Do you sometimes feel discouraged because the work you are doing seems insignificant or goes unnoticed?

ALLISON GINGRAS

Seeing the Yoke for What It Is

A cheerful heart always finds a yoke easy and a burden light.

Venerable Fulton J. Sheen

After an overwhelming day, I kissed my husband goodnight. As I was headed up to the bedroom, I passed a crucifix. I said out loud (to both Jesus and my husband), "I thought my yoke was supposed to be easy and my burden light!"

After all, wasn't I doing everything right? Just the previous Saturday, I had made a very good confession (long overdue) and was absolved of all my sins. As my eight-year-old daughter (who came with me) put it, "Mom, we got our grace back!"

I had been making an effort to say the Rosary (and my morning offering, consecration to Mary, and countless prayers muttered under my breath all day). So, if the graces were flowing and all was right with God, how could it be that my yoke felt so darn heavy and my burdens like crushing defeats?

My husband didn't answer, but I quickly realized how he had been lightening my load since the children's bedtime. He had patiently listened to my whiny venting as I gulped wine and tried to decompress from all the craziness. Then he held my hand as we watched the mindless TV programs of my choice. I suddenly realized (again) the gift that God has given me in my husband.

Then, as I closed my eyes after checking on my six beautiful children, my cheerful heart felt quite peaceful. In the morning, God willing, my body and mind would be refreshed and my yoke would once again (at least temporarily) be easy and my burdens light.

God, please give me the grace to remember your presence, especially when I feel weighed down.

To Ponder: How do you allow Christ and others to replenish you?

TRISH BOLSTER

SEPTEMBER 7

The Gift of Our Work

Work is fundamental to the dignity of a person.
Work, to use an image, "anoints" us with dignity,
fills us with dignity, makes us similar to God, who
has worked and still works, who always acts.

Pope Francis

Around Labor Day, it's always good to ponder our work. Instead of appreciating our work, we quickly get our work done so we can "get on with our lives." We count down the days to vacation, and this is true whether our work is done inside and/or outside the home. We can't wait to stop changing diapers or for our kids to eat without making a mess to clean up. I look forward to the days I don't have smudges on the refrigerator door.

But this calls to mind another image—Mrs. Lewis. She is pushing eighty. She has a smudged glass on her entryway door that she never cleans. When she was a young mother, she remembers complaining to her husband, children, and even God about those darn smudges that she constantly had to clean. "Can't folks keep their hands off the glass?" Now she longs to have little hands around to make messes.

Jesus worked as a carpenter. Mary changed dirty diapers. The work we have is ours, given to us from God.

Jesus, help me to see the dignity in my work. Help me to do it out of love for you and others.

To Ponder: Do you get tired and bored with your work? Can you see it as a way of serving others? Even if you suffer while doing it, can you turn the complaining into an offering to God?

TAMI KISER

SEPTEMBER 8
NATIVITY OF THE BLESSED VIRGIN MARY

Celebrating My Heavenly Mother

Thy birth, O Virgin Mother of God,
heralded joy to all the world.
For from thou hast risen the Sun of justice,
Christ our God.

Morning Prayer from the Divine Office

Today the Church commemorates the birth of the Virgin Mary. Tradition says that her parents, Anne and Joachim, were barren and had prayed long and hard for a child. Their great faith was rewarded. Their daughter would be chosen to be the Mother of God, and her Son, Jesus, the long-awaited Messiah.

As an adult Catholic convert, I encountered Mary a little late in the game. I wasn't raised with the Rosary, May Crowning, or a devotion to the Blessed Mother in any form. In many ways, she was a complete stranger to me when I entered the Catholic Church. For much of my early Catholicism, Mary remained an enigma to me—a symbol of the perfect wife and mother that reminded me of how I was woefully lacking in both areas.

In time, however, something remarkable happened. The Blessed Mother would become my mother. It began with my timid and awkward prayers asking for her intercession. The more I trusted my heart to her, the more she proved to be a powerful ally and a gentle friend. My only regret is that I didn't get to know her sooner.

Holy Mary, thank you for your patience with me as I stumble in gentleness, humility, and obedience. Wrap our family securely under the mantle of your protection and lead us ever closer to your Son, Jesus.

To Ponder: Can you do something special as a family today to honor the Blessed Mother's birthday? Consider baking a white cake with blue icing, decorating her statue or picture with flowers and candles, or praying a family Rosary or Memorare.

ELIZABETH FICOCELLI

Why Keep Learning?

We must make up our minds to be ignorant of much,
if we would know anything.

Blessed John Henry Newman

This fall I began my second year in an MA program in art therapy. As one of my friends, a fellow artist and educator, put it, graduate study is luxury and a pleasure. I feel this very keenly and am grateful for the opportunity to study.

For me, learning is a lifelong commitment. Perhaps this is because in my youth I wasn't able to study beyond high school because I entered a monastery. After discerning God was calling me from that life, I began to study and haven't stopped. My study has always been for a purpose: to serve.

For the follower of Christ, knowledge is not an end in itself but a means to know God and oneself, to understand better the reality and context of our fellows for the purpose of service. This is how we answer our calling, for whether we are lay or clergy we each must discern the way God is calling us to embody our gifts. That is why the Church must be a place where many gifts are welcomed and varied voices are heard. Each of us receives the Holy Spirit in Baptism, and we are confirmed and sealed with the holy oils of Confirmation. As the seven gifts of the Spirit rush upon us, God calls each one to a work and a way of life that enables us to serve others. The whole point of our discipleship and growing spiritually in the likeness of the Lord is so that we can be this presence of Christ to others in the world. In the context of our discipleship, lifelong learning is not only a luxury and a pleasure, but also a responsibility.

Lord, give me a generous heart and spiritual vision to love you in service to others.

To Ponder: To what has God called you? How have you used your knowledge and expertise for service?

JULIE L. PAAVOLA

SEPTEMBER 10
NATIONAL SWAP IDEAS DAY

Keeping the Saints from Crying

The saints cry over lost time.

Valerie Tripp

One of my favorite ways to "waste time" with my kids is to read with them. During a read-aloud of the book *Josefina Learns a Lesson* from the American Girls Collection, the kids and I learned that *dichos* is the Spanish word for "proverbs" or "wise sayings" used in Mexican culture. One *dicho* shared in the story was, "The saints cry over lost time." It was once a popular expression often said by parents to help keep their kids on task.

I immediately thought of an idea that had rolled around in my mind for some time, yet I hadn't mustered the courage to share it publicly. I also hadn't taken any steps to turn my thoughts into action. Had I given the saints reason to cry by not giving a voice to that potentially helpful idea? A few days later, a friend called and enthusiastically said, "I have an idea! Let's meet for dinner." Sure enough, she and I were pondering much of the same; her ideas complemented mine and vice versa. Together, we moved forward with confidence and purpose, while I hope giving the saints very little reason to cry.

Dear Lord, please set me ablaze with the fire of your Holy Spirit.

To Ponder: Have you been ruminating on an idea for some time but haven't mustered the courage to tell anyone? In honor of National Swap Ideas Day, share your ideas with a friend and ask for her thoughts in return.

LISA A. SCHMIDT

SEPTEMBER 11
What It Means to Be a Hero

All gave some; some gave all.

Howard Osterkamp

There are many themes to write about in connection with September 11. It's a day to ponder loss, faith, sorrow, unity. It's also a good day to reflect on what it means to be a hero.

On that awful day in 2001, we saw the worst that human beings can to do others, but we also saw the best. We saw it in the first responders who rushed toward the Twin Towers, trying valiantly to save others even at the cost of their own lives.

We saw it in Father Mychal Judge, the firefighters' chaplain who was the first registered death of Ground Zero. We saw it in the passengers of Flight 93, whose final act of defiance prevented the loss of still more innocent lives.

Kids idolize sports figures and musicians for their talent, and yes, talent is a gift from God. But maybe today, we can talk to our kids about true heroism. We can tell them that if rushing a football across a field is impressive, rushing into a burning tower should make us speechless with admiration. Jesus told us that there is no greater love than to lay down one's life for others. September 11 is a chance to honor those who gave their lives so that strangers might live, and to share their stories with the next generation.

Lord, be with the families and friends of those lost on September 11. May they know our compassion and our thanks.

To Ponder: What can you do to help your children recognize life's greatest heroes?

GINNY KUBITZ MOYER

SEPTEMBER 12
MOST HOLY NAME OF MARY

Put Your Hand in Mary's Hand

Let it be done to me according to Thy Word.

Luke 1:38

Because of her response to the Angel Gabriel's declaration of God's call to become the mother of her Savior, we honor Mary's name above all women with a special feast day, the Most Holy Name of Mary. Our eternal destinies were secured by her courageous acceptance of whatever being the mother of Christ entailed.

Where did Mary receive the graces she required to raise Jesus and nurture him for his mission on earth? From her immaculate soul, redeemed from original sin before birth. We had our original sin washed away at our Baptism, so like Our Lady, we can nurture the life of God in us by our fidelity to personal prayer.

"Mary treasured all these things and pondered them in her heart" (Lk 2:19). Her quiet time with Our Lord is when Mary processed the events of her Son's life and God molded her as his mother. In our own pondering, God reveals to us how the events of our children's lives are part of his plan for them and us.

Remember to ask Our Lady to walk with you on your own journey.

"Take Our Lady's hand and she will lead you to Jesus." This quote comes from a letter from Saint Teresa of Calcutta to me in 1991 as I sought her guidance about my vocation.

Mother Mary, take my hand as I walk through each day and lead me to your Son. Teach me to do whatever he tells me.

To Ponder: How has Our Lady been a role model and companion for you in your prayer life? Do you use the Rosary as a means to grow like Our Lady?

LETICIA VELASQUEZ

Where Is Your Strength?

Find out the secret of his great strength.

Judges 16:5

Sometimes I find myself fixated on what I *lack*, on what I'm sure I *need* but don't have. Things like cool stuff, money, influence, popularity—basically all the things your average half-hour of television will tell you are necessary to be happy. But weighed against that average half-hour of television is the story of Samson. All of the things that the world tells us we really need were pitted against Samson, one after another, as the Philistines tried to find the secret of Samson's great strength and subdue him.

Like technological marvels: the Philistines had iron, the Israelites did not. But with stone-age, anti-technology (the jaw bone of an ass, in fact) and God's help, Samson was able to defeat the Philistines and their iron weapons. Or money: the Philistines had it and used it to bribe people to betray Samson. But still, Samson prevailed with God's help. Or power: the Philistines ruled the Promised Land at that time, and when the Philistines talked, people listened (I'd love it if just my kids would listen to me, especially if I didn't have to count to three first). But even as one man alone, in the end Samson conquered with God's help.

The story of Samson shows that all of these other things, without God, are of no avail. But with God, even if you have nothing else, you have enough. And the amazing thing is that the source of Samson's great strength can be the source of our own strength. Even now he beckons.

Let me hear your beckoning and calling to me, Lord, and lead me to focus on you.

To Ponder: What in your life distracts you from the true source of your strength?

JAKE FROST

SEPTEMBER 14
EXALTATION OF THE HOLY CROSS

Releasing Perfectionism

To convert somebody, go and take them by the hand
and guide them.

Saint Thomas Aquinas

"Ohhhhh, fried chicken!" Nine-year-old Raphael's voice was gleeful. "I will *help* you, Mom!"

I sighed. I did not want help. I wanted to get the chicken breaded and myself out the door for my daughter's track meet as quickly as possible, but Raphael was already helping. He had washed his hands and was hard at work, dipping chicken into flour (all over the counter), beaten egg (spilling over the edges of the bowl), and the breadcrumbs (how did he manage to get so few to actually stick to the chicken breast?).

I am well-practiced at the frustrating art of cooking with children. I learned years ago to let go of perfectionism in the kitchen, and yet still I struggle sometimes. It helps to remind myself that my long-term goal is not efficient dinner preparation: it's to raise kids who have basic life skills and who are confident and natural helpers.

Kids learn best when we are right beside them, sharing the experience and guiding them through the tricky spots. This is true for cooking but also for their faith lives. We share our faith most effectively with others not when we lecture them but when we let our guard down, let go of perfectionism, and share from our heart our own experiences of God's love.

Help me to bring others to you, Lord, in my words and example, but most important, by taking them by the hand and guiding them toward faith.

To Ponder: Sometimes self-consciousness prevents us from sharing our faith with others more deeply. What is one area of your life where you can let your guard down, take someone by the hand, and share your experience?

DANIELLE BEAN

SEPTEMBER 15
OUR LADY OF SORROWS

A Heart of Courage

One cannot love without suffering or suffer without loving.

Saint Gianna Beretta Molla

I never realized how fragile a heart could be until the day I watched a group of four-year-olds tell my sweet three-year-old that she couldn't play with them. As I watched her lip quiver and her eyes swell with tears, I thought, "My heart can't take this. How can I possibly make it through her first breakup with a boyfriend or any pain that ever befalls her?"

Turns out I needed courage. Courage is the core of a mother's love, and if we are in need of it, all we need to do is to look to the one who is the perfect example of courage from the moment she is told that God has a plan for her life that will radically change the world.

From the moment of the Annunciation on, Mary lived with the greatest courage, because she lived with the greatest love. We can learn from and be nurtured in the virtue of courage by entering with her into that which embodies the greatest courage ever exhibited in one of God creatures—Mary's seven sorrows.

Through the seven sorrows comes the realization that God does not spare us from pain. Our pain, however, can coexist with God's peace when we trust him. God can use our pain to draw us closer to him and he can use it to save souls.

Lord, help me turn to Our Lady of Sorrows if I ever have difficulty trusting in you.

To Ponder: Mary experienced the greatest pain, yet she constantly believed in the will of God. Looking back, were there painful times that you now see as beautiful pieces of God's plan for your life?

KELLY M. WAHLQUIST

The Hurdle of Complacency

Unless there is a Good Friday in your life, there can
be no Easter Sunday.

Venerable Fulton J. Sheen

As hard as I was trying to possess a vibrant spiritual life, I was experiencing a lull. It was hard for me to admit, since I loved my Catholic faith, had just wrapped up my leadership of a flourishing moms ministry, *and* was speaking and writing to Catholic moms about working toward a faithful relationship with Christ. I was embarrassed to admit that I was subconsciously getting lazy in my spiritual life. I did not know what was wrong, but I felt spiritually numb.

Eventually, I sought a spiritual director. I wanted to feel a reignited passion for Our Lord and did not know how to proceed. After six months, it became obvious that there was a purpose for this dark part of my journey. The Lord works in ways we cannot fully comprehend. I still struggle, but new paths have been made clear, and I find them exciting and hopeful. I do not know how long this will last or when I will feel a lull again. But I learned such a valuable lesson already. Our Lord wants us close to him but he will not force a relationship with us. It is up to us to take stock of our relationship to him. Are we growing complacent? What should we do when this happens?

Lord, thank you for never giving up on me. Help me to consistently seek you and to never give up on you.

To Ponder: How satisfied are you with your spiritual life right now? How can you prevent or eliminate spiritual complacency?

MEG BUCARO

SEPTEMBER 17
SAINT HILDEGARD OF BINGEN

Our Intellectual and Spiritual Responsibilities

Do not use your freedom as an opportunity for the
flesh, but through love serve one another.

Galatians 5:13

Saint Hildegard of Bingen was the fourth woman to be made a Doctor of the Church, and she is an incredible role model regarding the value of lifelong learning. Of Saint Hildegard, Pope Benedict XVI said, "Let us always invoke the Holy Spirit, so that he may inspire in the Church holy and courageous women like Saint Hildegard of Bingen, who, developing the gifts they have received from God, make their own special and valuable contribution to the spiritual development of our communities and of the Church in our time."

Although at times in my vocation as a wife and mother I have questioned the financial investment of my college education or of buying educational books or CDs since then, I have never questioned their value in helping me to contribute to what Pope Benedict XVI lauds as "the spiritual development" of my communities and of the Church of my time. In those respects, I have always known that the more I know about God and his creation, the better prepared I am to raise my hand when the call goes out to serve in his vineyard, be that through parenting, home schooling, working as a paid professional, or being a simple pair of helping hands. When it comes to developing our God-given gifts, experience has convinced me that it is as important to be intellectually and spiritually responsible as it is to be financially responsible.

Father, thank you for the gifts of curiosity and intellect, and the opportunity to use them in your service.

To Ponder: What things do you really, really love to do? Have you ever thought about taking or teaching a class about those things?

HEIDI BRATTON

SEPTEMBER 18

Molded by God

Wonder is the desire for knowledge.

Saint Thomas Aquinas

September is the start of school and new beginnings. I am always looking to learn and grow, and I can often be found reading a self-help, nutritional, or cook book. Change does not scare me but not having any information to absorb does. I have a thirst to learn more about myself and the world around me.

As children, we learn through play and creation. A favorite pastime of children is Play-Doh. It is a squishy substance able to be shaped and molded at the control of their fingertips. God molds us daily. If we give him a little bit of control, he will only make us better. To have the wonder of a child is to search for the truth.

When I no longer have questions, I become stagnant. Children never cease to question and learn. They always have another question before their first one is even answered. That is what God wants of us. He wants us to thirst for knowledge and search for the truth. He is prepared to answer any question we may have. The more we learn, the more we grow as people.

Watch your children and observe how they learn through play. It gives us the reason to slow down and remember how to be a child freely exploring. God wants us to look to him as a father and mold us like Play-Doh. Let's be willing to be flexible and want to grow in our own skin.

God, teach me your ways and guide me. Help me to learn and grow through work and play.

To Ponder: Do you work or play more in terms of learning? Which way do you learn better?

TANYA WEITZEL

Something New Every Day

Education is the movement from darkness to light.

Allan Bloom

As a home schooling mom, I spend a great deal of time learning right along with my children. In the process, I've become even more aware of how little I know. Their interests have taken me places I never would have travelled on my own. Over the years with my two teen boys, I have become quite knowledgeable on *Thomas the Tank Engine* and *Star Wars*, and I have learned to play chess and trading-card games. Academically, I have delved into chemistry and algebra. We recently have begun to attend astronomy lectures at our local museum.

My little girl and I are only on the beginning of our journey, but she has a great interest in cooking and is forcing me to increase my culinary skills. I've also learned quite a bit about Disney princesses. With all three, I've read countless books aloud, exposing me to new ideas and new voices. I hope, in the process, my children have learned a few things from me as well.

Every day with my children is an educational adventure, which is as it should be. The world is so full of interesting things to learn, and I know that I can never learn everything I would like to even if I should live to be a hundred. I like to imagine a huge library in heaven with an eternity to discover new things. In the meantime, you'll find my children and me learning something new every day.

Thank you, God, for creating a wonderful world full of things to discover. May I always have a heart and mind eager to learn.

To Ponder: Is there something new you or your child(ren) would like to learn? Take one step to start learning it today.

PATRICE FAGNANT-MACARTHUR

SEPTEMBER 20

A Mind Is a Terrible Thing to Waste

With all there is, why settle for just a piece of sky?

Yentl

I retired at fifty-one. I was healthy, well-paid, and I worked with great people. But while I loved what the job had been, I didn't love what it was becoming.

At the time, my daughter was entering high school and I was ready to embrace the role of stay-at-home mom, writing and piecing together part-time gigs to reduce the looming college tuition panic.

A year later, I was hired to teach early childhood development at a local college. Though I'd lived the subject matter for nearly thirty years, I hadn't given serious consideration to it from an academic standpoint in, well, thirty years.

My first semester, I talked too much. Too much Power-Point, not enough personality. My second semester, I began digging up supplemental materials and integrating them into the course. Third semester, I entrusted them with more of their own learning. This semester, I changed textbooks. And a funny thing happened on the way to teaching these kids: I felt smart again. And it was lovely.

Don't get me wrong—it's still a lot of work. But I love it. I love knowing that the same mind I had in grad school is still in there, waiting to be activated by new information and ideas.

As it turns out, it's never too late to learn something new.

Lord, I can never learn all there is to know. Inspire in me a passion for knowledge and help me to discern what is true, what is good, and what is worthy of the time you have given me.

To Ponder: What have you always wanted to learn about? Take a baby step in that direction.

LISA LAWMASTER HESS

SEPTEMBER 21
SAINT MATTHEW, APOSTLE AND EVANGELIST

Inviting Jesus In

As Jesus passed on from there, he saw a man named Matthew sitting at the customs post. He said to him, "Follow me." And he got up and followed him.

Matthew 9:9

I wonder what Matthew's frame of mind was the day Jesus called him. Did he sense the emptiness of his dreary life of counting coins, gouging his fellow Jews, and keeping accounts for the brutal Roman army? Was he sick of being sneered at by his countrymen and longing to make amends? Or was his lust for financial gain in full flower when he beheld the eyes of the Savior and heard the voice of the God-Man commanding him to come, to follow?

Matthew immediately relinquished financial security to follow a stranger, and then he invited Jesus to dine in his home with a menagerie of social rejects: tax collectors, prostitutes, and other "sinners." Matthew was an outcast, like them, accustomed to making excuses for the darkness of his life. And yet, he exposed it all to Jesus. Perhaps Matthew sensed that to rid himself of the pall of spiritual death that hung over him, his life and his soul would have to be laid bare before the light of the world.

Every single one of us has something painful that we try our best to conceal, but inviting Jesus to love us as we are—wounded, frightened, and inadequate—is the gateway to incredible joy and transformation.

Jesus, help me to trust you with all the hidden sorrows, wounds, and secrets of my life. I need your help to be free of them and to follow you with all my heart.

To Ponder: Do you seek sacramental reconciliation and trust Jesus to love you as you are?

LISA MLADINICH

Actively Seeking Learning

Some people find oil. Others don't. Finding oil requires risk, patience, persistence, and hard work. Finding ourselves requires the same things.

J. Paul Getty

I'm a lifelong learning addict, a self-improvement freak, a female Brian Tracy. I'm on the outside of the bell curve for lifelong learners.

That doesn't mean it's a bad thing. There are benefits in actively growing your body, mind, and soul. If you are not yet a fanatic, here are some suggestions for how to get started:

* Join a book study, Bible study, or any group study at your church. You will become acquainted with new people and you will expand your mind as well as have a deeper understanding of who you are in Christ.

* Read an inspirational book twenty minutes per day. Finding time to be quiet and read twenty minutes a day slows you down so that *you* are directing your day, not the other way around.

* Plan for your next adventure. When you start tuning into the relevant information around you, you gain clarity on how much or how little your inspiration would really light your fire.

Normal, busy people can develop into to lifelong learners and manifest Holy Spirit-inspired visions. Carve out just a little space each day so that the Holy Spirit can squirt some relevant things into your consciousness for you to mull over and consider. Combine inspiration with downtime and let your unconscious get to work.

Mary, you watched and learned from every move Jesus made. You were a lifelong student of his way and his teachings. Help us to invest and absorb everything God wants us to know and learn in this beautiful world he gave us, and respond as good and trustworthy stewards.

To Ponder: How can you joyfully make room for learning more in the busyness of your life?

CHRISTINA M. WEBER

SEPTEMBER 23
SAINT PIO OF PIETRELCINA

Pray, Hope, and Don't Worry

The pope prays as the Holy Spirit permits him to pray . . . in a way in which . . . he can better fulfill his ministry.

Saint John Paul II

I was a seminarian when I first read those words of Saint John Paul II. At the time, I was preparing myself for a vocation of service to the people of God as a priest. Ultimately, God had different plans. But at that time I was praying as the Holy Spirit permitted me to pray. As a seminarian, I had the daily support of community in my prayer life, and my life was filled with ample opportunities for prayer: morning and evening prayer from the Liturgy of the Hours, daily Mass, the Rosary, prayers before and after meals, regular retreats, and other opportunities for both personal and communal prayer.

After four years in formation as a seminarian, God called me in a different direction and eventually matriculated me in the school of love known as the sacrament of Matrimony. Over the last sixteen years, I have been stretched and have grown in ways that I never could have foreseen. I wouldn't trade this vocation for anything. Clearly, God knew what he was doing with me.

At the same time, I struggled for years in the area of prayer. I tried to make the prayer life of a seminarian fit into my life of marriage and family. It didn't work. After years of feeling like I just didn't measure up, I finally remembered the words of Saint John Paul II. Let them speak to your heart today.

Holy Spirit, I open my life and my heart to you. Grant that I might be docile to your promptings and allow you to help me better fulfill my vocation.

To Ponder: Are you open to the Holy Spirit? Do you allow him to direct your prayer so that you can better fulfill your vocation?

JEFF YOUNG

Pausing in Reading, Pausing in Life

Punctuation saves lives.

Anonymous

On National Punctuation Day, I am reminded of how important punctuation actually is. A simple missing comma can completely change the meaning of an entire sentence, and run-on sentences will confuse and frustrate readers, causing them to glaze over the words and not take the time necessary to figure out what message the writer is trying to convey.

As each of my children learned to read, they had a blatant disregard for punctuation. Commas and periods were completely ignored, which caused great confusion when they tried to understand what they were reading. To help them work through the sentences, I taught them to take a breath whenever they saw a comma and to swallow when they came to a period. Taking this simple approach helped them navigate through their readings and gave them the pauses necessary to help them understand what they had read.

Lord, help me to remember to pause, to stop and take a breath, to settle my mind and my heart, and to redirect my thoughts toward you frequently throughout this day.

To Ponder: When was the last time you prayed your daily prayers slowly, pondering the words you were saying? How often do you go throughout your day as though it were just one run-on sentence? Do you remember to pause throughout the day to reflect on how your time is being spent and where you are headed?

CASSANDRA POPPE

SEPTEMBER 25

Married Friendship

If you need a friend,
Don't look to a stranger.
You know in the end, I'll always be there.

When In Rome

In 1988, the band When In Rome released its one-hit wonder, "The Promise." I was only seven years old, and my future husband lived more than fifteen hundred miles away. He was just a figment of my imagination—someone I had conjured in my daydreams or a fictional boyfriend-type based on a character from *The Babysitters Club.*

Ben and I never knew the other existed until we met—virtually, on a match website—in 2006. We had grown up on separate sides of the country, and yet we built an instant friendship that bridged the gap for nearly a year before our marriage. Because of the lack of geographical proximity, forging a friendship was natural for us. It built a solid foundation upon which our romantic love later blossomed.

When we were blissful and naïve newlyweds, we had no way of knowing what storms lay ahead for our marriage, especially raising two children with multiple special needs.

At times the intensity and stress in the daily tedium depletes our emotional reserve.

Like the lyrics of "The Promise," Ben and I make time to deepen our friendship each day—perhaps in small ways, like short and sweet text messaging, but often in grander ways, like savoring a glass of red wine together while chatting about life after the girls are tucked in bed.

Heavenly Father, thank you for blessing me with my husband, who is my lifelong partner and best friend.

To Ponder: How can you deepen your friendship with your husband today?

JEANNIE EWING

SEPTEMBER 26

The Grass Really Isn't Greener

The love of man and woman, capable of generating life, is a sign that points to God.

Cardinal Gianfranco Ravasi

My husband likes it when I go out with my girlfriends. It's not that he's trying to get rid of me for an evening. Actually, after twenty years of marriage, he *still* enjoys my company. No. It's not that he enjoys it when I'm gone. It's more that he enjoys it when I come back.

You see, when I go out with friends and we start catching up on our lives, inevitably, at least one of us will be unhappy with our spouse for a variety of reasons both large and small. It's part of marriage, I guess. All marriages go through trying times. Life is stressful. It's easy to get tired and grumpy. And that's usually when we start feeling misunderstood or taken for granted.

So, why does my husband like it when I spend time with disgruntled wives? Because when I do, I see all of the faults he *doesn't* have instead of the ones he *does*. I guess you could call it a reverse-grass-is-greener syndrome. Hearing other wives complain about their husbands makes me realize how small my complaints really are. In the end, I come home more appreciative of the wonderful husband I have rather than yearning for the perfectly fictitious husband of my imagination.

Mother Mary, help me to be the loving and appreciative wife that you were to Joseph. Remind me in times of weakness of the admirable traits of my husband and help me to communicate my love and admiration each day to the man I've chosen to spend my life with.

To Ponder: Do you gloss over your husband's good attributes while focusing on his faults? Do you unfairly compare him with other husbands? Do you spend more time criticizing than admiring the man you love?

LAURA B. NELSON

A Healthy Circle of Friends

Whoever walks with the wise becomes wise, but the companion of fools suffers harm.

Proverbs 13:20

A small group of women sat at the table eating salads, sipping iced tea, and talking. I'd been a part of the conversation many times before, but on this occasion I simply listened. One mom complained about a boss who had treated her unfairly. Another gossiped about a neighbor who was going through a difficult time. And several women traded negative stories about their husbands—trying to one-up each other with the shocking nature of their revelations.

I realized I was surrounded by unhappy women, and they were bringing me down with them. They weren't seeking comfort, encouragement, or healing in sharing their tales. Instead, they were enjoying the group therapy they found in their circle of discontent.

I decided I no longer wanted to be a part of the group. I didn't want to hang out with the cool kids anymore if it meant I had to gossip and complain all the time. So I set an intention to seek out the companionship of Christian women who would lift me up rather than drag me down. I prayed for divine intervention and a new circle of friends.

Lord, please help me to choose my friends wisely and to spend time with people who lead me closer to you. Please send people into my life who will help me fulfill your purpose.

To Ponder: With whom do you spend the most time? Are your closest friends helping you become a better Christian? Is it time to seek out the companionship of others who will bring you closer to God?

THERESA CENICCOLA

SEPTEMBER 28

Engage with God

Have no anxiety about anything, but in everything
by prayer and supplication with thanksgiving let
your requests be made known to God. And the peace
of God, which passes all understanding, will keep
your hearts and your minds in Christ Jesus.

Philippians 4:6–7

You know how it is when you're trying to get somebody's input and he or she won't cooperate? I remember my mother giving my father driving directions: "Should I go straight or turn left?" "Oh, either one." My father didn't want to be told, "Either one." He wanted to be told to go straight or turn left. Daily life is the same: "What would you like to have for lunch?" "Oh, I don't know." "What would you like to do tonight?" "Whatever you'd like to do, dear."

It's annoying on two grounds. First, you want to make your partner happy, and he isn't helping. And second, he is refusing to engage. (Fair disclosure: I have been the husband in this scenario.) You want him to engage and make his wishes known.

Every Christian at some time asks, "You know, Jesus just asked for his Father's will to be done. The Lord knows what I need; should I do the same? Should I just pray, 'Lord, your will be done,' rather than ask for things?"

The scripture above says no. Ask him for what you need. Ask him for what you want. Engage actively with the Lord and, yes, trust him and also ask for his will to be done. Because what he really wants is for you to engage with him.

Lord, help me to bring everything to you in prayer.

To Ponder: How can you begin to bring all the little things to God as they come up, in the middle of what you're doing?

WILL DUQUETTE

SEPTEMBER 29
SAINTS MICHAEL, GABRIEL,
AND RAPHAEL, ARCHANGELS

Knowing Who I Am

You are never too old to set another goal or dream
another dream.

C. S. Lewis

"All of us are called to meditate deeply on our own true selves," says Father James Martin, S.J., "to embrace the reality of our vocations, and to let God transform our true selves into sources of new life for others."[9]

The archangels—Michael, Gabriel, and Raphael—whose feast we celebrate today, tell me again who I am. Michael helps me remember I am not God. Gabriel announces God's call for me to be co-worker with him. Inspired by Mary's yes to Gabriel's announcement, her Magnificat becomes my, "With God all things are possible" (Lk 18:27). Challenges may attend my desire for lifelong learning. Raphael brings me God's healing and strength to persevere.

Each day I learn to entrust God with my yes, allowing him to heal any hesitancy toward my personal growth (Jer 30:17; Ps 147:3; Is 53:5). I know God will transform my life into new life for others.

I praise and thank you, Lord! Through Baptism I am a cooperator in your divine work of ongoing creation, redemption, and sanctification. I am how you choose to be present in this world.

To Ponder: "When the student is ready the teacher will appear" (proverb). How can you say yes to God's will for your life, starting with today?

MARGARET KERRY, F.S.P.

SEPTEMBER 30
SAINT JEROME

One Woman's Treasure

What you are is God's gift to you, what you become
is your gift to God.

Hans Urs von Balthasar

Waving goodbye to my daughter in her father's arms, I walked out of the door with a thermos full of coffee and dinner leftovers stashed in Tupperware.

Night after night as I clocked in for work as a night-shift nurse at our local hospital, I prayed that God would protect me through the twelve hours before me and the sleepless day to follow, that he would show me the path to take. Because the truth was, I was exhausted—physically, emotionally, and spiritually—and I wondered if the stirrings in my heart were true. *I went to school for this job,* I thought. *Surely God would just want me to be grateful.* Even after other opportunities presented themselves, I struggled with leaving my work as a nurse. The guilt overwhelmed me as I thought of leaving my patients or never welcoming a new life into the world.

But like the great parent who sees the unique abilities of his children, God does not wish misery upon us in work or in life. Honoring our God-given abilities can bring great joy in our own lives and in God's eyes.

Let me learn to foster my children's growth as children of God and model to them the gift of using our talents and abilities in testament to his goodness.

To Ponder: Do you ever feel guilty for the way you are using the gifts that God has given you? How can you evaluate your own life to ensure that you are not overlooking the God-given desires of your heart that can align with his greater good?

CHAUNIE MARIE BRUSIE

October

THEME: LIFE

The Difficult Little Way

Our Lord does not come down from heaven every
day to lie in a golden ciborium. He comes to find
another heaven which is infinitely dearer to him—
the heaven of our souls.

Saint Thérèse of Lisieux

I grew up being taught that Saint Thérèse of Lisieux, spiritual
giant and a Doctor of the Church, was a distant relative on
my great-grandmother's side. As a girl, I loved my chosen
patroness for her "little way." The idea that my small acts of
love, offered as intentional gifts, could constitute prayer was
appealing in its simplicity.

Only in adulthood have I come to truly understand the
profundity of Thérèse's spirituality. Confined within her Car-
mel, she lived out her passion for the gospels and her desire
to be a missionary in ways that were prescribed by her supe-
riors. Her faithful obedience has been a bright beacon for me
in moments when my duties as wife and mother conflicted
with the secret desires of my heart to travel, to volunteer,
and to evangelize.

During October we are called to reflect on the gift of life.
Is not the greatest way to champion human life by giving
my consent to God's plan for our family? How much easier
it might be to stand, placard in hand, before a women's clinic
than to wipe the runny noses or clean the dirty diapers of my
own little tribe. How tempting to study scripture and yet to
neglect seeing the face of Christ in my husband. How alluring

the call of the adoration chapel when my mission territory should instead be my kitchen.

Thérèse's "way" may be little, but it is never simple.

Saint Thérèse, help me to love Our Lord in the faces and needs of my family.

To Ponder: What are the challenges of your own little way?
LISA M. HENDEY

OCTOBER 2
THE HOLY GUARDIAN ANGELS

Bodyguard

With such bodyguards, what are we to fear? They can neither be subdued nor deceived; nor is there any possibility at all that they should go astray who are to guard us in all our ways. They are trustworthy, they are intelligent, they are strong—why, then, do we tremble?

Saint Bernard of Clairvaux

I can't think of a more comforting symbol of God's deep, personal, and ongoing love for us than a guardian angel. Imagine a beautiful celestial companion that is ours from the moment of our conception until we draw our last breath on earth. A forever-friend to guide us, strengthen us against temptation, and protect us from harm.

When my children were little, I used to take solace in the notion that a big, strong angel was at their side when they slept in their bedrooms, played in the yard, or ventured off to school for the first time. I find it even more consoling as my children reach teenage years, develop an attraction to members of the opposite sex, learn to drive, and leave for college.

Late at night when I find myself beginning to worry about my children's safety and well-being, I resort to the prayer we used to say together when they were little:

Angel of God, my guardian dear, to whom God's love commits me here, ever this day be at my side, to light and guard, to rule and guide.

To Ponder: How often do you look for ways to show your love, honor, and thanksgiving for the invaluable friend your guardian angel is? Celebrate this feast day with your family by reciting the Angel of God prayer together. Consider serving angel hair pasta tonight followed by angel food cake.

ELIZABETH FICOCELLI

OCTOBER 3
SAINT THEODORE GUERIN

Responding or Reacting?

If we are intended for great ends, we are called to great hazards.

Cardinal John Henry Newman

Sometimes life is messy and tumultuous and nonlinear.

And life with kids? All those things and more.

For me, the worst part about this messy, tumultuous, crazy life is not the difficult situations with which I must sometimes deal. For me, the worst part is my *reaction* to the mess and the tumult and the nonlinear.

It can be bad, like when I yell and stomp my feet like a two-year-old whose cookie was taken away because the two youngest children "entertained" themselves by overturning all the mattresses in one of the bedrooms.

Or when I flip at the kid who used the hose to create gigantic mud puddles into which he submerged his entire person, completing the messy disaster by pooping in his pants. My reaction? Yeah, it was bad.

In my early years of motherhood, I would get stuck on my poor responses to annoying or disruptive kid stuff. Instead of seeing my impatience as a weak moment and an area for improvement, I thought of myself as a perpetual failure, destined to ruin my children forever. I'm slowly realizing that just because I lose it doesn't mean *all* is lost. The truth is, I have ample opportunity to do it right the next time—to act in love, not impatience. Practice makes perfect, and if there's one thing I get, it's lots of patience practice.

Mother Mary, give me courage to try again after I behave poorly with my children. Inspire me to follow your perfect example as a mother and to respond with love instead of react in anger.

To Ponder: What types of parenting situations cause you to react most poorly? Where do you succeed in responding in love to your family?

COLLEEN MURPHY DUGGAN

An Instrument of Love

I beg you, Lord, let the glowing and honey-sweet
force of your love draw my mind away from all
things that are under heaven, that I may die for love
of the love of you who thought it a worthy thing to
die for love of the love of me.

Saint Francis of Assisi,
quoted by Ubertino da Casale

Bicycling home from work, I remembered the words of the
"Prayer of Saint Francis" hymn I had sung a thousand times
growing up in Catholic school. Here I was, fresh from college,
jumping into service work, and only now were the song's
words starting to make sense to me.

I was lonely. Work with the homeless was hard. Living
in a foreign country was exhausting. But the words of Saint
Francis's prayer circled stubbornly as I cycled: *Grant that I
may never seek so much to be consoled as to console.* In the midst
of that volunteer year, I was learning what it meant to give
of myself in love.

When I was younger and bolder, I resisted the idea of
being an instrument—too passive for the big plans I envisioned. Now I see that in becoming an instrument in God's
hands, we become bigger in love as we are shaped by
humility.

Today is the feast of Saint Francis of Assisi, a saint who
understood the sweetness of service. We know this truth as
moms, of giving and not counting the cost. Yet we find that

our service is repaid a thousandfold by the One who calls us to faithful love.

Lord, let me remember Saint Francis's humility as I seek to be your instrument. May you always use my life for your love.

To Ponder: How is your life an instrument of God's love?

LAURA KELLY FANUCCI

OCTOBER 5
SAINT FAUSTINA KOWALSKA

Lord, Have Mercy!

Surely goodness and mercy shall follow me
all the days of my life,
and I shall dwell in the house of the Lord
my whole life long.

Psalm 23:6

Sister Mary Faustina was an apostle, a twentieth-century "apostle of divine mercy," as the Vatican website refers to her. One excerpt of Faustina's famous diary shows God's longing to lavish mercy on us: "I sent prophets wielding thunderbolts to my people. Today I am sending you with my mercy to the people of the whole world. I do not want to punish aching mankind, but I desire to heal it, pressing it to my merciful heart."[10]

Can you imagine the Lord Jesus pressing you close to his merciful heart? What a place to be!

Praying with the imagination can lead to intimate encounters with the Lord. Try to use all five senses as you allow Jesus to draw your weary head upon his chest.

What can you hear? His heartbeat? Breathing? What else?

Where are you and Jesus, as you sit enfolded together? What can you see around you?

What can you feel? Are Jesus's garments rough? Soft? Scratchy? How are his arms holding you?

Can you taste anything? Have you and Jesus been sharing a meal together, perhaps?

How does Jesus smell? Mothers know how newborns respond to the familiar scent of their mothers. What happens when you inhale deeply, cradled against Jesus's chest?

Cozy moments like this with Jesus can strengthen our relationship. With love, we can pray:

Jesus, I trust in you.

To Ponder: Is there any part of you—your history, pastimes, feelings about yourself or others—that you keep hidden? How do you feel about inviting Jesus into your secret shame to shine his mercy there?

GRACE MAZZA URBANSKI

OCTOBER 6

Making Ourselves Present to God

For me, prayer is an aspiration of the heart, it is a simple glance directed to heaven, it is a cry of

gratitude and love in the midst of trial as well as joy;
finally it is something great, supernatural, which
expands my soul and unites me to Jesus.

Saint Thérèse of Lisieux

Personal prayer is our conversation with God. My time for it is early morning, before the sun is up; the only time I'm alone in the house, and the best time for me to find that unification with Jesus that Saint Thérèse talks about. But wherever we are, whatever time it is, God is present to us. And all prayer is our acknowledgement of his presence. We can be certain that God is listening. We can tell him anything without worry because he's madly in love with us.

Still, for some, prayer is difficult. It takes a humility we haven't been willing to give. It takes the acceptance that despite the books, advice, and general hype about being totally independent, we know somewhere deep inside us that we can't go it alone. We need another's hand. Prayer is our side-by-side walk with God. Yes, he is always present to us, but in prayer we make ourselves present to him. And in doing so we unite ourselves to him.

Jesus, may I make myself present to you, as you are always present to me. Draw me constantly into dialogue with you in prayer, no matter how simple or insignificant a subject I may bring to you. And then, may I be quiet. May I listen to what you've brought to me.

To Ponder: Do you truly realize how much God loves you?

KAYE PARK HINCKLEY

The Joy of Baptism

You can be at all fronts, wherever there is grief, in the
power of the cross. Your compassionate love takes
you everywhere, this love from the divine heart.

Saint Edith Stein

As Christians we celebrate giving thanks for the gift of life
in abundance (Jn 10:10). Pope Francis says that abundant
life begins in Baptism, a living reality that pertains to every
moment of our lives.

"There are two great days in a person's life," said scripture scholar William Barclay. "The day we are born and the
day we discover why." Eternal life begins here and through
Baptism has set deep roots in us. Jesus promises that whoever partakes of the Eucharist has eternal life (Jn 6:54). We
remain in Jesus and he remains in us. "All the way to heaven
is heaven," Jesus told Saint Catherine of Siena, "because I
am the Way."

On this feast of Our Lady of the Rosary we find particular
celebrations in the mysteries. Praying the third joyful and
first luminous mysteries of the Rosary (the Nativity and the
Baptism in the Jordan), we thank God for the gift of life and
Baptism. We pray for those children awaiting birth and for
those awaiting new life in Baptism. We pray for first com-
municants, for those returning to confession to renew their
baptismal promises, for people struggling to find serenity in
life, and for the dying that they may enjoy eternal life in God.

My Baptism day was a joyful and luminous day. Thank you for the gift of abundant life.

To Ponder: Do you know the date of your Baptism? Do you know the Baptism dates of your family and friends? How do you celebrate?

MARGARET KERRY, F.S.P.

OCTOBER 8

Can't Take My Eyes Off of You

We love because he first loved us.

1 John 4:19

I catch myself looking at them when they are not aware. I marvel at how beautiful, how miraculous they are. I am lost in these moments of love. When they are reading or eating or watching a show or sleeping. When they are doing nothing out of the ordinary, and yet they are doing miraculous things because everything a miraculous being does is miraculous. God's awe-inspiring creation. My children.

And then it hits me. This is the way God looks at us. This must be his constant gaze toward each one of his children. We don't see him there. We don't hear him or feel him. We go about our business every day, and we have no idea someone is watching us, not just to keep track of us or make sure we aren't breaking any of the rules but to fill up our every split second with his love. There he is—delighting in who we are, because we are his. Though I know God can do anything, I like to think that he "can't" take his eyes off of us.

Dear Lord, never let us forget how much you love us.

To Ponder: How often do you stop to consider how captivated God is in his loving gaze toward you? How would this change your actions and reactions if you could remember it throughout your day?

SHERRY BOAS

OCTOBER 9

One Tablespoon of Hope

When things come to the worst, they
generally mend.

Susanna Moodie

It was one of those days. Before breakfast, one child bit two others. Another "accidentally" colored the wall. A third, inconsolable, would not be put down for even a second. Struggling to make breakfast with him on my hip, I discovered we were out of milk. Sighing heavily, I abandoned my plans to just give them cereal and opened a cabinet. A falling tea cup narrowly missed my head and shattered on the floor.

It was the last straw. I crumbled, sobbing under the strain of caring for four little ones. *Jesus, how can I possibly meet all these needs?* I prayed silently. My children gathered around sadly as I swept up the china, patting me and telling me it was okay. Touched by their empathy, I began gathering things to make muffins. My eyes rested on the set of measuring spoons my aunt had given me. The biggest one read, "One Tablespoon of Hope."

One tablespoon of hope doesn't seem like much, but using that spoon to measure the baking soda lifted my spirits. The children came to help mix and pour, sniffing the cinnamon and sharing scent-filled memories: Christmas, sticky buns, monkey bread, French toast. Gradually, their happy chatter and the smell of baking muffins soothed me.

Jesus, thank you for loving me even at my worst. Help me remember that nothing is too lost for you to redeem.

To Ponder: On tough days, we don't always cope well. Jesus loves us in even our worst moments. He cares about how we feel. We have his assurance that he is with us always. No problem is too small to bring to Jesus. If you encounter a stressful situation today, try asking Jesus to help you handle it, and trust him to do it.

ABBEY DUPUY

OCTOBER 10
WORLD DAY AGAINST THE DEATH PENALTY

Our Duty and Freedom to Protect All Life

In modern democracies, which no longer refer to a higher moral law, upright citizens have an innate duty to aspire to laws that reflect what they believe is best for society: that is the only duty incumbent

upon them, and the only freedom which they
still possess.

Servant of God Dr. Jérôme Lejeune

Thirty years ago my family suffered a terrible loss. My cousin Ralph was a talented saxophone player who played with Tommy Dorsey in his heyday. He taught music in a high school. Ralph's students, his wife, and his three kids loved his gentle nature and sunny disposition. Tragedy struck in the form of an argument between his teens and those of his next-door neighbor. It enraged their father so much that he ran out of his house with a shotgun and shot Ralph dead in front of his family. The neighbor served seven years for the murder. However, for the past thirty years, Ralph's family has mourned him. The injustice of this seemed to demand the death penalty for the murderer.

During that time, Saint John Paul II said the death penalty was not necessary in developed nations, and I accepted his opinion, although it was hard for me to see my family suffer.

If a guilty man's life is to be protected by society, so much more should we protect innocent life: the baby in the womb, the disabled, the sick and elderly. All life is precious because God has a plan for each of us to live our lives on earth until he calls us home, to be together with him in heaven forever.

Lord, help me to show respect for the lives of others in the respect with which I treat them, no matter how sinful or inconvenient they are.

To Ponder: How do your attitudes and actions show respect for life of these vulnerable members of society? Do you vote to protect life?

LETICIA VELASQUEZ

OCTOBER 11

A Vibrant Life

I have set before you life and death . . . choose life.

Deuteronomy 30:19

Some people embrace life while others seem to merely exist. Those whose lives are vivacious carry a rare and infectious joy that seldom falters, even in the sorrowful events of life. Those who merely exist seem to hover in a perpetual apathy and acceptance of mediocrity in their lives.

In my youth, I secretly elected to reject mediocrity and instead chose a vibrant life. I knew this would entail a lifetime of overcoming obstacles, tackling challenges, and facing fears, but the alternative was too bleak and macabre for me. A life void of color and meaning obviously led to a hollow and shallow reality, and I knew that love and apathy did not coexist. Apathy meant death, and love equaled life.

In a jaded and tainted world, opting for the easy way out is a constant temptation. Concupiscence taunts us with worldly enticements and pleasures or even just distractions, often in the form of multiple stimuli competing for our attention. It is hard to love. It is difficult to *choose life*, because death (sin) is already a natural part of our humanity.

Choosing to live a life rich with exuberance and generosity requires intentional effort on our part and God's grace to carry us through the lulls and setbacks. We lead joy-filled lives when we reject sin and its consequences. Perhaps that translates into advocacy or other actions for the good. Perhaps our call is more contemplative. No matter, we are called to choose life over death, love over apathy, greatness over mediocrity.

Lord, you have given me the beautiful gift of free will. Grant me the grace to choose love today.

To Ponder: How can you live a vibrant life today?

JEANNIE EWING

OCTOBER 12

Heaven on Earth

How sweet are your words to my taste, sweeter than
honey to my mouth.

Psalm 119:103

What a long day, a long week! I felt worn down by the daily grind.

Like many moms, my days include running errands, washing laundry, reading stories, giving baths, and counseling tweens. I offer my work to God, but sometimes I feel the weight of my responsibilities and wonder if I am making a difference.

At the end of this particular day, all I wanted to do was unwind with a good book before falling asleep. I wished my husband were home so he could tuck the kids into bed. But this one last task fell on my shoulders, so I slowly made my way to each of my six kids' beds.

As I tucked in my youngest daughter, I kissed her and blessed her forehead with the sign of the cross. Then, she gave me a big hug, breathed in deeply, and said, "Mmm . . . Mom, you smell like heaven!"

My entire being melted into the tiny arms that wrapped around my neck. The stress in my shoulders subsided, and the heaviness in my heart lifted. I immediately knew that God used my child to speak words of consolation to my weary soul.

My days remain long, and my responsibilities still weigh me down. But the Lord's message through my daughter remains close to my heart, reminding me that being faithful to my work as a mom brings me closer to God, closer to heaven.

Gracious God, thank you for soothing words of consolation that give me strength.

To Ponder: When you are weary from the daily grind, what restores your soul? Carve out some time today to receive the refreshment God wants to give you.

SARAH DAMM

How Mothers Make Space for Life

Don't lose heart. I will never forsake you. My
Immaculate Heart will be your refuge and the way
that will lead you to God.

The Blessed Mother to the visionaries at Fatima

The oldest known prayer to Mary, dating back to the year AD
250, is a plea for her motherly care: "We fly to thy protection,
O Holy Mother of God; despise not our petitions in our necessities, but deliver us always from all dangers."

In 1917, Fatima, Portugal, needed a mother. World War
I was raging, faith was attacked by anti-Church government
officials, and living conditions were poor. This is what the
Blessed Mother entered into. On this date in 1917, the "Miracle of the Sun" occurred and the sun appeared to dance.
This touched the lives of the three children, Lucia, Jacinta,
and Francisco, giving them and the world assurance of her
motherly care.

Deep down we need to know someone will care for us.
Women carve a unique space into the world—a space of comfort, acceptance, and love. It is a woman's special gift to make
the world receptive to personal dignity and beauty, to bring
life into the world and allow it to grow.

Motherhood is not merely human. It is, in a sense, divine.
God wanted us to have a mother who would nurture and
nourish our lives in the spiritual realm, be the relief for our

pain and our recourse in hopelessness. Moms create the space in the world for love, and our heavenly Mother Mary does that for all of us.

Heavenly Father, thank you for the gift of motherhood and of our Blessed Mother Mary. Help me to be a holy, caring mother and to nurture life in everything I do.

To Ponder: How can you create a space of acceptance, beauty, and the assurance of love in the lives of those you care for and cherish?

MARC CARDARONELLA

OCTOBER 14
WORLD STANDARDS DAY

God's Hand in My Life

Without standardization, communication and collaboration between people, machines, parts, and products would be extremely challenging on an international level.

American National Standards Institute

Who even knew that such an institute existed? I guess without these organizations all over the world working on standards, particularly in the area of technology, we couldn't swipe a credit card or make a phone call when traveling out of the country. In fact, those Legos we bought recently for our kids would have had a little more difficulty getting to our local store.

How many other things in our life do we take for granted? Flush toilets? Sliced bread? The list goes on. Perhaps the biggest and most ignored "standard" in our lives is God's presence. Yes, he is there doing many marvelous things for us, but most of the time, we don't even acknowledge a single one. The philosopher John Piper once wrote, "God is always doing ten thousand things in your life, and you may be aware of three of them."

Did you see that smile on your child's face? Did you hear that bird sing a song as you walked out your door? Did your toddler get that extra hour of sleep today so you could finish paying your bills? All these things are the unseen work of a Father in heaven done just for you.

Dear heavenly Father, help me to be the faithful child that sees her father's care in matters big and small, and then completely gives her life over to that loving care.

To Ponder: Where can you expect to see God's work in your life today?

TAMI KISER

OCTOBER 15
SAINT TERESA OF AVILA

Even the Saints Struggled

She was always afraid no matter what she did, she was going to do everything wrong.

Saint Teresa of Avila

As a teenager, Saint Teresa admits she cared only about boys, clothes, flirting, and rebelling. That sounds awfully familiar. At sixteen, her father sent her to a convent. How many times did my father threaten the same thing in the classic "clean up your act or you're going to the convent" manner? I can't believe Teresa's father actually did it.

While there, Teresa contemplated becoming a nun because she thought the convent was a safe place for *someone like her*. Ironically, it did not help her spiritual life. However, in a twist only God could engineer, she would become a nun and later the catalyst to the reform of such places.

At forty-one, although a nun, Teresa had fallen away from prayer. A priest convinced her to return to prayer. At first, she found it difficult, saying, "I would rather have a heavy penance than the practice of prayer." However, she persevered and eventually received great spiritual delight.

For me that delight comes in the form of peace and joy regardless of my circumstances, and the freedom—if only for a moment—from the fear that I am doing everything wrong.

Saint Teresa, how I adore that you were so much like me. I love that you struggled with holiness in your life and yet still attained sainthood. Please pray for me to remain steadfast in my desire to do the same.

To Ponder: How many of us struggle to pray in our day-to-day life? Examine your prayer practices. How would you assess your current spiritual state? Do you need to return to prayer?

ALLISON GINGRAS

The Humus of Humility

To the Sacred Heart of Jesus, I give myself . . . my
person and my life, my actions, pains and sufferings,
so that I may . . . honor, love, and glorify the Sacred
Heart. This is my unchanging purpose, namely, to be
all His, and to do all things for the love of Him.

Saint Margaret Mary Alacoque

Today's feast reminds us of the powerful love Our Lord Jesus
has for us. His Sacred Heart was described by this beautiful
saint as "inflamed by love" and a "burning furnace of charity" for souls. He showed himself to Saint Margaret Mary
Alacoque in this way because of her great humility.

The word *humility* comes from the Latin word *humus*,
which literally means "soil." Humus is the organic component of that soil. It is the combination of the dying and the
living—the dead plant parts and the living plant parts—the
decomposition of materials and the living microorganisms.
In this unnoticed place, what was buried comes alive. In this
deep, dark, wonderful place, new life grows in silence.

The grace of humility. A place where one dies to oneself.
The humble walk silently through life, decidedly unnoticed.
Saint Margaret Mary Alacoque made herself the humus from
which Jesus could grow his seed. She made herself available
for the living word he spoke to her. Her mission then became
to sow the field.

Jesus, I pray for the grace of humility, to die to myself so that you might create new life in me. May I always recognize the powerful love you have for me, which consumes your most Sacred Heart.

To Ponder: What opportunities have you had to be open to the gift of humility? How have you seen humility as a way to grow in holiness?

CINDY COSTELLO

OCTOBER 17
NATIONAL MULLIGAN DAY

Confession

Every time you go to confession, immerse yourself entirely in My mercy, with great trust, so that I may pour the bounty of My grace upon your soul. . . . Tell souls that from this fount of mercy souls draw graces solely with the vessel of trust. If their trust is great, there is no limit to My generosity.

Saint Faustina, Diary

Knotted stomach. Whispered prayers. Apprehension. I turn hot as I kneel and trip over the words in the ancient script for confession. I lay down all my many faults, words pouring out in a wave. Advice and encouragement comes from God through the priest, like a balm to my open wounds.

From somewhere in my foggy brain, I pull out the words of the Act of Contrition and wait for the words of freedom: "I absolve you from your sins, in the name of the Father, and of the Son, and of the Holy Spirit." A tear rolls down my cheek as I stand to exit the confessional, do my penance, and ponder God's unending mercy.

We aren't guaranteed a tomorrow, but God in his mercy always offers us a second chance. In honor of National Mulligan Day, let us take a spiritual mulligan from Christ's generous fount of mercy.

Dear Lord, thank you the gift of your mercy! Though I am but a poor sinner, you shower me with love and mercy. Help me to fully trust in you. Let me be a reflection of your mercy to others and enable me to be as generous as you.

To Ponder: Today, resolve to take advantage of the mercies that God offers to us. Find a time to experience the graces of Reconciliation and make arrangements to go regularly.

JEN STEED

OCTOBER 18
SAINT LUKE THE EVANGELIST

Exactly the Right Person

I too decided, after investigating everything carefully
from the very first, to write an orderly account
for you.

Luke 1:3

Saint Luke, the physician, played an interesting role in the writing of the Bible: it was his job to report the miracles that his professional expertise would have made him, of all disciples, most likely to pass off as purely natural occurrences.

The Gospel of Luke reports two mirror-image miraculous conceptions. Saint John the Baptist was the child of his parents' old age; God gave the gift of fertility to a couple who had given up all hope of it. Mary, meanwhile, was presumably perfectly able to conceive naturally but instead was overshadowed by the Holy Spirit.

Saint Luke's medical knowledge made him exactly the man to understand and attest to God's intervention in these events.

We, too, have a testimony to give. We are able to see God working in ways that other people might not understand. We see miracles that other people might pass off as purely coincidental or natural occurrences. *But you don't understand. You don't know how impossible it was for this to have happened without the grace of God.* Our willingness to share that testimony is one way God uses us to bring the Gospel to the world.

Lord, fill me with courage. Let me never be afraid to tell others about the wonder of your work in my life.

To Ponder: What has God been doing in your life? What are the miracles you can see but that others might not understand unless you find a way to tell them what has happened?

JENNIFER FITZ

The Faith of Martyrs

We (missionaries) begged God to accept our lives
and our blood and unite them to His life and His
blood for the salvation of these tribes.

Saint Isaac Jogues

Today we remember the lives of the North American martyrs. With our open churches and adoration chapels all around us, it can be hard to imagine that we are the spiritual children of martyrs. It is easy to forget that holy men shed their blood for the faith we profess so openly today. But this is our history. It is also our calling. If we look to the world around us, we know that giving your life for your faith is not a thing of the past. Daily, men and women are being tortured and put to death for professing Christ as Lord and Savior.

And we are supposed to be cultivating a faith that strong in our own hearts, a faith ready to be tried and tested in the most dangerous of fires—a faith that will hold in the face of the ultimate sacrifice. How do we grow that kind of faith in our own lives? A daily life of authentic prayer, real intimacy with God our Father, and loving sacrifice are the keys. Prayer draws us near to God and reminds us why we live. Sacrificial love trains our spirits in how to live and say yes to God even when the cost feels high.

Together they remind us that this life here is not our final destination, that we have another goal. The hope of heaven and desire to see Jesus face to face is the driving force that gives us the courage to embrace our faith in the most difficult circumstances.

We may not face the threat of martyrdom like Saints René Goupil, Isaac Jogues, Jean de Lalande, Antoine Daniel, John de Brébeuf, Charles Garnier, Noël Chabanel, and Gabriel Lalemant, but we are all asked to live and walk in hard things in our lives, to die to ourselves and take up our crosses daily to follow Christ. We find the strength to do that in prayer, in the sacraments, and through the open doors of our churches, where the prayers of the martyrs ascend on our behalves.

Saint Isaac Jogues and companions, pray for us.

To Ponder: How can you honor the sacrifice of the North American martyrs today? Take the time to stop in a church and pray for faith like theirs. Then ask their intercession.

COLLEEN CONNELL MITCHELL

OCTOBER 20

Small Things with Great Love

We can do no great things, only small things with great love.

Saint Teresa of Calcutta

For my family, October is a weigh station. By now we have readjusted from summer sleep habits back to the regular school routine. But we are also adjusting to new schedules for school, work, and extracurricular activities. The first report card is soon to be on its way and as a family we need to take stock: How are we doing? Have we taken on new things and managed to grow as a family nurturing our potential and gifts? Have we overextended ourselves yet again? Do we have enough time as family, as a married couple, and for our own spiritual growth?

I am no more successful at this than many other parents and married couples. What I do know is we often put our trust in organization and enforcement. But that does not simplify life or reduce stress. Instead, if we attend to the value of simple things, we actually can succeed more.

Our lives are filled with so many repetitive actions that can become unifying rituals in the home. Replacing toilet paper or taking out the trash, placing dishes nearer to the sink, and tidying up the entryway are all actions that go toward creating a shared space that says we care for one another. And this helps everyone to be able to get beyond that distraction to focus on the more important things. But it only works if it isn't any one person's burden. Know the value, respect the person.

Gentle hand of God
Touch our family
So that your will
May dwell in our home.

To Ponder: How can we help each other with life's big things by finding the small things that lead to great joy?

JAY CUASAY

Making Cleaning Fun

"Happy Windsday, Piglet. I see you're sweeping leaves." "Yes, Pooh. But it's hard. This is a very unfriendly wind."

Winnie the Pooh and Piglet

Fall is one of my favorite seasons: the cool crisp air, the leaves changing colors on the trees, and the smell of pumpkin candles. The problem comes when I just want to curl up with my scarf and oversized sweater and sit on the couch by the fire with a book instead of attempting to clean my house, which looks like it's been hit by a storm.

Usually, when it's time to clean, I think of something I'd like to clean, then I begin prioritizing and decide that item should wait, choosing instead to just sit and whine about the chores I don't want to do. One of the best pieces of advice I've received was from a friend who said, "If you start with the chore you want to do, you'll feel accomplished and be more motivated to tackle the rest of the cleaning." So now I start with the fun or easy chore.

Another way I get past my lack of motivation to clean is to call a girlfriend, put her on speakerphone or use my earbuds, and talk to her while I clean. Of course, when I do that, I have to do more stationary things like folding laundry or scrubbing the bathroom, but as I'm talking I forget I'm cleaning and when the conversation is over, I feel fulfilled by our conversation and accomplished because I completed a task.

Dear Jesus, help us to find ways to push past our desire to be lazy and instead find joy in serving and caring for our families.

To Ponder: What is one thing you can do to make cleaning more entertaining?

COURTNEY VALLEJO

OCTOBER 22
SAINT JOHN PAUL II

More than Useful

A person's rightful due is to be treated as an object of love, not as an object for use.

Saint John Paul II

When my boys were younger, they loved Thomas the Tank Engine and his friends. Like many parents, I became very familiar with Sir Topham Hatt's words of high praise: "Thomas, you're a really useful engine!"

It's good to be useful, no doubt about that. It's also nice to compliment others for their contributions to our community. But as a friend of mine once pointed out, isn't there something lacking in Sir Topham Hatt's signature phrase?

One thing I value so much about my Catholic faith is its insistence on the dignity of every human life. I admire Saint John Paul II for his commitment to sharing the truth that every life matters: poor, unborn, elderly, disabled, prisoners. Many of these people are not useful in the traditional sense of the word, but our faith shows that the world's understanding of usefulness is not the measure by which we should judge another's right to live. Every life has dignity. Every life is a reminder of the God who sees not as we see, and who invites us to view other people through his loving eyes.

Lord, help me to recognize your love for everyone, no matter what they do or are unable to do.

To Ponder: Are you too hard on yourself when you are sick, tired, or not being "useful"? Next time this happens, rest in the knowledge that you don't need to do anything to deserve God's love.

GINNY KUBITZ MOYER

OCTOBER 23

The Joy of Family

Brotherly love is a dewy freshness and aridity in the monotony of personal and community life.

Cardinal Gianfranco Ravasi

Growing up, I thought everyone had thousands of cousins and aunts and uncles. I loved spending Sundays in Houston: going to Mass followed by playing at Grandmother's house in the backyard, fresh fried chicken, eggs Benedict, tamales, grits, bacon, and orange juice. Every weekend, it seemed to my child's mind, was a feast. The only thing I hated was the car ride. Lying down in the back of the station wagon, I'd know we were close to my grandparents' house when I'd see trees lacing branches, creating a tunnel of oaks.

After my grandparents passed and we grew up, reunions happened less and less frequently. However, whenever we'd get together, there'd be food, someone would pull out a guitar and begin playing, and the songs and stories would flow faster than the wine. The stories got told and retold and retold, but they never grew dusty. We'd all laugh recalling the fire at the beach house or the bus ride to Denver during an ice storm. It's always a moment of sacred time, when the years and miles that seemingly separate the aunts and uncles from the cousins and the generation beyond melt away in a singalong, a meal, or a prayer.

What I thought began as a family ritual by my grandparents—to see all their children and grandchildren—is, in fact, a very Catholic ritual. We gathered, we shared stories and memories of our history, we prayed, we sang, and we ate. This is also what we do at Mass. Our own faith teaches us, "Do this in memory of me." The celebration of the Eucharist is, was, and will be when Mass is celebrated again.

Thank you, Lord, for the joy that comes from family.

To Ponder: What's one thing you can do today to show your appreciation for your biological family or your parish family?

SHERRY ANTONETTI

OCTOBER 24

Letting Ourselves Be Found

God became man to turn creatures into sons: not simply to produce better men of the old kind but to produce a new kind of man.

C. S. Lewis

Growing up in New Orleans with nine siblings and a gaggle of other children, hot summer evenings usually found us playing hide-and-seek using an entire city block as our playground. On occasion, we could hide so well that it took the one who was "it" great effort and skill to find us. The signal that the priceless discovery of a "hider" had been made came forth when the magic words, "Olly, Olly, oxen free," rang through the night air. Upon hearing this, we knew could return to home base victoriously and without fear of penalty for another round of hiding and being sought. Sometimes, when we were flat weary, we would simply let ourselves be found, surrendering to the seeker in order to take a rest.

Child's play often illustrates the greater truths of the human experience. To be sought after—and found—is the cornerstone of our relationship with God. Though we often think of ourselves as looking for God, it is God who relentlessly pursues us, searching for us endlessly until he finds us—that is, until we let ourselves be found.

God's first words to human beings after the fall were, "Where are you?" The pinnacle of God's creation, made for an intimate love relationship with their Creator, had taken cover behind fig leaves. The hiding game had begun.

Where are you? God continually asks each of us that all-important question. His great desire is that we unveil our best disguises and let ourselves be found.

Father in heaven, unveil my heart and give me the grace to surrender freely to your love.

To Ponder: Are you hiding your heart from God so well that it can't be found?

JUDY LANDRIEU KLEIN

Make Time to Be Together as a Family

That which is truly great grows unnoticed, and silence at the right moment is more fruitful than the constant activity that degenerates into spiritual idleness.

Pope Benedict XVI

One Saturday afternoon not too long ago, our family scarfed down a late lunch after a long and busy morning. Lately, it seemed we were all going in different directions. Between school, work, sports, and everything our family was involved in, it felt like our family life was frayed and quickly unraveling.

After lunch, I was determined to finally clean the sticky puddle of orange juice in the fridge before it became a permanent fixture. Just as I was getting down on all fours and rolling my sleeves up, my two younger sons came barging in, their faces flush from playing outside.

"Mama, will you play outside with us? Pleeeeassssee?" I tried to avoid their pleas and remain focused on the sticky orange blob on the fridge shelf. I reasoned that my husband was out there and could play with them. I paused and looked at my sons waiting for my answer, their eyes filled with guarded hope.

"All right," I sighed, "for a little while." I grabbed my sneakers and joined the rest of the family in the yard. Before long, we were all chasing each other around, laughing and smiling together. I glanced back at the house knowing what waited for me inside. There would always be something to clean but my family would not always be here together like this. I knew I needed to cherish these moments while I had them.

Dear Saint Martha, pray for me, that I may give more of what really matters to my family today.

To Ponder: How can you foster more family time together?
ERIKA MARIE

OCTOBER 26

Deployed

Mankind will not have peace until it turns with trust
to My mercy.

Saint Faustina, Diary

"Slippery rail season," they call it. My husband is a train commuter. Fall leaves coat the tracks, and when it rains, the soggy leaves become slicker than ice. The rails get sanded each morning before rush hour, but some days—like this one—the rain and leaves both fall heavily throughout the day. I got the text from my husband: he'd be at least an hour late coming home. In order to get the passengers home safely, the trains had to slow to a crawl. This was after a long day of children snippy from being trapped indoors. Self-pity threatened.

I reached out to a friend of mine, a military wife, for perspective. I admitted I felt I needed God's mercy today and felt I wasn't getting it, and then I felt guilty for not having it nearly as tough as the spouses of our deployed military. She cheered me up by saying that she didn't mind deployments half as much as that "I'll be home late" text. I realized that it was all about resetting expectations, about placing our spouses' safety in the Lord's merciful hands, about knowing that God will provide the grace to keep fighting, even when our own fight has slipped away.

Father God, you deployed your only Son to be our Savior. Help us keep faith in your plan, no matter where we find ourselves called to serve. Help us offer our discomforts for those who offer their lives to keep us free.

To Ponder: Do you know a mom whose spouse is serving abroad in the military? Think of one act of kindness you can do for her today.

ERIN MCCOLE CUPP

OCTOBER 27

Keeping the Fire of Youth

The greatest challenge of the day is: how to bring about a revolution of the heart, a revolution which has to start with each one of us?

Dorothy Day

When I imagined life as an adult my primary thought was that it would be almost perfect because I would be in charge of it myself. No longer doing what my parents or teachers wanted me to do, following rules that seemed random and constricting, or having to work so hard to get along with people. My life and relationships with others would be mutually supportive and my needs taken care of by myself or those who loved me. Talk about delusional, but I suppose youth need those thoughts to have a point from which to begin when starting out as an adult.

Eventually I learned that no one would meet all my needs, rules are necessary for order rather than chaos, and there is always someone who wants you to do something you'd rather avoid. Part of being an adult is realizing that God has gifted us in so many ways and that sharing those gifts with others is what makes life beautiful, not perfect. God's grace gives us the supernatural ability to handle the idiosyncrasies of life and people. Relying on God's grace makes self-sacrifice a reality for us and helps drudgery become a joy. The naiveté of youth becomes wisdom through the power of God, the giver of life, love, and grace.

Father, thank you for my life and all the people you have given me to love. Help me to keep my youthful spirit while becoming the person you call me to be. I pray that you pour out your grace so I continue to grow in wisdom and learn to share what you have given me.

To Ponder: Is your adult life different from what you thought it would be like? How does God's grace help with un-met expectations?

DEANNA BARTALINI

Never Alone

Because Jesus is the Light, you too become light
when you proclaim him.

Saint John Paul II

So many of our loved ones turn away from the faith. It can seem hopeless as we watch them fall deeper in love with the values of the secular culture. Only God can draw a heart back to himself, but we are asked to lend our own love into the mix. With our prayers and sacrifices, we cooperate with the unseen work of the Holy Spirit. And as we seek to image the virtues of Christ in our own lives—especially humility and purity—we become more and more radiant in our witness to the faith.

Along the way, it's important to seek out holy friendships and community. Make sure you stay in touch with others who love Jesus and who encourage you along the path of virtue. Do what you can to love and support their walk with God, too. Even the apostles did not set out on their journeys alone. The feast of Saints Simon and Jude is a testament to the power of faith and friendship. Empowered by the Holy Spirit, they brought many souls to conversion. Together, they even accepted martyrdom, imitating Christ to the end—out of love for those who were spiritually lost.

Jesus, in the immensity of your love and mercy, help me to follow you with all my heart, mind, body, and soul. Though I am often afraid, use me, your frail daughter, to draw others back to your Sacred Heart.

To Ponder: What is holding you back from evangelizing? This week, do something sweet for a fallen-away loved one without expecting anything in return.

LISA MLADINICH

OCTOBER 29
BLESSED CHIARA LUCE BADANO

Inspired by the Bright Light of Youth

I have nothing left, but I still have my heart, and with that I can always love.

Blessed Chiara Luce Badano

In high school, I had the life-changing experience of a teacher who inspired me to want to become a teacher myself. I remained gung-ho even through college, and then I student taught. Long story short: I found myself *not* teaching.

Ironically, twenty years after earning the bachelor's degree in education that some thought went to waste as I entered the business world, I find myself up to my nose in educational matters. I'm a mom, yes, but I'm also very active in our parish's religious education program, and I've spent nearly fifteen years teaching classes, helping with Confirmation, and even leading adult groups. I've spoken to adults, too, but I find the most energy when I'm working with young people.

Young people have a courage and enthusiasm I can't help but appreciate. They draw me in with their bright motivation and desire to make a difference. They make me want to dig in and keep working, showing me that there is always hope. They are, in fact, the reason I am a teacher, though I'm not in a classroom in the traditional sense.

Thank you, Lord, for the gift of young people. Guide me so that I am a holy example to them and help me to be open to the excitement they can inspire in me.

To Ponder: Who are the young people in your life who could use your encouragement? Reach out to them today and don't forget to pray for them!

SARAH A. REINHARD

OCTOBER 30
The Mirror

You formed my inmost being; you knit me in my mother's womb. I am fearfully and wonderfully made. Your works are wonderful, I know that well!

Psalm 139:13–14

I once did a group devotion called a prayer labyrinth. In lieu of an actual pilgrimage, which they were rarely able to undertake, medieval Christians walked elaborate labyrinths set in marble in their cathedral floors as a type of pilgrimage. In our day we might travel to Rome or to the Holy Land, but not often, if ever.

The prayer labyrinth I walked was a sort of substitute for a pilgrimage. At varying points there were prayer stations, and at one of them there was a station called The Mirror. At the foot of a full-length mirror there were written directions.

If you are able, right now, go to a mirror. When you look in the mirror, what do you see? Do you, like the psalmist, see someone who is "fearfully and wonderfully made"? Spend a few moments looking at your reflection. Then finish reading today's meditation, the instructions for The Mirror: "Stop to feel your pulse. Life is running through you. Life is a gift from God. Feel your fingertips. Look carefully at their print pattern, a pattern shared with no other living being. Uniquely, fearfully, wonderfully made. Made in God's image. Loved for it. Look again at the mirror. Ask God to show you the real you, the you without image, *the you that God sees*."

Thank you for the gift of my life, Lord. Help me use it as you desire me to use it and grant me the grace to appreciate it as it is.

To Ponder: Does what you see make you want to sing or to look away? What is the *you* of you? What might your spirit look like without your body? What did Jesus mean when he said to love others as we love ourselves?

SONJA CORBITT

OCTOBER 31
HALLOWEEN

The Joy of Becoming

If you are what you should be, you will set the whole world ablaze!

Saint Catherine of Siena

As tiny ballerinas and beautiful ice princesses, brave pirates and spooky skeletons run happily from door to door tonight, we are reminded of the joy of *becoming*. Our kids take such delight in picking out their costumes and transforming into something different—*better*—for the night.

As adults we are tempted to think that our lives are locked in, our futures all but written, because we are married and settled with jobs and children and responsibilities. If we fall into that temptation, though, we would simply be putting in our time and watching ourselves age. We would be dying slowly, a day at a time.

Our children's joy reminds us that even though our futures aren't as mysterious as they were when we were kids, we are not yet "finished." In fact, we've just begun growing. We're still in the process of becoming more fully the children of God that we were made to be.

Saint Catherine, please pray for me that I never stop striving to grow into the person that God has made me to be.

To Ponder: What is an area of your life that is stunted? What can you do to help foster the type of growth that God is calling you to?

MEG MATENAER

November

THEME: GIVING THANKS

My Path to Sainthood

In all circumstances give thanks, for this is the will of
God for you in Christ Jesus.

1 Thessalonians 5:18

Today, I'm pondering my own path to sainthood as we
embark on a month oriented toward giving thanks. Remembering my favorite saints, I wonder how they felt in the midst
of their own spiritual journeys. How were they capable of
offering up even their greatest sacrifices, seeing those things
as a path to sanctity?

As I age, I'm trying to remember to proactively offer gratitude for the crosses I'm being called to bear. But I'll admit to
often failing, falling into "Seriously, God?" pessimism. Rather
than seeing the chance to come to the aid of a loved one as
another step toward holiness, too often I miss grace because
I'm blinded by selfishness. But a deeper consideration of the
saints we celebrate today, the canonized but also those known
only in our own lives, reminds me that seeing the hand of
God in all things—perhaps especially those we wouldn't
choose for ourselves—bears witness to the truths we profess.

Let's give thanks this month not only for the Norman
Rockwell moments, but also for the trials. Let's embrace the
chance to nurse an infant in the wee hours or to discipline the
teen who just broke curfew. Let's appreciate the budget that
needs balancing, the roof that leaks, the layoff from work,
or Nana's health-care needs. In all circumstances, especially

those that demand that we lean more deeply into God's loving arms, let's give thanks.

God, source of all bounty, allow me to embrace every moment of my path to knowing and loving you.

To Ponder: What struggles in your life require your gratitude rather than your grief?

LISA M. HENDEY

NOVEMBER 2
ALL SOULS' DAY

Praying in Hope

> For now we see in a mirror, dimly, but then we will
> see face to face. Now I know only in part; then I will
> know fully, even as I have been fully known.

1 Corinthians 13:12

The first year after my father died was full of emotional potholes. I was at Mass on All Souls' Day of that year when, during the prayers of the faithful, the reader said, "For all those who have died in the hope of rising again, especially for any of our own family members who have died this past year; may they see God face to face. We pray to the Lord." As the entire congregation responded, "Lord, hear our prayer," I was slammed into an emotional pothole. "Dad!" my heart cried out. "Just look! Every Catholic around the world is praying for you today!"

You see, both my parents were raised in the Catholic faith, but neither of them felt particularly at home in the

Church. My father's story included his own father's struggles with alcoholism, which not only tarnished my dad's personal image of our Father God but also warped all of his interactions with the Church.

Sadness for my dad's earthly experiences commingled with great hope for his heavenly experiences on that first All Souls' Day after his passing. As I fought to steer a course of emotional stability that morning, I was profoundly grateful to belong to a Church that habitually organizes its members to pray in hope for one another.

Thank you, Father God, for the hope of heaven you have gained for us by your Son's life, death, and resurrection.

To Ponder: Do you have deceased family members for whom you can pray today? Have you thought about lighting a candle or having a Mass said for them?

HEIDI BRATTON

NOVEMBER 3

Praying with
the End in Mind

Prayer is like a great love. When you start dating the silence can be awkward, but as you grow to know each other you can sit in silence for hours and just being with each other is a great comfort.

Matthew Kelly

It has been a busy couple of days! With All Saints' Day on November 1 and All Souls' Day on November 2, today could be our day! Have we given much thought to our state in the Church as one of the fledgling pilgrims on earth, one day perhaps a soul in purgatory awaiting eternal life in heaven, one day actually counted among the saints?

The *Catechism of the Catholic Church* explains the three states of the Church (954). The Church comprises the pilgrims on earth (that's us), those who have died and are being purified (in purgatory), and those who are in heaven, basking in God's holy presence as saints.

What are we doing as pilgrims on earth? Are we trying to evangelize, reminding others that we can have a personal relationship with Jesus? Does it show that we are Christians through our actions, our words, and our love? Are we in it for the long haul, knowing that while we struggle, we can struggle for God; we can unite our suffering to his for the intentions of our loved ones, for those we've heard about who are hurting, and even for ourselves to draw closer to Jesus? Do we pray especially for the souls in purgatory, particularly those who have no one praying for them? Do we identify with this congregation of the living, determined to follow God, pursue his plan, and walk slowly and steadily toward his kingdom, our eternal life?

Inspired by your saints and offering our prayers and struggles for the souls in purgatory, help us to be a light for one another in service and in love as we plod toward the narrow gate.

NOVEMBER 4

Love Your In-Laws

Do not waste time bothering whether you "love" your neighbor; act as if you did. As soon as we do this we find one of the great secrets. When you are behaving as if you loved someone you will presently come to love him.

C. S. Lewis

As Halloween comes to a close and your child's candy is calling from the closet, Thanksgiving is just around the corner. It is a time to reflect on the blessings in our lives as we sit around a table with extended family and loved ones enjoying the company that the holiday brings.

While Thanksgiving is one of my favorite holidays, it has its challenges. Strengthening family ties is probably something we can all work on, especially if there are past hurts that linger. Being vulnerable and letting others in is a difficult thing to do, especially with in-laws. When will in-laws ever feel like blood-related relatives? Truth is, I don't think they ever will. But with that knowledge, blood is not the only thing that binds us to one another. After all, we are not related by blood to our own spouses. Love is the truth that holds our relationships together.

Love is a choice that we make. It is a gift of our time, money, or talent in order to help out a family member. If we act out of love, we will love. If we wait to feel love, we might never make the chance to show that person how we truly feel.

Lord, help me to be aware of the efforts my in-laws make to reach out to me and teach me the loving way to respond to their gestures, no matter how small.

To Ponder: What is one way you can touch the heart of an in-law going through a difficult time?

TANYA WEITZEL

NOVEMBER 5

The Art of Thankfulness

Dear Mom and Dad, this was a very hard thing to do. Most parents would probably hire a person to do it, but the BEST parents ever would do it with the help of the kids. You are helping us be prepared.

A thank-you note from my
seven-year-old daughter

Our family pitched in together and did some heavy labor around our house. Anticipating some reluctance from certain quarters, my husband and I prayed before proposing the family project to our five children. With only minor resistance, and despite some early-onset adolescent fatigue, we accomplished our goal.

Frankly, I was just relieved to get the whole project out of the way. What surprised me was the response of our youngest child. She decorated some construction paper and wrote the note quoted above. A few days after we finished our work, she left the card under my pillow.

My daughter's gratitude was a direct gift from God. I'm not remotely tempted to take credit for her thoughtfulness; her thank-you note came out of the blue. She inspired me to reflect: How thankful am I for the work I have to do? How do I demonstrate my thankfulness to others?

It's easy (and appropriate) to be thankful for gorgeous weather, good health, and functioning cars. It takes some creativity to give thanks for the blessings born out of hardship. Our loving Father can bless us in any circumstance. He didn't spare his own Son from torture and death, because he knew he could create life out of what seemed like utter destruction.

Father, I thank you . . . (Jn 11:41).

To Ponder: Who could use a thank-you note today? Don't let the day end before you send a quick card.

GRACE MAZZA URBANSKI

NOVEMBER 6

Blessed to Be Blended

We love because he first loved us.

1 John 4:19

I am a stepmother. And a stepchild as well. The latter has helped me to be a better stepmother, or at least I hope so. Still, living in a blended family is not easy for anyone. It is very complicated. Love needs to be nurtured and tended carefully.

Years ago, as grandchildren started coming into our lives, we needed to figure out how to see my husband's children and their families during the holidays without them having to "take turns" or drag their children everywhere. We all decided to get together in one place.

For many years now, my family has celebrated Thanksgiving at my oldest stepson's home. Many generations of us gather together for an entire weekend of celebration of giving thanks and spending time with family. My husband and his ex-wife and I all attend, along with my stepchildren, our children, and our many grandchildren. And everyone's relatives, no matter how distant.

We also get together for a Christmas party on Christmas Eve for all the grandchildren. And we have dinner on Easter Sunday. Still, Thanksgiving continues to draw the largest crowd.

Perhaps it is because, deep down inside, we know we are blessed to have enough love to be able to overlook our disagreements and separations and come together this one day and give thanks to the One who makes it all possible.

Dear Lord, thank you for helping us to know your love and share your love with others.

To Ponder: As a parent and/or stepparent, how can you help your children to feel loved and secure? What are you thankful for today? Write a gratitude list every day and give thanks.

COLLEEN SPIRO

Name Your Battles

I know what it is to have little, and I know what it is
to have plenty. In any and all circumstances I have
learned the secret of being well-fed and of going
hungry, of having plenty and of being in need. I can
do all things through him who strengthens me. In
any case, it was kind of you to share my distress.

Philippians 4:12–14

One way you can approach your day is to name your battles.
The tasks may seem impossible and they may well be—for
you. But God does the impossible—through you. Because
he lives in your heart, every characteristics of his nature is
available to your nature.

Circumstances turn on a dime, but what is your constant?
What no-matter-what tool do you have? Praise—in all things.

Balance that list of looming battles by listing the characteristics of God you need to help you through today. Then
praise him for each attribute. Many were bestowed on you
at your Baptism, Confirmation, or in the sacrament of Matrimony. They increase with every Reconciliation and Eucharist.

If you start the day sleep-deprived, take a deep breath
and praise him for perseverance. If you face a battle with
gluttony, praise him for the self-control that will be there
when you need it. Doubting God's providence in financial
matters? Thank him for trusting in his provision for you
today. Discouraged? Praise God for his courage within you.
Confused? Praise him for wisdom. Frustrated? Praise him for

patience. Your praise for God will grow immensely as you continue to keep praising him as you win today's battles.

Lord, I praise you for being present in every circumstance of my life and providing me with every grace I need.

To Ponder: How can naming your battles and praising God change your daily circumstances?

NANCY H. C. WARD

NOVEMBER 8
NATIONAL CAPPUCCINO DAY

Taking Time for Community

It is requisite for the relaxation of the mind that we make use, from time to time, of playful deeds and jokes.

Saint Thomas Aquinas

One of my favorite activities is Friday-morning coffee with my prayer group. We laugh, we pray, and sometimes we even cry together. I had a friend who once made the case for sainthood for people who pick coffee beans: "They raise the dead to life every morning!" she said. It's true that I feel much better after my morning cup of joe: coffee is a drink for which I am truly grateful. It's not just that it energizes me but that it offers a touchstone for togetherness, a moment to pause and reflect on friendships. When someone says, "Let's have coffee," they aren't really looking for coffee so much as community. These moments provide *time* most of all: time to minister to one another, time to be two or more gathered in his name. So raise a cup of coffee with frothed milk with a friend today. Pray for one another and share the gift of a moment with friends. They are God's gifts to us.

Dear Father, thank you for the gift of friendship and the gift of time to share with friends. Help us through our sharing in friendship to grow in virtue and grace.

To Ponder: How can you be a better prayer support for your friends? Is it time to share a cup of coffee and a good laugh?

KATIE O'KEEFE

NOVEMBER 9
DEDICATION OF THE LATERAN BASILICA

The Mother
of All Parishes

Today's feast celebrates a mystery that is always relevant: God's desire to build a spiritual temple in the world, a community that worships him in spirit and truth.

Pope Benedict XVI

The Basilica of Saint John Lateran is the oldest church in the West, built in the time of Constantine. It is the cathedral of the Diocese of Rome and therefore the official parish of the Holy Father. As such, this historic basilica is referred to as the "mother and head of all the churches of the city and the world."

What does this ancient church have to do with me, and why should I consider celebrating it today? The reason is that as a Catholic I am connected to this basilica in a special way. Saint John Lateran is the mother of all parishes—including my own—which connects me with a vast network of Catholics around the world, both past and present.

She likewise is the mother of my home, the "domestic Church," in which I strive to live out my faith with my family. And, to be really specific, she is the mother of me because I, too, am called to be a living dwelling place for the Holy Spirit.

Lord, your church buildings are sacred and important because they are where we celebrate you in praise, worship, and sacrament. I thank you for my local parish, for those who came before me to make this building possible, and for the freedom to worship here—a privilege many in the world today do not have.

To Ponder: How do you support your parish in terms of time, talent, and treasure? Are you a vital member? Do you understand and appreciate its history and significance? Pray in a special way today for your pastor, the staff, and the members of your parish.

ELIZABETH FICOCELLI

A Deeper Look at Thanksgiving

I appeal to you therefore, brethren, by the mercies of
God, to present your bodies as a living sacrifice, holy
and acceptable to God, which is your
spiritual worship.

Romans 12:1

For Americans, the term *thanksgiving* conjures up images of
turkey and cranberry sauce, parades and football games.
But in the New Testament, *thanksgiving* is simply the English
translation of the Greek word that also means Eucharist.

The great central prayer of every Mass is introduced with
these words: "Let us give thanks to the Lord our God." And
we respond, "It is right and just." During the Eucharistic
Prayer, I always silently add thanks for my personal blessings. I think of the natural blessings of home and work, of
food on the table and the health of my family. I also thank
God for my own salvation history, especially for plucking me
out of the dangerous crowd I was running with in my youth.
I thank him for my loving spouse and wonderful children. I
thank him for our own family's salvation history.

But true thanksgiving is not just a matter of words and
warm sentiments. Gratitude for a gift means offering a gift
in return. He gave his whole, entire self. The only adequate
response would be to offer *ourselves*. Thanksgiving cannot
be separated from sacrifice. The Mass is a celebration of his
love and the freedom it won for us through his sacrifice.

Through it, the love of God is poured into our hearts and enables us to love with his love. In the power of that love, we offer ourselves back to him and enter into that sacrifice that we celebrate.

True thanksgiving means self-giving.

Jesus, make my entire life an unending Eucharist.

To Ponder: What percentage of your prayer is thanksgiving?

DR. MARCELLINO D'AMBROSIO

NOVEMBER 11

The Gift of Attention

Love begins at home and it is not how much we do,
but how much love we put into that action.

Saint Teresa of Calcutta

My girls stopped napping at age two. Three times now, this has thrown my entire life as a stay-at-home mom off course. Life had been going along just fine with as much routine and order as possible with young children. There were busy mornings and then "resting time" after lunch. Mommy was able to have some much-needed alone time to help her recharge for the rest of the day.

And then, without warning, my daily routine came to an end. At age two-and-a-half , my girls did not yet have an interest in watching a TV show with their siblings. So I found myself with a buddy who wants to sit in my lap, type on the computer, make lots of demands, and utterly distract me from anything "worthwhile."

I know that I should enjoy these priceless moments. I know that I will miss them. But the minutes tick by as my tank quickly drains empty. When "resting time" is over, I have nothing to offer anyone except for critical comments, general impatience, and everything else that comes with burnout.

What pulls me through (not always soon enough, unfortunately) is realizing that my child (I hope) got the attention that she needed. Her little heart and tank should be quite full. I imagine how rare hours of undivided Mommy attention might bless her little heart, mind, soul, and developing personality forever. At least, I can hope. And, it gives me a little perseverance to get through this stage.

Jesus, pour into this empty shell whatever is needed by others in the present moment.

To Ponder: What can you do today to show your children how much you love them?

TRISH BOLSTER

NOVEMBER 12
PESTERING THE JUDGE

Can our prayers sometimes push God too much?

We must pray without ceasing, in every occurrence and employment of our lives—that prayer which is

rather a habit of lifting up the heart to God as in a
constant communication with Him.

Saint Elizabeth Ann Seton

Jesus gives a lesson on praying always without becoming weary in Luke 18. He speaks of a widow who has a just request. What she's asking for is a righteous thing. It isn't answered in a timely fashion.

Another meditation thought: the one being asked to render a judgment (we would think of this as God) is holding back for some reason. Why, we might wonder?

We are heard. Immediately. Consider Daniel 10:12: "Then he said to me, 'Fear not, Daniel, for from the first day that you set your heart to understand and humbled yourself before your God, your words have been heard, and I have come because of your words.'"

In Hebrews 10:36–37, we find these words: "You need endurance to do the will of God and receive what he has promised. For, after just a brief moment, he who is to come shall come; he shall not delay."

God's timing isn't our timing. His will may not be in accord with our determined prayer. God may be sharing a teachable lesson with us. We may not know the purpose of any of this until eternity. Delay may be a test of your patience. In all things, put him first.

Lord Jesus, some of the things I ask for I have set my own timetable on. Please accept my apology for giving you my will, which I set before you. Teach me the patience of the Old Testament leaders who waited for freedom from exile. They waited for a Messiah, not for days or years but for generations.

To Ponder: Do you ever feel like you're asking too much with your prayers? You're not. Keep asking.

DEACON TOM FOX

NOVEMBER 13

Giving Thanks

The measure of love is to love without measure.

Saint Francis de Sales

I spent most of 2009 waiting to travel to China to add one adorable, three-year-old girl to our family. While waiting for our travel approval, I had a particularly difficult night. I felt unprepared and worried about so many things: would we be able to give her the best care and language access (she is deaf)? I worried about the transition.

The doubts were heavy and people were not really helping me feel better. I went to Jesus in prayer and then picked up Saint Faustina's *Diary*. I opened to a "random" page and found these words, which I have paraphrased: "You are right, you are misery itself but do what you can, and I will do the rest." I laughed out loud. I loved that first Jesus agreed, then reminded me that I could do only so much. He would do the rest.

Some of my fears were founded: communication was difficult at first and she had some very tough days during the transition, but Jesus was faithful. We did what we could and were so grateful for the outpouring of grace that accomplished the rest. Sometimes doubts and obstacles overcome us, and we think only of our limitations. Thankfully, Jesus does not have limits and he is always willing to pick up our slack.

Thank you, Jesus, for helping me recognize what I've been gifted with and what I have to rely on you for. Thank you for the limitations that keep me humble and reliant on your boundless love. May I always open my heart to life's possibilities knowing I am supported in everything by you.

To Ponder: Pour your heart out to Jesus, accept what you cannot do, and thank him for doing the rest.

ALLISON GINGRAS

NOVEMBER 14
WORLD DIABETES DAY

Healthy on the Inside . . . and the Outside

You haven't been praying? Why, because you haven't had time? But you do have time. Furthermore, what sort of works will you be able to do if you have not meditated on them in the presence of the Lord, so as to put them in order? Without that conversation with God, how can you finish your daily work with perfection?

Saint Josemaría Escrivá

Saint Josemaría Escrivá had diabetes for over ten years. On April 27, 1954, he suffered a near-fatal anaphylactic shock. Not only did he inexplicably survive the incident, but he was also cured of his diabetes. For this reason, he is the patron saint of diabetes. His lifelong message to everyone was to sanctify their daily work and to become saints.

Although Type 1 diabetes cannot be prevented, there are many ways to radically decrease one's chances of getting Type 2 diabetes. These preventative measures include healthy living habits that we have heard before: not being overweight, following a healthy diet, exercise, proper sleep, less stress, and not smoking. Not only will these lifestyle patterns prevent diabetes (and other diseases and illnesses), but we also know that when we practice these habits, we are better moms.

It's difficult for moms to find the right balance of taking care of themselves along with taking care of the other people in their lives. Moms need to be healthy in order to do this well. Even more important than our physical well-being is our spiritual health. As the saying goes, if you are too busy to pray, you are too busy.

Jesus, help me to find the wisdom to know how to take care of myself physically as well as spiritually.

To Ponder: If you received a physical checkup, how would you be doing? How about a spiritual checkup?

TAMI KISER

Father, Daughter

Feelings come to us, passively; love comes from us, actively, by our free choice.

Peter Kreeft

For many years I struggled with scruples. I only want to do your will, Lord, I thought, and just don't let me upset you!

My fear of upsetting God was neither proper reverence for the Almighty nor a healthy fear of sin. Instead, I was so wrapped up in trying to discern God's will perfectly in all the minutia of my life that I didn't feel free to *live* life.

Much of this stemmed from my view of God as a top-down authority figure: he'd tell me what to do, I'd listen and obey. Done. I wanted justification more than I wanted a relationship.

As I've grown in my faith and in self-understanding, God has showed me that he wants me to exercise the use of my free will. Ours is not a relationship of bondage, of indifferent master and unthinking slave. Ours is a relationship of freedom. He is my Father; I am his daughter.

I need not fear upsetting God by the "little decisions" in my life. Indeed, even in making life's big decisions I need not fear, for he's genuinely interested in hearing my opinion on the matter, whatever it might be. Sometimes he even lays out many choices for me and says, "What do you think, Rhonda?"

Heavenly Father, you sent your Son so that I might know freedom. Release me from the traps—spiritual, physical, or emotional—that prevent me from experiencing the fullness of your joy.

To Ponder: "Perfect love casts out fear" (1 Jn 4:18). Are you afraid of God? If so, what about? Why?

NOVEMBER 16

The Ultimate Thank-You Note

A real happy new year and many thanks for everything, mostly for being.

Flannery O'Connor

Just days before she wrote the above note, Catholic novelist Flannery O'Connor had experienced a disconcerting turn in her health. When she was fifteen, she lost her father to lupus, the same disease that would eventually claim her life. Flannery lived with a deep awareness that her years might also be shortened. With this possibility ever before her, she sought solace in the redeeming love of Christ as well as through friends near and far with whom she corresponded in letters that flowed forth fluidly from her typewriter until her death in August 1964. As Flannery came closer to the end, her friendships became even more precious, to the point that on that New Year's Eve just several months before her death, Flannery had boiled down her feelings toward the life-giving relationships around her to one word: gratitude. Gratitude not for the things the people in her life gave her, but for their very *being*—the most priceless "thing" of all. What a wonderful gift to take along into eternal life, and what a beautiful gift for us to have here and now!

Dear Lord, thank you for helping me see that what matters most isn't what I can hold in my hands but the people you've put on my path that I can hold in my heart, not just now but forever.

To Ponder: For whom are you most grateful on this day of your precious life? Why not send them a thank-you note to tell them they matter, not because of anything they've done, but simply because they are?

ROXANE B. SALONEN

NOVEMBER 17
SAINT ELIZABETH OF HUNGARY

Bread Baskets

The commandments . . . are summed up in this word, "Love your neighbor as yourself." Love does no wrong to a neighbor; therefore, love is the fulfilling of the law.

Romans 13:9–10

Years back I mistook our church statue of Saint Elizabeth of Hungary as Mary our Queen. The elegant posture, the robes, and the crown drew me in. Then I noticed she carried a basket of bread. Learning Elizabeth's story, I discovered this regal woman to be a loving servant to her family and the poor.

Elizabeth was a thirteenth-century wife and mother, and her father was the king of Hungary. Married to a nobleman when she was fourteen, she and her husband enjoyed a happy home. Despite their abundance, Elizabeth chose simplicity, penance, and almsgiving as her way. Her husband agreed with her. She often gave royal robes to peasants, and she served bread daily to the needy at the gates of her estate. An interesting note: this bread distribution is why Elizabeth is considered a patron saint of bakers.

Sadly, at the death of Elizabeth's husband, pressure from his family mounted. Fearing she would squander the family fortune, Elizabeth and her children were dispossessed and suffered their own trials of poverty. A bishop, Elizabeth's uncle, is said to have intervened and the extended family recanted. Yet by then Elizabeth had fully renounced riches. She took up residence in a small house and later founded a hospital. She cared for the sick and needy there until her own death at the tender age of twenty-four.

Jesus, draw me to know you as the bread of life
and to share your bread with my neighbors.

To Ponder: Are you a bread baker? Double your recipe and share with another family. Not a baker? Find ways to contribute to a local food bank this week.

PAT GOHN

Thankful for the Good and the Bad

Give thanks in all circumstances; for this is the will of
God in Christ Jesus for you.

1 Thessalonians 5:18

It's so easy to be thankful on a good day. At times we even question why the Lord is so good to us—a rather rhetorical question from the security of our comfortable circumstances. But then comes a bad day, and this question of why arises from the sincerest depths of our hearts. We plead for an answer, but we don't always listen. We want reasons, but we are so shortsighted. We feel an ache, a thirst, we want more, and God knows. Oh, how he loves us!

Only a true Father is willing to watch his children suffer a little in order that he may one day be reunited with them. Only a true Father gives real meaning to the word love, the kind of love that humbles the proud and turns sinners into saints. The kind of love that uses *all circumstances* to turn his children's faces toward his own. How quickly we forget that it is he who breathed life into us, he who gifted us with all that we have, he who sustains us just one day more. And how thankful we are, when he brings us to our knees with tears on our cheeks and an ache in our heart, as he reminds us that all of our strength comes solely from him.

Dear God, please increase my trust in you, that I will have the courage to surrender everything to your loving care.

To Ponder: Do you remember to thank God for the challenges you face? Trust in his craftsmanship as he shapes you into a person worthy of heaven.

CHARISSE TIERNEY

NOVEMBER 19
WORLD TOILET DAY

Thankful for the Overlooked

Be thankful for the least gift, so shalt thou be meant
to receive greater.

Thomas à Kempis

When someone asks me what I'm thankful for, I usually respond with the typical things that most of us say: family, friends, good health, and maybe the occasional random blessing like a new job or kind deed received. I can *guarantee* that I've never added "toilets" to my list of blessings. Sure, I'm glad I have one, but do we really need to talk about it? After all, it's gross and smelly and that's just not something people bring up in polite conversation.

But, after today, that may change. You see, today is World Toilet Day, a day dedicated to building awareness of the sanitation problems that plague many parts of the world because of a lack of access to toilets and sewage systems. According to WorldToilet.org, in 2013, one thousand children died *each day* from diarrheal diseases due to poor sanitation. Suddenly, toilets seem like something to be thankful for, and their lack in much of the world something to be concerned about.

I guess we only appreciate something as humble as a toilet when we don't have it. But toilets aren't the only things we forget to be thankful for. Our lives are full of things and people we take for granted. The things we use the most and the people we depend upon the most are often the ones we overlook when we count our blessings.

Holy Spirit, fill our hearts with gratitude for the blessings in our lives. Instill in us a thankful heart that always remembers the goodness of Our Father in heaven.

To Ponder: Are you grateful for the things that seem small but are so important to those who don't have them? Do you forget to appreciate the people who have both large and small roles in your life? What can you do today to thank God for these blessings?

LAURA B. NELSON

NOVEMBER 20

Daily Examination of Thanks

If the only prayer you ever say in your whole life is "thank you," that would suffice.

Meister Eckhart

Saint Ignatius of Loyola recommended that everyone make an examination of their day. The examination consists of five steps: asking God for the light to see oneself clearly, giving thanks, reviewing the day, facing one's shortcomings, and looking ahead to the day to come. For whatever reason—genetics, brain chemicals, hormones, etc.—I am not naturally an optimistic, upbeat person. The clouds often loom; my cup is usually half-empty. I often wish I wasn't that way, but it has been part of my lifelong cross.

This evening ritual forces me to be thankful on a daily basis, to find the good things that I don't always see or acknowledge, even though I should. My relationships are definitely one of those things. It can be easy to take the people who share our lives for granted. I am extremely thankful for my family and friends, both the ones I see in real life and the ones I interact with through the gift of social media. I am especially thankful that there are people who care enough about me to pray for me. I hope there are people out there who are thankful for me as well.

Dear God, thank you for my wonderful friends and family. Please help me to always appreciate the gift of the people you have placed in my life.

To Ponder: What and whom do you have to be thankful for today? Be sure to take a moment to count your blessings and offer gratitude to God.

PATRICE FAGNANT-MACARTHUR

Motherhood: A Great Compliment from God

The house does not rest upon the earth but upon
a woman.

Italian proverb

Can you imagine being Jesus's mother? Can you fathom changing the Creator of the universe? Have you ever wondered what grace sounded like before their family dinners in Nazareth?

God could have come on a chariot. He could have been dropped off by angels. God could have come in a myriad of ways, but he chose the safest option: through a woman. And if heaven came through a woman, wouldn't it make perfect sense that God's plan for us to return to heaven would also go "through" a woman?

Whether you are a mother through natural birth, adoption, marriage, or fostering, or you are a spiritual mother, God anointed you for this vocation. Your motherhood is the highest affirmation God could pay you. Beyond the sacraments, there is no greater invitation to intimacy God could offer you than your motherhood. He even offers you his own mother and presents her, to you, as a spiritual guide and intercessor. In taking Mary as your own Blessed Mother, you both invite her to pray with you and bid her to pray for you. You are not only being embraced but also, by extension, ensuring that the Blessed Virgin's mantle is wrapped around your own children as well.

Lord Jesus, entrust me to your Blessed Mother's care. Help me to need the only soul you chose to need so intimately and so profoundly.

To Ponder: When is the last time you thanked God the Father for the gift of Mary? When did you last pray a Rosary out of joyful desire as a daughter of God and not merely as his follower or his disciple? Climb up onto the Father's lap today and invite Jesus's mom to be your mom again.

MARK HART

NOVEMBER 22
SAINT CECILIA

The Power of Music

Music is the exaltation of the mind derived from things eternal, bursting forth in sound.

Saint Thomas Aquinas

Two-year-old Gweneth was one of my first early-childhood music students. Before classes began, her mother began to play the CD of the class music to familiarize the family with the songs. One of the songs was an original Latin Gregorian chant, the "Magnificat." The first time Gweneth heard the chant, she walked over near the CD player, knelt down, and folded her hands. She'd never heard chant before. She doesn't speak Latin. She simply knew from deep inside her that the song was a prayer and it called her to join.

Today is the feast of Saint Cecilia, patroness of music. Music is an amazing gift from God. It connects us with heaven and our spiritual selves. One legend connecting Saint Cecilia to music tells that she could hear heavenly music from the angels. I love that we celebrate her feast so close to Thanksgiving. Thank God for music.

Dear Lord, thank you for the gift of music; may it lead us to you. Saint Cecilia, pray for us.

To Ponder: Music has great possibility to connect us with God. Singing, dancing, praying in song, and even listening to the right song can stir our souls. What can you do today to musically connect yourself and your family to heaven?

KATE DANELUK

NOVEMBER 23

Catching Gratitude

The most deadly poison of our times is indifference.
And this happens, although the praise of God should
know no limits. Let us strive, therefore, to praise
Him to the greatest extent of our powers.

Saint Maximilian Kolbe

The practice of cultivating gratitude by counting the gifts and blessings of my days is a bit like catching fireflies in a jar. These little flashes of glory streak across the ordinary mess of my days, sparks of beauty in the midst of my darkness. If I train myself to notice, to be attentive, I see more and more these moments in my days—God present, loving me in a thousand little ways.

Gratitude can sometimes feel like a lesser virtue to dedicate ourselves to, as if we are meant to just smile and pretend in our darkest moments that the sky is lit with rainbows and butterflies. But authentic gratitude is just the opposite. It is the discipline of spirit that seeks God present in the hard moments, in our suffering, and in our brokenness. It rests in the relief of knowing that even then, God is there, gifting us with his goodness, his loving kindness, his hand at work on our behalf.

God, we give you thanks out of genuine joy that even when all seems dark, we can look out upon the night and wait in joyful expectation for the little flashes of light that show us that you are near.

To Ponder: Today, look for the lights that like a thousand fireflies will streak across your day, lending you a glimpse of glory, a glimpse of God present, right there in the middle of your ordinary, messy life. Take note of them. Hold them in your heart and mind. Let them remind you of how deeply loved you are, and be grateful, truly grateful.

COLLEEN CONNELL MITCHELL

Let a Smile Be Your Standard

It is not fitting, when one is in God's service, to have a gloomy face or a chilling look.

Saint Francis of Assisi

"Momma always said nobody could come inside her house unless they was smilin'." The old Cajun dipped his paintbrush in the can. "I hold my children and grandchildren to the same standard. If you can't smile, go someplace else."

We were standing in the cemetery, this old Cajun and me, and neither of us should have been talking. I was on retreat and he and his wife were cleaning graves for All Souls' Day.

"Good philosophy." I jotted his astuteness in my notebook. His wife balanced her broom's yellow handle on her hip as she shot a stream of ant poison at a nearby ant pile. She dusted off the old headstone. The old man dipped his brush in the paint again and went back to his job and his eulogy.

"Life's too short," he continued, "for long faces and bad attitudes. Life's hard on everybody. We all have our troubles. Life's too short to let somebody bring you down. Why even bring it into your house? Don't invite it in and you'll live a good, long, happy life. That's the secret."

God, remind me that having a good attitude can be a wonderful gift of thanks.

To Ponder: Think of the company you keep and the homes you visit. Whose presence blesses you the most? Practice leaving smiles of hospitality wherever you go.

NOVEMBER 25

Walking the Holy Apple Peel of Life

I am the way, the truth, and the life.

John 14:6

The captivating story of our spiritual ancestors, the children of Israel, and their difficult, desert journey out of the slavery of Egypt, around and around and around Mount Sinai to the Promised Land, is related repeatedly throughout both testaments of the Bible. When God repeats himself this way in the scriptures, could it be because he is stressing the importance of something?

The story of God's children works a little like the way my grandfather used to peel apples with his pocketknife. He would start at the bottom and work his way up, around and around the apple he would go, very slowly, in order to offer me one unbroken peel.

Isn't life's journey like the Israelites' and like that apple peel: an upward-directed spiral leading straight into God's arms? Alternately trudging, flying, crawling, and dancing, the way seems to be a journey of repeated revolutions around the center. Where are we going? How will we make it?

Sometimes the way is lush and green and watered, full of nodding wildflowers. Sometimes it's barren and dry, where the wind sounds like howling demons. I may grow discouraged by how I seem to tread the same ground over and over, but the story of the Israelites teaches me I am really making upward progress in small degrees. My destination is the safety of God's bosom.

You can be gentle with yourself. You're doing the best you can.

You, Lord, are my way. I do not need a map.

To Ponder: Do you struggle with a need for direction in your life? Have you stopped to see how far you have come lately? Have you encouraged someone else to press on?

SONJA CORBITT

NOVEMBER 26

An Attitude of Gratitude

The unthankful heart . . . discovers no mercies, but the thankful heart . . . will find, in every hour, some heavenly blessings.

Henry Ward Beecher

After years of teaching in difficult settings—the south side of Chicago, a barrio in the Philippines, and a gang-ridden neighborhood in Los Angeles—I had come to the dismal conclusion that nothing I did would make any positive difference. The challenges of this world were too great, the wounds too deeply embedded. I felt sick with despair. But then I met an extraordinary woman who, though of a different faith, was able to help me do something very important. She challenged me to fill a notebook page every day with things that I was grateful for. She wanted to see the notebook every week, and though I could repeat some things, it was to be as honest and varied as I could make it.

There were days I racked my brain trying to think of something to write down. I ended up listing things like the chair I was sitting in, the floor that was holding me up, the clean painted walls, and the way the light slanted across the floor at dusk. I got pretty creative—as my friend knew I would have to. Her brilliant scheme forced me to look at everything around me in a new and more grateful light. But I had to will myself to see it. I had to force myself out of my grumbling and be glad. Amazing how it worked. Before a month was over, I was a transformed person. The world had not changed. I had.

Thank you, Lord, for all of it: the things that make me smile, the things that I take for granted, and the things that make me scream.

To Ponder: What does the world gain by our despair? What does it gain by our gratitude? When everything seems to be going wrong, which will you choose?

A. K. FRAILEY

An Advent
of Thank You

Let gratitude be the pillow upon which you kneel to
say your nightly prayer.

Maya Angelou

The end of November has Americans thinking about Thanks-giving and Christians the world over thinking about Advent. November is also a traditional month for remembering the dead. November's endings and beginnings can be a source of anxiety (forget Advent; a busy Christmas season is almost upon us!) or hope. The difference might just be gratitude.

Writing in the early 1300s, Meister Eckhart says, "If the only prayer you ever say in your entire life is 'thank you,' it will be enough." A lifetime feels like a long time to concentrate on one prayer. But what about Advent? What would happen if we dared to make "thank you" the foundation of our prayers this season? If in the middle of all the busyness we learned to say our nightly prayers kneeling on the "pillow of gratitude"?

Dear Jesus, as November comes to a close, we remember again those who have died and we thank you for the gift of their lives. We thank you for the many blessings with which our lives are filled. Thank you for Advent, for the chance at new beginnings. For promises of deliverance and salvation, thank you. For these next few weeks, if in your kindness you would grant us one grace, grant us the grace of a grateful heart. Thank you that you hear our prayers and for your boundless love and compassion.

To Ponder: What concrete change can you make to adopt gratitude as "the pillow on which you kneel" this Advent? How can you cultivate the prayer of thank you? How can you share your gratitude with others?

MICHELLE JONES

NOVEMBER 28

The Gift of Family

What can you do to promote world peace? Go home and love your family.

Saint Teresa of Calcutta

Christmas was my grandmother's birthday. After Mass on Christmas Day, we would travel to her home to celebrate the holy day and exchange gifts. In the evening, we would return. This time we celebrated her birthday. Everyone would be there: her seven children, all her grandchildren, her two sisters, Grandpa's brother, all their children, and their children's children. All of us—aunts, uncles, cousins, second cousins, third cousins, and some neighbors—jammed together in a little duplex. The love of Christmas seemed to me all the more real surrounded by so much love and joy. It is my favorite childhood memory.

My grandparents have since passed. I rarely see my second and third cousins; however, I enjoy any opportunity I get to see and catch up with them. Still, all my aunts, uncles, cousins, and their children come together to celebrate important holidays. I revel in the fact that I am providing my own children with the wonderful opportunity to make the fond memories that I have.

Extended family provides us with a familial history. We discover that we are a part of a picture larger than our own little world. We become aware of the bigger family of which we are all a part: God's family.

Father God, creator of family, thank you for my family. Help me to always love them, reach out to them, and share in their joys and sorrows.

To Ponder: In our busy world, losing track of extended family is easy. How can you keep in touch with family members: make a call, send a little letter or e-mail, make a lunch date, or plan a family reunion?

KELLY GUEST

NOVEMBER 29
NATIONAL DAY OF LISTENING

Listen Up

And I want to repeat these three words: please, thank you, sorry. Three essential words! . . . Let us say these words in our families!

Pope Francis

A man of few words, my grandfather once remarked that the best conversationalist is a good listener. Listening shows courtesy and respect. It requires focused attention and a slower pace.

Today, on the National Day of Listening, let's reflect on how well we listen to others and how courteously we communicate with them. If you're anything like me, every third sentence is a panicked interjection: "Eat!" or "Find your shoes!" or "Don't you dare stick a tomato in the light socket!"

As improbable as it might seem, greater domestic peace might be achieved by phrases such as, "Please eat the dinner I cooked for you with so much love" or "Thank you for putting your shoes away now so you can find them later." Or even, "I'd be happy to listen to the reasons why you thought sticking a tomato in the light socket was a good idea."

Moms really do set the tone and pace of the household, even though it feels sometimes like those things are beyond our control. Words like please and thank you and sorry show that we care about the person we're talking to. And that, more than anything else, might just make them more willing to listen.

Open my ears to hear your will, O Lord, and open my lips to speak your words.

To Ponder: Have you forgotten about common courtesies in the hullabaloo of daily life? Try to say please, thank you, and sorry a little more often and see what effect it has on the people around you.

KAREE SANTOS

Remembering to Thank God

Gratitude is not only the greatest of virtues, but the parent of all the others.

Marcus Tullius Cicero

In our home, Thanksgiving dinner is the most anticipated meal of the year. Everyone loves turkey and all the trimmings, not to mention the various dishes I make with the leftovers. Friends shared with us that they love to make Thanksgiving dinner more than once a year, and that got us started on a new tradition: multiple Thanksgiving dinners to share with friends. The number of Thanksgiving meals we have each year varies, but what we do does not.

For each of the meals, we invite some friends over, break out the good china, and I cook an entire Thanksgiving meal—a big turkey and all the trimmings from my father's stuffing recipe to homemade mashed potatoes to fresh-baked rolls. We share our home with our friends, relaxing and talking over dinner the way we cannot on real Thanksgiving when people tend to travel to visit family.

What this does for us is that it reminds us to always be thankful to God for his many blessings. While we still observe Thanksgiving on the fourth Thursday of November, this new tradition makes it much more purposeful. We stop everything else and center an entire day on giving thanks for our blessings.

Father in heaven, help me to be more thankful for your many blessings. Teach me how to notice even the smallest blessings in my life so that I may always be reminded of your love for me.

To Ponder: Do you give thanks each day for your blessings? What can you do to make it a more purposeful act?

CHRISTINE JOHNSON

December

THEME: GIFTEDNESS

Gifts, Given and Received

God asks little, but he gives much.

Saint John Chrysostom

I smile today, thinking of the little ones who can't wait to peel back that cardboard door marked 1 on their Advent calendars and be rewarded with the very first of those twenty-four morsels of chocolate. Advent may have already begun, but for most of the world today marks the start of the Christmas countdown.

We moms often get so caught up in the frenzy of this season that we miss its tiny treasures: the toddler lighting the Advent wreath for the very first time, the handwritten greetings from afar, or even those handmade gifts of pine cones and papier-mâché. We fixate on our lists, crossing off our acquisitions and keeping our appointments. The swirl of this month, its busyness and bounty, threaten to overwhelm us.

Today, as we remember the true reason for our Advent preparations, let's linger in the giftedness that is all around us:

The scent of the greenery reminding us of new life . . .

The deep violet harkening penitence to prepare our hearts . . .

The star and the flames pointing us toward the Light of the World . . .

And yes, even the presents, given and received with intentional love.

In our giftedness, we are given the opportunity to serve as stewards for those who go without sustenance, shelter, or even love. In giving, we receive.

Father, source of every gift, help me to embrace this Advent season. Thank you for the incredible gifts you pour into my life, especially for my precious family. May I journey toward you mindfully, grateful at every turn for your love.

To Ponder: How can you be more mindful of the gifts you give and are given this month?

LISA M. HENDEY

DECEMBER 2
INTERNATIONAL DAY FOR
THE ABOLITION OF SLAVERY

Boundaries Aren't Bad

Boundaries help us to be the best we can be—in God's image. They let us see God as he really is. They enable us to negotiate life, fulfilling our responsibilities and requirements.

Dr. Henry Cloud and Dr. John Townsend

When people rose to abolish slavery, they formally acknowledged the universal truth of the dignity of all human persons. Slavery is an extreme boundary violation of this dignity. God endows each person with unique gifts to fulfill his or her personal mission. But when we operate in this world with poor personal boundaries, we tarnish our gifts and compromise our dignity.

Pleasing others, lacking clarity about who we are and what we want, allowing others to enter our homes or psyches with ill effects weakens us and the entire Body of Christ. Poor boundaries make it increasingly difficult to authentically love others. Our sense of self can become so fragmented that there is not enough left to gift to another. We've let the world and others "pick our orchard." Then there are no apples left when we want to give one to a person of our choosing.

Isn't that a self-imposed form of modern-day slavery?

Breaking free starts with self-knowledge. God gives us knowledge of ourselves when we seek our fulfillment in him. Slave owners tried to break down their slaves by dehumanizing them. We must stop dehumanizing ourselves by ignoring the unique callings and needs of the soul God has given us. By letting God show us who we truly are, we respect our time, our thoughts, our feelings, and our desires, and we start establishing boundaries to protect them. From that place, we are free persons able to give authentic love to another.

Jesus, so many people wanted a piece of you in your journey on this earth. You modeled how to love others while also staying connected to your Father. Help us have the right balance between being generous and taking needed time for ourselves.

To Ponder: How healthy are your boundaries? What can you do to improve them so you can authentically love the people God has put in your life?

CHRISTINA M. WEBER

Finding Joy Inside Myself

He walked with a joyful, calm face. . . . Everywhere
he went he went with laughter in his mouth.

An Observer of Saint Francis Xavier

Saint Francis Xavier (1506–1552) is regarded as one of the
greatest missionaries in Christianity, baptizing tens of thousands in his widespread travels. Despite language barriers,
inadequate funding, and resistance from European officials,
Saint Francis Xavier spread his Christian faith in lasting ways
throughout the Far East.

Total confidence in God kept this evangelist from being
discouraged in the face of obstacles. Instead, he was filled
with a sense of ongoing joy and enthusiasm. Living among
the poor, sharing their food, and administering to the sick,
Saint Francis Xavier preached the Gospel by living it joyfully.

As Christians, we, too, are called to "go and preach to all
nations." We may not be called to distant shores like Saint
Francis Xavier. That's okay. There's more than enough mission territory right where we live, among our family, friends,
co-workers, and neighbors. But what Saint Francis Xavier
teaches us most poignantly is that the spirit of joy must per-
meate all our efforts.

Joy is something that can slip quickly through my fingers, despite having a loving husband, great kids, good
health, and rewarding work. It's so easy for me to focus on

minor irritants and setbacks and on what I don't have instead of on what I do.

Saint Francis Xavier, you discovered that emptying yourself for others cheerfully is the secret to spreading the Good News. Infuse me with the joy you radiated in sharing your love for Jesus.

To Ponder: What words would people use to describe you? Joyful and calm? Would others want to be Christian because of your disposition? Today, pledge to find an opportunity to bring someone else a little bit of joy.

ELIZABETH FICOCELLI

DECEMBER 4

Seek Negative Space

Build an oratory within yourself, and there have
Jesus on the altar of your heart.

Saint Paul of the Cross

It's getting noisy out there, isn't it? The music, the commercials, the shopping malls . . . it can quickly result in sensory overload. It seems as if every space is filled. For me, it doesn't take long to crave negative space, space that is filled with *nothing*.

In music, we recognize negative space as silence. When musicians remove noise and strategically incorporate silence, they also add emphasis and lend definition to their work. Can you imagine an arrangement of "Let All Mortal Flesh Keep Silence" performed by an ensemble of four vocalists, a horn section, three guitars, bass, and congas? No, because that stands in direct contrast to the song's very message—standing in awe and meditating on the fact that God has become man.

Such an ensemble is also inappropriate for Advent, a time when we remember and reflect that Christ came to us as a baby in the silent night—meek and humble in the unlikeliest quarter of a small town. No fanfare, no trumpet blasts, no procession. What sense would it make to prepare to reexperience this event by filling our lives with noise on top of noise? That stands in direct contrast to this season's very purpose. Let's allow this Advent to be memorable not for how we try to supersize it, but for how we don't. Seek negative space. Savor the silence. De-clutter your heart. Make room to receive Jesus when he comes.

Lord Jesus, remove from my heart all that separates me from you.

To Ponder: Take a look at your calendar. What nonessential activities can be removed so you can savor a bit more silence this Advent?

LISA A. SCHMIDT

DECEMBER 5
INTERNATIONAL VOLUNTEER DAY

Hearing the Call

The call of God is not just for a select few but for everyone. Whether I hear God's call or not depends on the condition of my ears, and exactly what I hear depends upon my spiritual attitude.

Oswald Chambers

"I'm looking for a volunteer."

Do those words fill you with dread? Do they remind you of school days when you didn't know the answer and were terrified you'd be called on? For me, that panic always hit in math or science class. While I'd confidently raise my hand elsewhere, I wanted to shrivel up and disappear when my algebra teacher or, heaven forbid, my physics teacher asked a question.

Once I got to college, the fear subsided. By then, I knew my own strengths and could focus my studies on subjects where I was eager to join the discussion.

God has called us all to join the discussion. Toward that end, he's given each of us gifts—gifts he wants us to share with other people. He needs butchers, bakers, and candlestick makers, *and* singers, lectors, and religious-education teachers.

But that's not the whole story. If the only thing that mattered was expertise, he'd have made a lot more experts and many fewer lay people. While every ministry needs someone knowledgeable to lead it, it also needs people who are gifted with eagerness to help, to participate in the community, and to join the discussion with the goal of spreading God's word.

Lord, help me to hear your call with open ears, an open heart, and a willingness to join the discussion.

To Ponder: God has made sure that we all have something to contribute, even if we haven't quite figured it out for ourselves. What volunteer opportunities will enrich your life and spirit as well as help others?

LISA LAWMASTER HESS

Don't You Tell a Single Soul

We humbly implore your mercy, Lord:
protect us in all dangers
through the prayers of the Bishop Saint Nicholas,
that the way of salvation may lie open before us.

Prayer on the Feast of Saint Nicholas

Why is the story of "jolly old" Saint Nicholas so compelling? We're not certain how many of his legends are factual. Did he really seize the sword of an executioner poised to punish three innocent men? Did he really leave bags of gold for three daughters of a poor man?

Even if legends prove to be thin on facts, they often communicate some truth. In the case of Saint Nicholas, we celebrate the goodness of a bishop who tried to live the gospel message of Matthew 6:1–4: "So whenever you give alms, do not sound a trumpet before you, as the hypocrites do in the synagogues and in the streets, so that they may be praised by others. Truly I tell you, they have received their reward. But when you give alms, do not let your left hand know what your right hand is doing, so that your alms may be done in secret; and your Father who sees in secret will reward you."

Do we love doing good deeds in secret? If I am the only one who bothers to clean the hair out of the bathtub drain, do I rejoice in my anonymity? Nope. The feast of Saint Nicholas just threw down a challenge.

Lord, help me "to labor and not to ask for reward" (Saint Ignatius of Loyola).

To Ponder: How would your attitude change if your thankless jobs became "secret good deeds"?

GRACE MAZZA URBANSKI

DECEMBER 7

Small Greatness

You will know your vocation by the joy that it brings
you. . . . You will know when it's right.

Dorothy Day

A friend of mine recently adopted a boy from Ukraine. She and her husband have two daughters and their lives seem full and blessed. Yet they accepted the challenge—physically, emotionally, and financially—of welcoming another child into their lives, a child with a traumatic past of neglect and abuse.

She's not the only mom I know with such selfless devotion. After adopting two children from Ethiopia, a colleague founded an organization that builds schools and medical facilities and provides clean water to small villages in Ethiopia.

If I took a mental inventory of my friends and associates, I'd find countless examples of women—busy moms just like me—who are making a *real* difference in the lives of others. I know this should be an inspiration to me, but sometimes I can't help but feel inferior in their presence. After all, these women are truly following Christ. And here I am, the mom who can't remember to fill the brown paper bag I got in church for the holiday food drive. Why are those moms destined for greatness, while I'm floundering in mediocrity?

The truth, I remind myself, is that we are each destined for greatness in our own way. And that God is just as pleased with the small ways I serve him in my home as he is with the women who travel the globe to do his will.

Lord, please show me how I can serve you in some small way today.

To Ponder: Instead of wondering what amazing thing God has planned for you, think about how you can do something simple to glorify him right now.

THERESA CENICCOLA

DECEMBER 8
SOLEMNITY OF THE IMMACULATE CONCEPTION

Celebrating Mary as the Immaculate Conception

For I do not do the good I want, but the evil I do not want is what I do.

Romans 7:19

Mary the Mother of Jesus was both conceived free from original sin and preserved from sin throughout her life. That's the reason for today's feast, and for we who struggle with our sins, it can be an overwhelming feast. Keenly aware of our utter inability to hold it together for half an hour, let alone a whole lifetime, it can feel like today is the commemoration of an impossible standard.

There are three reminders that can help us who have difficulties grow more comfortable with this feast:

- Mary was prepared for her place in salvation history, not yours or mine. We who must wait for eternity to shake off the last vestiges of sin can trust that God has, all the same, made a way for each of us that is what our souls need most.

- Salvation is not a contest, it's a gift. Mary is not a disdainful victor, looking down on us losers. She's our very champion. We're on the same team, and we can be helped by those members who are stronger than ourselves.

- Sinlessness doesn't mean freedom from mishap. Though without sin, Mary lost track of her own Son for three days—and he was a boy without sin. Not all of our apparent failings are signs of guilt.

For those of us who find the Immaculate Conception easy to understand and contemplate, today is a good day to pray for those who have difficulties with the Catholic faith.

Mary, Mother of God, when I am sinful and weak, stand in my place for a while and pray that God would strengthen me.

To Ponder: What is your relationship with the Immaculate Conception? Is it easy for you? Comfortable? Consoling? Or does it challenge you in some way?

JENNIFER FITZ

Christmas Gifts—A Blessing or a Distraction?

It is more blessed to give than to receive.

Acts 20:35

What do we do with society's gift-giving extravaganza at Christmas? It's Jesus's birthday, but the presents under the tree are the real focus, especially for the kids. The first is unwrapped and then another and another, faster and faster. The scene resembles a school of sharks going into a feeding frenzy. Almost instantly the thrill is gone and the room is filled with crumpled wrapping paper even though it took so long to wrap them all.

Rather than following the Grinch and eliminating the gifts, our family set rules to make them more meaningful. First, we try to select at least some gifts or stocking-stuffers that will help people develop their relationship with Jesus: books, CDs, videos, Rosaries, etc. Then, on Christmas morning before we go to the tree, we gather at the manger, sing a carol, read a brief scripture, and thank God for Jesus, the greatest gift of all. Then we open one gift at a time, with everyone paying attention to what others get (this teaches patience!). And we don't open everything on the twenty-fifth. Rather, we leave some presents wrapped and under the tree for the other eleven days of Christmas (another lesson in patience!). We get more prayers, readings, and carols around the manger this way.

So we have three options: (1) just acquiesce to society's way; (2) say "bah-humbug!" with Scrooge; or (3) take the traditional Catholic approach and press the custom into the service of the Gospel. I say Catholics have more fun.

Jesus, you are the greatest gift of all. Let us honor you by giving of ourselves.

To Ponder: What can you do in your family to make Christmas gift-giving more meaningful?

DR. MARCELLINO D'AMBROSIO

DECEMBER 10

Imitating the Imitators

Children are great imitators, so give them something great to imitate.

Anonymous

I vividly remember being four years old and sitting on the bathroom counter watching my dad shave. He would put a tiny bit of shaving cream on my face and I would squeeze my lips together, squish my face to the left, push my tongue into my right cheek and shave with the toothpaste squeezer, doing every movement just like my dad. I was learning through imitation. (I hope, though, I will never have to shave my face!)

If we learn through imitation, then in our spiritual lives, too, we need to be great imitators. Imagine walking in the footsteps of one who loved God more than self, one who sacrificed everything to teach others of the Lord's love for each individual person, one who gave up everything to live the will of the Father.

How blessed we are to have many great saints whom we can imitate! As a wife and a mom, I look to the beautiful women saints who lived ordinary lives with extraordinary grace. These women allowed their hearts to be transformed so they could love like Christ. They did this through prayer, meditation on the Word of God, frequenting the sacraments, and receiving holy Communion with a fervent devotion.

If you can see yourself imitating wonderful women saints then you can see yourself imitating Christ.

Lord, help me imitate the virtues of the saints.

To Ponder: Today, ask Saint Catherine of Siena to help you to learn to love like Christ or spend five minutes meditating on Psalm 67 and, like Saint Gianna Molla, praise God for all your blessings. Or, take an extra moment before receiving holy Communion and follow Saint Mother Teresa and invite the Lord to increase your tender love for him in the Eucharist.

KELLY M. WAHLQUIST

DECEMBER 11

"He Give It to Me"

We should not accept in silence the benefactions of God, but return thanks for them.

Saint Basil the Great

My dad always told me, "It's lonely at the top." When I was younger I lived to do musical theater, and every year I had the leading role. This was my greatest joy, and at the same time, I would feel the jealousy from other girls. I was cut out from cliques within the cast, and I felt a real isolation. My greatest gift also became my greatest burden.

I find this is usually true in life. We are all blessed with different gifts—talents, brilliance, financial abundance, beauty—and often our greatest gifts have a flip side and become our heaviest crosses. The brilliant mind suffers the torment of incessant thinking to the point of compulsivity. The wealthy one must constantly question what to do with his money. The beautiful woman may be lusted after.

Yet all of these remain gifts from our heavenly Father out of his love and goodness. The question is always how can we embrace them with humble gratitude while joyfully carrying the crosses that coincide with them.

My little Columbian grandmother always had a beautiful response whenever we would compliment a gift she had. "Mina, you are so funny!" "Mina, you're such a good cook!" "Mina, we love your house!" No matter what it was we praised her for, she would simply look to the sky with a grin, then look us in the eye and say in her broken English, "*He* give it to me."

Thank you, Jesus, for the abundant gifts you have blessed me with in my life. Help me to embrace everything—my crosses as well as my blessings—in gratitude and joy.

To Ponder: Do you recognize the gifts that God has given you in your life? Just for today can you accept your burdens as being a natural part of life?

KARA KLEIN

DECEMBER 12
OUR LADY OF GUADALUPE

The Great Gift of Peace

Let not your heart be disturbed.

Our Lady of Guadalupe to Juan Diego

These earliest days of December can be such a manic time. We've finished with the great ordeal of Thanksgiving and have begun to shop for Christmas. The lists seem so long, the money only stretches so far, and the expectations seem so outsized. There are decorations to put up and parties to host or attend, and it all seems like so much.

At the same time, we have entered into Advent, a season that entices us toward quietness and reflection as we long, like a pregnant woman, for deliverance of our heavy burdens. "He shall be peace," says the prophet Micah, and we "wait in joyful hope" for the coming of something so extraordinary that it makes our efforts seem shortsighted and small: the great gift, peace beyond all understanding.

Peace—real peace—is the forever plea from a people in wounded exile, forever looking outside of itself for that gift. But what if the process of peace depends in part on our ability to recognize it? A gift that cannot be recognized as such can often seem disguised as a heavy load.

A willingness to remain undisturbed, trusting in Christ, is a necessary component of peace. It is a great gift.

Our Lady of Guadalupe, in this hope and expectation, help us to be open to the gifted grace of trust that we might begin to know peace and thus begin to better know Jesus.

To Ponder: Take a stroll through your everyday surroundings and see them through the eyes of someone as destitute as Saint Juan Diego before Mary spoke to him. Identify all of the gifts around you. Say thank you. Peace begins right there.

ELIZABETH SCALIA

DECEMBER 13
SAINT LUCY

Can Teens Hold on Against the Tide?

Foolish is he who follows the pleasures of this world, because these are always fleeting and bring much pain. The only true pleasure is that which comes to us through faith.

Blessed Pier Giorgio Frassati

Today, as part of the Church's liturgical cycle, we honor a young Italian teen named Lucy. She was martyred for faith and purity in the year 304. As the "new religion on the block," we can imagine the pressures and the manipulation that was going on between the pagan Romans, the Jews, and those adhering to true love and the call to a higher ideal. Given all the versions of twenty-first-century paganism in our world, you might say it's the same or maybe even worse today.

In the community where we live, we know younger families who have done their best to live their Catholic faith and pass it on to their teens ready to leave the cocoon. In a few cases, it doesn't take much to see apathy about faith in the teens: clothes worn that are a bit much and boyfriends who don't have nearly the same values as the family the girls come from.

Saint John Paul II spoke to men: "God has assigned as a duty to every man the dignity of every woman." And to questioning and restless young women he said, "The most beautiful and stirring adventure that can happen to you is the personal meeting with Jesus, who is the only one who gives real meaning to our lives."

Saint Lucy, pray for the young people in our lives. Appear to them in their thoughts and meditations. Speak to them when they are invited to surrender their body and emotions to someone outside of marriage.

To Ponder: What can you do today to help teens and young people? Really live the faith. Love the faith. Pray hard.

DEACON TOM FOX

Companion Planting for Life

The Church is nothing other than "the family of God." From the beginning, the core of the Church was often constituted by those who had become believers together.

Catechism of the Catholic Church, 1655

Companion planting is the practice of growing plants side by side where, together, they enhance each other's development. Some plant combinations will enhance mutual root development, others protect the pairing from harm by pests or diseases, and some combinations increase fruitfulness by attracting pollinators.

Companion planting has been an agricultural practice for centuries. The Benedictines developed our modern-day horticultural practices centuries ago when monastery land was often marginal at best for food production. If we look at our lives, we see that we have a lot of companions, too. Those whom God has planted in our spiritual garden to help develop our roots in faith, protect our minds and hearts from evil, and increase our fruitfulness at being Christians. These companions are our spouses, parents, children, friends, and acquaintances who, each in his or her own way, help us to grow.

It's easy to see how our God planned for things to work together for the good of all—in plants and people.

Thank you, Lord, for the Church family that helps me to prosper for your good.

To Ponder: We have human companions and spiritual companions. Who in your life now, and who in the past, has been significant in your becoming who you are today? Who have you companioned—children or adults—on their faith journey? How have you done it and how has it affected your life?

MARGARET ROSE REALY, OBL. O.S.B.

DECEMBER 15

Preaching with Your Living

Preach the Gospel at all times; when necessary use words.

Attributed to Saint Francis of Assisi

We've all heard someone say, "I try to share my faith by the way I live," and there's an important truth there. We are told that the early Christians were notable for their love and care for one another; if we are aiming to follow Christ as we should, people will notice the effect of it in our lives. If we are not aiming to follow Christ people will see that, too, and it won't matter what we say because they won't see any reason to listen to us. At best we will be ignored, and at worst we will cast doubt upon the faith because of the difference between what we say and what we do.

But suppose we are aiming to follow Christ, we are praying, and we are trying to show God's love and mercy to those around us. Eventually, someone is going to notice and ask about it. "How do you always stay so calm?" "You're always so helpful." "Thank you for letting me vent—you're so good about that." "Things are so hard for you, but you keep going. How do you manage it?" "You go to church, don't you?"

It is easy to respond to comments like these by hemming and hawing and saying nothing to the point, but Saint Peter tells us to always be ready to give an answer. If you can't think of anything else, try a simple, "God is good!"

O Holy Spirit, teach my heart to know what to say when I'm called upon to give an answer.

To Ponder: Have you recently remained silent when you could have used words? What could you have said?

WILL DUQUETTE

DECEMBER 16

Love Beyond Measure

Celebrate the feast of Christmas every day, even every moment in the interior temple of your spirit, remaining like a baby in the bosom of the heavenly Father, where you will be reborn each moment in the Divine Word, Jesus Christ.

Saint Paul of the Cross

All acts of love require a sublimation of the will. Sometimes it is easy: the baby cries and the mother picks her up, holds her, and offers food or comfort. Sometimes it is not: climbing the stairs one more time at the end of the day without gritting my teeth can be a challenge, even if it is because I didn't get to kiss them good night. What I have to do to save souls may mean climbing the stairs, washing the dishes, or running the extra errand. It doesn't feel like love or the means by which a soul is saved, except if we consider that perhaps the soul being rescued from sloth or indifference is our own.

Family life requires daily sublimation of the soul for the good of others, and it frequently includes tedium like folding socks, plunging toilets, and redoing work done yesterday. If it is not done for love's sake, the person doing it will become bitter, feel used, and grow resentment where love should be.

Preparing for Christmas can feel like one long to-do list if we forget the reason why the gifts, celebrations, cards, decorations, and music exist.

Love makes sacrifice possible. Perfect love makes it a joy.

Lord, let me be an instrument of love beyond measure during this crazy holiday time.

To Ponder: In Jesus, God humbled himself to become a helpless child. That is the reason for Christmas. Mary's obedience, her *fiat*, is also a gift to us of untold beauty and a reminder that all we do for others, we do for Christ. Therefore whatever we do should be done out of love.

SHERRY ANTONETTI

DECEMBER 17

Redeemed by Love

Motherhood changed from a role into a calling . . . a nameless something so enormous that a great deal had to be sacrificed for it.

Anna Quindlen

A favorite expression of mine is "I'm slow but I get it eventually." That colloquialism played out with motherhood. We were married seven years before we had children. I believed I had no maternal instinct. All around me our cousins were having children. I felt left out, wanting to be a part of that club, but I also felt pressured. I was still too much of a child myself to take on motherhood. I had goals to accomplish and, if all happened according to plan, then I'd have children by the time I was twenty-nine. Right on schedule I announced to my husband that it was time.

When Stephen was born I fell in love. Totally. Nothing existed except for this baby. I still count those first six weeks as one of the happiest periods of my life. I was amazed how easy it was to put away everything for which I had worked so hard. Nothing else mattered.

I had been given a gift of love. Sacrificial love. I had been wandering aimlessly in a spiritual desert for years, still attending Mass but leaving God behind in church. But he never left me. Even though I did things my way all those years he still poured his love into me, unlocking a fierce mothering instinct.

I would spend nine more years in that desert. But the road back home had already been laid out.

Thank you, Lord, for the gift of children and the love they release in the world around us all.

To Ponder: How have your children brought you close to God?

SUSAN BAILEY

DECEMBER 18

O Adonai

All blessings come to us through Our Lord. He will teach us, for in beholding his life we find that he is the best example.

Saint Teresa of Avila

Because I'm a teacher, Christmas, especially Christmas with small children, stressed me almost to the breaking point. The struggle with work responsibilities at the end of a school term plus home responsibilities and the children's schooling conflicted with any expectations of a lovely and peaceful Advent. Christmas wasn't likely to look like a greeting card, either. By the time I was ready to focus on Advent, it had almost passed. Blessedly, my Christmas vacation often started in time for the O Antiphons. I always felt that last week of reflection helped me to catch up with Advent.

Today's antiphon, O Adonai, calls to mind not just deliverance from slavery under the Pharaoh but our own deliverance through the coming of Christ. Just as the Lord, Adonai, redeemed the people of Israel from the bonds of slavery with outstretched arms, we look forward to the birth of the Christ Child, who comes with outstretched arms, seeking our embrace, and foreshadowing the day when those same arms will be stretched upon the cross for us.

O Adonai, thank you for the precious gift of you.

To Ponder: This season is filled with so many distractions that take our focus away from Christ in Christmas. What can you do as a family that reminds you of the best gift, Jesus?

MARIA MORERA JOHNSON

DECEMBER 19

Aim for Heaven

Aim at heaven and you will get earth thrown in. Aim at earth and you get neither.

C. S. Lewis, Mere Christianity

Scripture tells us, "Set your minds on things that are above, not on things that are on earth" (Col 3:2). Are our minds occupied with heaven? Could this be an impractical or ridiculous question for a mother who needs to be uncompromisingly mindful of her present moments with her children as she vigilantly cares for them?

Without doubt we mothers need to live fully in our present moments to focus on our family. But all the while we naturally yearn for heaven. We teach our children that heaven is the destination we strive for. Everything we do and say, the very way we live our lives, must add up to that.

In this Advent season of hope and anticipation, we set our sights on the joys and the beauty that is to come in our eternal life, and we do our best to fully live out our vocation as Catholic mothers raising our little saints to heaven.

Dear Lord Jesus, please grant me the graces to be ever mindful of the true purpose of my life: to grow in holiness and help others so that I may meet you face to face one day.

To Ponder: Are you "aiming" at earth alone? Are you "attached" to the world and its allurements so that you neglect to make the needed changes in your life to get closer to God? What steps can you take to avoid getting caught up in worldly affairs?

DONNA-MARIE COOPER O'BOYLE

DECEMBER 20

Refusing to Juggle

First do what's necessary; then do what's possible,
and suddenly you are doing the impossible.

Attributed to Saint Francis of Assisi

It's almost Christmas, and the fact that you found the time to actually open this book and take a few moments for prayer and reflection is pretty impressive.

These last couple of pre-Christmas weeks really test a mom's ability to juggle.

I learned to juggle in college, spending hours upon hours tossing tennis balls in the air in the hallway of the freshman dorm. When juggling, in order to keep those balls in the air, you have to be willing to let them go. To keep things in perpetual motion, you can only have one ball at a time in your hand.

The art of juggling proves that multi-tasking doesn't work. The more you try to do all at once, the more likely it is that you will drop a ball or three.

In these last days of hectic preparation, take a moment to set your priorities as Saint Francis advises. Figure out what's necessary and do that first. Then move on to what's possible—and suddenly, you may find yourself accomplishing those things you never thought would get done.

Lord, guide me through these busy days. Help me to keep my priorities firmly in line with my family's needs and following your will.

To Ponder: Are you overwhelmed by your to-do list as you prepare to celebrate Christmas? Can you let go of some things or curb your impulse to multi-task so you can approach the coming holiday with wonder, joy, and gratitude?

BARB SZYSZKIEWICZ, O.F.S.

DECEMBER 21

Gifts for the Kingdom

We have gifts that differ according to the grace given to us.

Romans 12:6

I wonder what the grand tally would be if I added up all the minutes I've spent wishing I had someone else's gifts. I'm sure the number would be big. Even when I recognize the gifts God has given me I still compare. I find myself wishing

I had her sophisticated charm or his writing talent or her slim little thighs. Sometimes I have to stop and remind myself that comparison is the thief of joy and that I have other gifts.

The truth of the story is that God not only gives us gifts and graces but he also gives us exactly the ones we need to do the work he has for us in the time and place he has chosen. I think the part that trips us up is the "he has chosen" part. We have to remember we are a part of his divine plan, not the star of the show. If we were to trade comparison for gratefulness we would be overwhelmed with contentment. God doesn't hand out gifts as if they are gold stars or extra credit for his favorite students; he blesses us with gifts in order to help further his kingdom here on earth. The gifts he gives are meant to be returned to him through loving service to others in his name.

Loving giver of all gifts, help me be grateful and proud of the gifts you have blessed me with. Help me be a humble steward of your gifts and graces.

To Ponder: What are your gifts? Make a list and then offer a prayer of thanksgiving for them. Next to each gift on your list write down the ways you can use that gift to further God's kingdom.

SHERI WOHLFERT

DECEMBER 22

The Gift of Yourself

We must become cradles of silence, meditation, and contemplation so that the Word may find our hearts

ready to receive him—our souls and minds ready to
hear his message of love. And, hearing it, may we
arise and go forth and live it!

Catherine Doherty, Welcome Pilgrim

Although Advent and Christmas seem to bring out the best
in people, it can also bring out the worst when people are
scrambling around to buy last-minute Christmas gifts, getting
annoyed that this gift or that gift isn't available.

Sometimes the gift of ourselves can be the most important
gift we can offer others. How do we give of ourselves? In
our family, we've tried to create new traditions like singing
Christmas carols, giving toys to children whose families are
in need, donating to the food bank, volunteering to assist
seniors during the holiday season, and visiting rest homes
or hospitals. These all help to strengthen family ties and
increase virtue, which can help us to make our hearts ready
to "receive him," the babe who came to save us all.

*Thank you, God, for the gift of your Son, Jesus, whose birth we will
celebrate in a few days.*

To Ponder: What gift of yourself can you give in these last
few days before Christmas?

ELLEN GABLE HRKACH

Longing to See His Face

My soul thirsts for God, the living God. When shall I
come and behold the face of God?

Psalm 42:2

My sister's three-year-old woke in the morning and said, "I
want to go to Grandma and Grandpa's house." Only problem: Grandma and Grandpa live a thousand miles away.

"I'm sorry, honey," my sister said, "it's too far for us to
go for a visit right now. What do you like about Grandma
and Grandpa's house?"

"Their backyard," her daughter said, "and their books.
And their toys. And . . . I miss Grandpa's face."

I thought that captured perfectly this season of Advent.
After the fall, God promised a messiah. Israel waited for the
promised one to arrive through the ages, through the long
ages of Israel's captivity in Egypt, in Babylon, and under
various foreign overlords in the Promised Land. Israel looked
always with yearning for their redeemer to come. Simeon
waited in the Temple to see the face of his Savior. And then,
one day, he arrived. Finally Simeon could look upon that face
that he and all the Israelites had been waiting to see for so
long: the face of our Redeemer, our Savior, our God.

With the arrival of Jesus, a new day dawned, hope came
into a forlorn world, truth came into a world dark with lies,
and love came into a world where human hearts had grown
hard as stone. That day, that momentous day that changed
the world forever, is almost upon us. We have only a little
time left to prepare to see the face of God.

May I have the grace to see you, Lord, in the midst of all that's going on.

To Ponder: What can you do today to prepare to meet God?

JAKE FROST

DECEMBER 24
CHRISTMAS EVE

The Gift of Life

Silent night, holy night, Son of God, love's pure light.

"Silent Night"

Maybe you've spent the last few weeks thinking about gifts. You've made shopping lists, visited the mall, wrapped and tagged, and stocked up on batteries. Perhaps all this gift-giving or the other traditions of the season have made you feel exhausted or depleted.

But now, on this silent and holy night, give yourself a gift. Take a moment to recall the arrival of your child or children into your life. Was it the culmination of a long labor, a C-section, an endless tussle with an adoption agency or the foster-care system? Maybe the process itself made you feel exhausted or depleted.

But recall the feeling of seeing that child for the first time. Think about all that has happened in the days, weeks, months, or years since then. Ponder all the ways that this child has been a gift to you, cracking open your worldview and making you understand things about life and faith you never knew before.

Think about Mary, on this holy and beautiful night, holding her newborn son. Her exhausting journey and search for shelter are over, and she's looking at her child for the first time. Admire the baby boy with her. He's her gift; he's your gift, too.

Merry Christmas.

Lord, I have received so many gifts. Thank you.

To Ponder: Your children are precious gifts from God. How will you let them know that they are?

GINNY KUBITZ MOYER

DECEMBER 25
CHRISTMAS

The Songs of Christmas

The Church never tires of singing the glory of this night.

Catechism of the Catholic Church, *525*

Love songs stir our hearts. Maybe we've sung or danced to a favorite with our husband or father. Perhaps we've sung memorable songs with children or good friends. We understand Saint Augustine's preaching, *"Cantare amantis est"* ("Singing belongs to one who loves").

Consider the very first Christmas songs.

A dark Bethlehem night with shepherds in a field watching their sheep, when a sudden beat of wings shatters the quiet. A surprise messenger lights up the sky: "Behold, I bring you good news of a great joy." An astonishing host of angels—a majestic choir—sings across the cosmos. "And suddenly there was with the angel a multitude of the heavenly host, praising God and saying, 'Glory to God in the highest heaven and on earth peace among those whom he favors!'" (Lk 2:13–14).

Imagine the wonder of the shepherds privy to the love song of heaven. After which they went in haste to Bethlehem "and found Mary and Joseph, and the child lying in the manger" (Lk 2:16). When they arrived at the stable, they might have heard a mother's voice singing a lullaby. How often throughout their lives did the shepherds replay the memories of that night, of those songs? How often do we sing the songs that mean the most to us?

Singing belongs to one who loves.

Jesus, help me to love you with a song in my heart.

To Ponder: What Christmas hymns and carols are most meaningful to you? Listen to them and prayerfully linger over the verses. Ponder their meaning. Then bring your heart to Bethlehem and sing to Jesus.

PAT GOHN

DECEMBER 26

Stooping for God's Gifts

Everyone is gifted. Some just never open their package.

Wolfgang Riebe

The definition of gifted means having exceptional talent and natural ability. In reality, we are gifted in every ordinary way.

In her book *One Thousand Gifts*, Ann Voskamp tells how she found receiving God's gifts a gentle, simple movement of stooping. Her inspiration was a quote from F. B. Meyer: "I used to think that God's gifts were on shelves one above the other and that the taller we grew in Christian character, the more easily we should reach them. I find now that God's gifts are on shelves one beneath the other and that it is not a question of growing taller, but of stooping lower and that we have to go down, always down to get his best ones."[10]

We all hunger for more, something more, something other, and may miss the gifts we have. Voskamp tells us that the miracle of joy follows naming everyday gifts and giving God thanks: "Is there a greater way to love the Giver than to delight wildly in his gifts? . . . God gives gifts and I give thanks and I unwrap the gift given, joy."[11]

There are natural gifts and there are charisms, gifts given by the Holy Spirit. Saint Paul talks about charism as gifts given to each person for the building up of the Body of Christ (Eph 4:7–13; 1 Cor 12:4–11). Saint Peter reminds us to "use whatever gift you have received to serve others, as faithful stewards of God's grace" (1 Pt 4:10).

Jesus, help me use these gifts I have received so that I may pass on the love that has been given to me.

To Ponder: What are some creative ways you celebrate your "awed adoration" of all God's gifts?

MARGARET KERRY, F.S.P.

What's in the Box?

Those who seek applause for their gifts do not really give at all—they buy. They are not surrendering— they are purchasing. They are less impressed with the need of others than they are with the heed that will be given to them.

Venerable Fulton J. Sheen

Each of us holds in our hands a beautifully wrapped box. Inside this box is our own special, God-given talents, bestowed upon us to help us grow in holiness and bring others to God as well. But for some, pride distorts the purpose of this gift and they begin to believe the beautiful gift is for themselves. They hold tight to their gift because it brings them appreciation, friends, and flattery, and they never consider the One from whom it came.

Others, however, see this beautifully wrapped gift as something to give away to benefit others and bring them joy. Instead of holding tight to their gift because of what it offers them, these people freely pass their gifts along to others. In the end, they learn that it is through giving that they truly receive.

Lord, you have blessed me with great gifts. Show me how to use them to bring you glory always.

To Ponder: Many times our talents allow us to fulfill one or more of the corporal or spiritual works of mercy and help us to know, love, and serve Our Lord. Have you considered how your talents may fit into God's larger plan for your journey to holiness?

CASSANDRA POPPE

DECEMBER 28
HOLY INNOCENTS

Great Joy, Deep Sadness

To become a Catholic is not to leave off thinking, but to learn how to think.

G. K. Chesterton

Great joy is often preceded or followed by deep sadness. Seeing the positive lines on a pregnancy test is often followed by heavy nausea. The joy of that first ultrasound is quickly followed up with increased swelling and back pain. The pangs of labor precede the joy of holding a miracle. Think back to the joyful pride you felt walking your little angel to the kindergarten door and the tears streaming down your cheeks as you walked away.

Christmas unleashes great joy but possibly also loss or anguish over a missing loved one, sorrow after a hard year, or the stress of extended family. In God's creative wisdom, tears can communicate both joy and sadness.

The cries that emanated from the manger were, not long after, replaced by the cries of the Holy Innocents, the first martyrs whose lives were taken by King Herod. On this day, we recall that sometimes grace comes violently. Grace often comes through difficulty. God hears our cries the same way you hear your kids cry and seek to respond. The Lord and Our Blessed Mother hear our cries and respond.

Lord Jesus, your manger lay in the shadow of the cross. May we have, this day, the grace not to flinch but to praise you both in the joys and the sufferings.

To Ponder: Has your joy departed with the Christmas wrapping paper? Have the carols turned to lamentations? Is there anyone in your life who, now that Christmas Day is over, might need a kind word, an invitation, or a reminder that God's love is very much available through you and your family?

MARK HART

DECEMBER 29

Receiving Christ

When we give each other our Christmas presents
in His name, let us remember that He has given us
the sun and the moon and the stars, the earth with
its forests and mountains and oceans and all that
lives and moves upon them. . . . And to save us from
our own foolishness and from all our sins, He came
down to earth and gave himself.

Sigrid Undset

Christmas is the season of giving. Sure, we have to face a labyrinth of crowded malls and furious preparations before we finally enjoy the delighted faces on Christmas morning, but it's worth it, right? Or is it? What if Christmas is not only about giving but also *giftedness*?

Stores want to sell stuff and the holidays are characterized by an enormous retail push to begin the season earlier and earlier, jumpstarting us to begin worrying about being ready for Christmas on Halloween. It makes sense that we want to be ready for guests and family to celebrate the holidays. However, the Church calendar calls us to celebrate spiritual realities that take precedence over the physical details of the holiday season, and at Christmas we celebrate the greatest gift God has ever given: his Son.

Giftedness means that in Christ we already have all we need. We are already blessed and prosperous. We are already ready.

If we are honest, it is our sense of not being ready that makes us run around at the holidays. We can only rest when everything is bought and wrapped and baked. This psychological feeling of lack is what makes us feel urgency. What would it be like if we understood fully and deeply that *we already have all we need*?

Christmas is meant to help us receive Christ more fully. Out of this fuller reception, we can give to others as we ought. Our giftedness as people of faith, hope, and love, imbued with the gifts of the Holy Spirit, enables us to give the gift of spiritual joy in the Lord whom we possess and who possesses us.

Lord, help me see you as my greatest gift, given to me by the Father.

To Ponder: Do you see yourself as gifted or lacking?

JULIE PAAVOLA

A Marriage Checkup

All the wealth in the world cannot be compared with
the happiness of living together happily united.

Blessed Margaret d'Youville

I know exactly where I was standing in my kitchen when I
heard about the *third* couple in the same day to announce
their divorce. All three couples were friends of ours who did
not know each other.

My husband and I were well aware of the complexities
of even a happy marriage. Just a few years into our marriage, financial struggles and the demands of having children all added stress to the relationship. Even so, this news
surprised us.

That night, I started to ask my husband questions: "What
can I do to make this marriage work better? How can I be a
better wife?" We knew that we should use this news as an
opportunity to do a health check on our own relationship.
God certainly gave us a sacred gift when calling us to marriage. The challenges of daily life can force autopilot on us,
and our marriage can be the first thing to get pushed to the
back burner.

We talked for hours that night about what we both want,
for our marriage and family. This never would have happened in between shuffling kids off to soccer practices. We
learned the value of making time for a marriage checkup
because, as with any gift from God, we must treat our marriage with utmost respect.

Dear Lord Jesus, thank you for the gift of my spouse and the blessing of our marriage. Help us to grow together, in union with you, always.

To Ponder: What is something that you can do for or with your spouse this week in the hopes of nurturing your marriage and each other?

MEG BUCARO

DECEMBER 31
NEW YEAR'S EVE

God Is with You Now

Few souls understand what God would accomplish
in them if they were to abandon themselves
unreservedly to him and if they were to allow his
grace to mold them accordingly.

Saint Ignatius of Loyola

Tomorrow begins a new year and, for most people, a new round of resolutions. There is something built into us that makes us yearn for *more*: more joy, more happiness, more peace, more health (and less weight!), more time with family and friends, more savings (and less spending). At heart, this desire for *more* is really a desire for God, who alone can satisfy all of our longings.

We long for God, yet God is right here with us. God is our goal, yet he is also our constant companion. God is with you right now. God has brought you to this moment in your life.

I like to run. Running for me is like prayer, and I can feel the presence of God. As I was running one evening a couple of weeks ago, I became aware of the stream of my thoughts. It was as if I was watching myself think. And God was right there with me. My thoughts mainly were about things that happened to me the day before or the week before or years before. And they were about the future, worries about to-do list items and upcoming events. With amazing clarity I recognized that God was with me in the *now*, in the present moment. He was not in the concerns of the past or the worries of the future. And in that present moment I felt peace. What a great lesson for me! What a wonderful, all-encompassing New Year's resolution: to live with God in the present moment.

Father, thank you for being with me right now. Please help me to be present to you now and at every moment.

To Ponder: What specific actions help you to become aware of God's presence? How can you use those actions to become more present to God in the new year?

JEFF YOUNG

Contributor Biographies

DR. MARY AMORE speaks nationally on the Eucharist, sacraments, and women's spirituality; she is a published author of DVDs and serves as the executive director of Mayslake Ministries in Downers Grove, Illinois.

SHERRY ANTONETTI works as a contributor to *Catholic-Mom.com* and a columnist for multiple Catholic publications; she is wife to Marc Antonetti and mother to their ten children.

SUSAN BAILEY is the author of *River of Grace: Creative Passages through Difficult Times* and *Louisa May Alcott: Illuminated by the Message*. She writes for *CatholicMom.com* and *The Catholic Free Press* (Diocese of Worcester newspaper), and on her blogs, *Be as One* and *Louisa May Alcott Is My Passion*.

DEANNA BARTALINI has a master's degree in pastoral administration from Loyola University-New Orleans. She works as a faith formation director, serves her parish in youth ministry, and teaches others how to use Web 2.0 tools and social media in ministry.

MARIANNA BARTHOLOMEW is an award-winning journalist, podcaster, and blogger who reports on Catholic missionaries and their people. She podcasts *Missionary Moments* for

SQPN-affiliated CatholicVitamins.com, contributes *Catholic Womanhood* and *Worldview Wednesday* posts for Catholic-NewsAgency.com and *CatholicMom.com*, and explores living a balanced life in a technological world on her blog, FinerFields.blogspot.com.

DANIELLE BEAN is publisher of *Catholic Digest* and author of *Momnipotent*, a book, a study, and a movement to reclaim a vocation (MomnipotentStudy.com).

CELESTE BEHE, wife to Michael Behe and the mother of nine home-schooled children, is a humorist, writer, speaker, and storyteller. She is also a recovering Mompostor™ who, after spending decades worrying that she'd one day be found out as a substandard mother, is on a mission to help other moms struggling with similar feelings of self-doubt. Follow her at CelesteBehe.com

Novelist **SHERRY BOAS** is a special needs adoptive mother to four amazing children and owner of Caritas Press, a Catholic publishing company founded to shed light on things eternal in a culture that has become increasingly blind to the wonders of God's works and numb to his boundless love.

TRISH BOLSTER grew up in Massachusetts but now calls Harrisburg, Pennsylvania, home. After a few years of infertility, she and her husband Ryan have been abundantly blessed with six children in seven years! Her *Seasons* blog chronicles her crazy yet wonderful journey as she attempts to raise up saints.

HEIDI BRATTON is a *CatholicMom.com* contributor, an educational consultant, and the author of nearly twenty books including *Finding God's Peace in Everyday Challenges* and the Celebrate series of children's board books. Heidi and her husband, John, are hilariously attempting to keep up with their half-a-dozen children spread over eighteen years in age. Catch up with Heidi at HeidiBratton.com.

CHAUNIE MARIE BRUSIE is a freelance writer, mom of four, and author of the book *Tiny Blue Lines: Reclaiming Your Life, Preparing for Your Baby, and Moving Forward in Faith in an Unplanned Pregnancy.*

MEG BUCARO is a professional speaker, communication coach, and mom to three energetic children. She works with women who desire to communicate more confidently and live with more soul-filling peace through a fulfilling spiritual life. Follow Meg at MegBucaro.com

MARC CARDARONELLA is one of the few but proud Catholic dads on *CatholicMom.com*. He writes on spirituality, evangelization, and raising faith-filled kids at MarcCardaronella.com. He also serves as director of The Helmsing Institute for Faith Formation in the Diocese of Kansas City, Missouri.

THERESA CENICCOLA is "The Christian Mompreneur"—a mentor to moms who are running a business that supports their values of faith and family. As president and founder of the International Christian Mompreneur Network (ICMNetwork.com), she empowers and equips moms to build profitable businesses while putting family first.

DONNA-MARIE COOPER O'BOYLE is the mother of five and a new grandmother. She is the best-selling and award-winning author of twenty books, including *The Miraculous Medal*, *The Kiss of Jesus*, and *Feeding Your Family's Soul*. She is host of EWTN's TV series *Everyday Blessings for Catholic Moms* and *Catholic Mom's Cafe*. Find her at DonnaMarieCooperOBoyle.com.

Southern scripture evangelist **SONJA CORBITT** (PursuingtheSummit.com) connects the Bible and its powerful scriptural tools to everyday life and experiences through her speaking, Real Life Radio broadcast (search the app), Catholic television series, and multimedia Bible studies. Her most recent study, *Unleashed*, was released in 2015.

CINDY COSTELLO, coordinator of marriage ministry in the Diocese of Paterson, New Jersey, is a speaker and writer on the theology of the body and other Catholic topics and is a graduate of the Theology of the Body Institute in Pennsylvania.

JAY CUASAY is a freelance writer on religion, interfaith relations, and culture and is reachable at TribePlatypus.com. He works for a bilingual Franciscan parish in northern Virginia and raises a daughter with his Jewish wife.

ERIN MCCOLE CUPP is a wife, mother, and lay Dominican. Information about her novels, nonfiction, and speaking can be found at ErinMcColeCupp.com.

Husband and father of five, Catholic theologian, speaker, media personality, and best-selling author of hundreds of articles and books including *When the Church Was Young: Voices of the Early Fathers* and *40 Days, 40 Ways: A New Look at Lent*, **DR. MARCELLINO D'AMBROSIO** can be found at DrItaly.com, @DrItaly on Twitter, and on Facebook.

SARAH DAMM is a wife and mother of six children. She writes for *CatholicMom.com* and at her own blog, SarahDamm.com, and also serves as the book club specialist for WINE: Women in the New Evangelization.

KATE DANELUK is a wife and mother of six, founder of Making Music Praying Twice, and writes and speaks in various venues on Catholic life, education, music education, and home schooling.

COLLEEN MURPHY DUGGAN is a writer and photographer. You can find her on the web at ColleenDuggan.net.

ABBEY DUPUY is the mother of four young children and is perfecting the art of flying by the seat of her pants. She writes about practicing gratitude, parenting with intention, and living the liturgical year with her family at SurvivingOurBlessings.com.

WILL DUQUETTE is a lay Dominican, software engineer, prolific reader, father of four, and husband of a woman who is better than he deserves. He writes at Patheos.com about Catholicism, the interior life, technology, and pop culture, all with a fair dollop of whimsy.

JEANNIE EWING is a grief recovery coach and author of *Navigating Deep Waters: Meditations for Caregivers* (CreateSpace) and *From Grief to Grace* (Sophia Institute Press). Find her at LoveAloneCreates.com and FromGrieftoGrace.com.

PATRICE FAGNANT-MACARTHUR has a master's degree in applied theology and is editor of TodaysCatholicHomeschooling.com as well as author of *The Catholic Baby Name Book*.

LAURA KELLY FANUCCI is a wife, mother of three, and the research associate for the Collegeville Institute Seminars. She blogs at MotheringSpirit.com and is the author of *Everyday Sacrament: The Messy Grace of Parenting* and the coauthor of *Living Your Discipleships: 7 Ways to Express Your Deepest Calling.*

ELIZABETH FICOCELLI is an international speaker, radio host, and author of fifteen books, including *Thérèse, Faustina, and Bernadette: Three Saints Who Challenged My Faith, Gave Me Hope, and Taught Me How to Love.*

JENNIFER FITZ is the home-schooling mom of four children and author of *Classroom Management for Catechists*. She blogs about the Catholic faith at Patheos.com/blogs/JenniferFitz.

In addition to active parish and community ministry, **DEACON TOM FOX** has been active in Internet evangelization using written and audio reflections for nearly a dozen years. Tom and his wife Dee started the *Catholic Vitamins* podcast almost seven years ago. Someplace between coffee and chocolate, you can reach Deacon Tom at CatholicVitamins@gmail.com.

A. K. FRAILEY is a teacher with a bachelor of science degree in elementary education and is the author of six books: *The Road Goes Ever On*, The Deliverance Trilogy, and *Georgios I & II*. She has eight children, and she home educates them while maintaining a rural home.

JAKE FROST is a lawyer in hiatus, having temporarily suspended his legal career to raise his preschool-aged children. He is the author of *Catholic Dad: (Mostly) Funny Stories of Faith, Family, and Futherhood.*

CAY GIBSON is a director of religious education in her parish; author of *Catholic Mosaic*, published by Hillside Education; and writes on education, spirituality, and family life. She lives in Louisiana with her husband, Mark, their children, and three grandsons. She blogs at CajunCottage.blogspot.com.

ALLISON GINGRAS founded Reconciled to You ministries, developed the Words with Jesus daily devotional app, and is the host of *A Seeking Heart with Allison Gingras* on BreadboxMedia.com.

PAT GOHN is the award-winning author of *Blessed, Beautiful, and Bodacious* and is the host of the *Among Women* podcast.

KELLY GUEST is a former Nashville Dominican and is now a wife and mother of ten children. She is coordinator of youth ministries at Saint Bartholomew Parish in Manchester, Maryland.

MARK HART is an award-winning Catholic author, radio host, and sought-after speaker. The executive vice president for Life Teen International and a twenty-year veteran of youth ministry, Mark's DVD Bible studies, podcasts, and books are known around the world.

LISA M. HENDEY is founder of *CatholicMom.com* and author of *The Grace of Yes* and the Chime Travelers children's series. She employs television, radio, social media, and her writing to share her passion for her faith. Lisa speaks internationally and resides in California with her husband, Greg.

LISA LAWMASTER HESS is an adjunct professor of psychology at York College of Pennsylvania. A blogger at L2Hess.blogspot.com and contributor to Tech Talk and STYLE Savvy at *CatholicMom.com*, Lisa is also the author of numerous articles, two nonfiction books, *Acting Assertively* and *Diverse Divorce*, and two novels, *Casting the First Stone* and *Chasing a Second Chance*.

In the past few years literary fiction writer **KAYE PARK HINCKLEY** has emerged as a major talent in what Paul Elie calls "the literature of belief." She is the author of *A Hunger in the Heart*, *Birds of a Feather*, and *Mary's Mountain*.

ELLEN GABLE HRKACH is a best-selling, award-winning author of five books and is also a speaker, publisher, book coach, natural family planning teacher, and the mother of five sons. You can find out more about her at her EllenGable.com.

CHRISTINE JOHNSON is a wife, home-schooling mother, and lay Dominican who blogs at DomesticVocation.wordpress.com and is a regular contributor to *CatholicMom.com*.

MARIA MORERA JOHNSON, author of *My Badass Book of Saints: Courageous Women Who Showed Me How to Live*, blogs at DomesticVocation.com and CatholicMom.com.

MICHELLE JONES is a writer, teacher, cook, chauffeur, wannabe farmer, wife, and mom who loves God, kids, good food, and the great outdoors. She writes to think, pray, imagine, laugh, and love.

SISTER MARGARET KERRY is a member of the Daughters of Saint Paul, religious sisters who participate in the new evangelization through all forms of media. She is a writer of books and social media and speaks on the vocation and mission of the laity.

TAMI KISER is founder of CatholicConference4Moms.com, CatholicFamilyCelebrations.com, and Smart Martha Ministries. She shares her experience as mother of ten in her book *Smart Martha's Catholic Guide for Busy Moms*.

JUDY LANDRIEU KLEIN, a theologian and inspirational speaker, is the founder of Memorare Ministries and the author of *Miracle Man* and *Mary's Way: The Power of Entrusting Your Child to God*. Her blog, *Holy Hope*, can be found at MemorareMinistries.com.

KARA KLEIN is a six-time award-winning recording artist, international speaker, and author, and is passionate about calling others to discover authentic joy in Christ. Her website is KaraKlein.com.

ELENA LAVICTOIRE is a graduate of Baker College in Flint, Michigan. Her flute can be heard on CDs with the Peace Together Choir at HopefulMusic.com. Elena has been married to her high-school sweetheart for more than thirty-five years. They have six children. She blogs about Catholic married life at MyDomesticChurch.com.

ERIKA MARIE is a simple Catholic wife and mama. She writes about faith, motherhood, and marriage for *Catholic-Mom.com* and at her personal blog, OneSimpleMama.com.

MEG MATENAER is a wife, mom of five, weekly contributor to *CatholicMom.com*, and author of the blog *Heaven's in Your Corner* (HeavensinYourCorner.wordpress.com).

MONICA MCCONKEY is a mother of five who creates craft kits, books, and quizzing cards to help celebrate and teach the Catholic faith in fun new ways. She blogs about Catholic

activities and family traditions at EquippingCatholicFamilies.
com.

COLLEEN CONNELL MITCHELL is a wife, mother, missionary, and cofounder of the missionary nonprofit Saint Bryce
Missions. She writes about faith, family, social-justice issues,
and the missionary mandate of the Church at BlessedAre-
theFeet.com.

LISA MLADINICH is the author of *True Radiance: Finding
Grace in the Second Half of Life*, the founder of AmazingCate-
chists.com, and a speaker at catechetical and women's conferences around the country.

GINNY KUBITZ MOYER is the author of *Taste and See: Experiencing the Goodness of God with Our Five Senses* and *Random
MOMents of Grace: Experiencing God in the Adventures of Motherhood*. She lives in the San Francisco Bay area and blogs at
RandomActsofMomness.com.

LAURA NELSON is a happy, goofy, busy, (and just a little
bit tired) wife, mother of three, Catholic blogger, writer, and
speaker who also happens to be the coordinator for children's
catechesis at her parish in Grapevine, Texas. Pray for her!

KATIE O'KEEFE—mother, grandmother, and blogger—holds
a bachelor of arts degree in philosophy from Ohio Dominican
University and is a great fan of nifty new tools and dusty
old books.

RHONDA ORTIZ is a Catholic convert, a writer and graphic
designer, and a wife and mother of three. She is a regular
contributor *to CatholicMom.com* and is the art director and
web editor for *Dappled Things*. The Ortizes live in Michigan,

where they wear long johns seven months out of the year. Follow her work at www.RhondaOrtiz.com.

JULIE PAAVOLA, author of *The Mother's Calling*, speaks on prayer and offers spiritual direction in the Ignatian tradition. She has a master's degree in religion and is pursuing a degree in art therapy.

CASSANDRA POPPE is a convert to the Catholic faith, a wife, and a home-schooling mother of seven children. She is also a writer and speaker specializing in marriage, prayer, parenting, and redemptive suffering.

MARGARET ROSE REALY, OBL. O.S.B., is a lay hermit, master gardener, and retreat leader. The author of three books, she also writes garden columns, is a monthly columnist at *CatholicMom.com*, and blogs about gardening and spirituality at *Patheos.com*.

When she's not chasing kids, chugging coffee, or juggling work, **SARAH REINHARD** is usually trying to stay up to read just one . . . more . . . chapter. She's the editor of *Word by Word: Slowing Down with the Hail Mary*. You can find her online at SnoringScholar.com.

ROXANE B. SALONEN, wife and mother of five from Fargo, North Dakota, coauthored the spiritual memoir *Redeemed by Grace: A Catholic Woman's Journey to Planned Parenthood and Back*. An award-winning children's author and columnist, Roxane also enjoys her work as a Catholic radio host and speaker. She gathers her ruminations and writings at RoxaneSalonen.com.

KAREE SANTOS is the founder of the *Can We Cana?* blog and the coauthor of *The Four Keys to Everlasting Love: How Your Catholic Marriage Can Bring You Joy for a Lifetime* with her husband, Manuel P. Santos, MD.

ELIZABETH SCALIA is a Benedictine oblate, a popular speaker, and the author of *Strange Gods: Unmasking the Idols in Everyday Life*. Her book *Little Sins Mean a Lot* was released in spring 2016.

LISA A. SCHMIDT is sought as a speaker and radio guest on a variety of topics including motherhood, spiritual friendships, and family spirituality. She writes at ThePracticing-Catholic.com with her husband, Deacon Joel Schmidt.

COLLEEN SPIRO is a Benedictine oblate, author of *The Third Floor Window*, and loves to share her faith through her retreats and her website, Catholic-PrayerLife.com.

JEN STEED is a Catholic wife and mother to three whose nose can usually be found buried in a book learning once all the work is done (or not!). You can find her blogging about the top five priorities of women at HappyLittleHomemaker.com.

BARB SZYSZKIEWICZ, O.F.S., writes at FranciscanMom.com, shares family-friendly diabetic recipes at Cookand-Count.wordpress.com, and is an editorial consultant for *CatholicMom.com*.

CHARISSE TIERNEY is the assistant editor for Catholicap.com. She writes about her family's faith journey from a theology of the body perspective at

PavingthePathtoPurity.wordpress.com and on her Facebook page, "Paving the Path to Purity."

GRACE MAZZA URBANSKI teaches high school English at Brookfield Academy in Wisconsin. She previously served as children's ministry director with the Apostleship of Prayer. She speaks at conferences and gatherings around the country.

COURTNEY VALLEJO is a convert to the Catholic faith and an adoptive mother of two. She enjoys speaking and writing on a variety of topics, including conversion, adoption, youth ministry, marriage, and theology.

LETICIA VELASQUEZ is the author of *A Special Mother is Born* and contributor to several books and Catholic websites. She advocates for the human rights of those with Down syndrome in the international media.

KELLY WAHLQUIST is the founder of the Catholic women's ministry WINE: Women In the New Evangelization and is the author of *Created to Relate: God's Design for Peace & Joy*. She is the assistant director for the Archbishop Harry J. Flynn Catechetical Institute, a Catholic speaker and evangelist, a contributing writer for *CatholicMom.com*, and can be found online at KellyWahlquist.com as well as CatholicVineyard.com.

NANCY H. C. WARD, journalist, convert, speaker, and author of *Sharing Your Faith Story*, writes about Catholicism, conversion, and Christian community at JoyAlive.net. She is also a contributor to *CatholicMom.com*, SpiritualDirection.com and *Shalom Tidings* magazine. She loves to tell her conversion story to Catholic groups and help others tell theirs.

CHRISTINA M. WEBER, coach and family therapist, teaches Christian women entrepreneurs how to confidently follow God's will by changing messages and patterns blocking them from earning more in less time and embracing the various roles in their lives. Christina founded ChristianWomens-Guide.com, speaks, and authored *The Catholic Women's Guide to Healthy Relationships: 12 Supernatural Keys to Make Good Relationships Great and Improve Difficult Ones*.

TANYA WEITZEL is a busy wife, mother, home-school teacher, and library assistant, and who spends her days writing, walking, reading, and cooking. She writes at CatholicSimplicities.com and is a contributing author at *CatholicMom.com*. She loves learning more about her Catholic faith.

SHERI WOHLFERT is a Catholic wife, mom, speaker, writer, and schoolteacher. She combines those experiences with her sense of humor and her deep love of God into a ministry designed to help others love and serve the Lord.

DR. CAROLYN Y. WOO is CEO and president of Catholic Relief Services, the official international relief and development agency of the United States Conference of Catholic Bishops.

JEFF YOUNG, author of *Around the Table with The Catholic Foodie: Middle Eastern Cuisine*, is the founder and producer of *The Catholic Foodie*, where he offers Catholic culinary inspiration to help families grow in faith around the table. Jeff is the host of *The Catholic Foodie Show* on Real Life Radio, and many of his recipes and Catholic culinary inspiration can be found at CatholicFoodie.com.

Notes

1. Cf. Matthew 13:47; Romans 6:11, 14; Procatechesis, 5.

2. Natasha Geiling, "The Real Johnny Appleseed Brought Apples—and Booze—to the American Frontier," Smithsonian. com, http://www.smithsonianmag.com.

3. Saint Margaret calls Our Lord "Jesu" in the Middle English fashion.

4. The date for National Day of Prayer changes each year.

5. The date for National Cancer Survivors Day changes each year.

6. The date for the feast of Corpus Christi changes each year.

7. The date for National Cancer Survivors Day changes each year.

8. John Sullivan, O.C.D., *Edith Stein: Essential Writings, Modern Spiritual Masters* (Maryknoll, NY: Orbis Books, 2002).

9. James Martin, S.J., *Becoming Who You Are: Insights on the True Self from Thomas Merton and Other Saints* (Boston: Paulist Press, 2006), 70.

10. Saint Maria Faustina Kowalska, *Diary* (Stockbridge, MA: Marian Press, 2014), 1588.

11. Ann Voskamp, *One Thousand Gifts: A Dare to Live Fully Right Where You Are* (Grand Rapids, MI: Zondervan, 2010), 171.

LISA M. HENDEY is the founder and editor of *CatholicMom.com* and the bestselling author of *The Handbook for Catholic Moms*, *A Book of Saints for Catholic Moms*, *The Grace of Yes*, and The Chime Travelers children's fiction series. She serves at editor-at-large at Ave Maria Press. As a board member and frequent host on KNXT Catholic Television, Lisa has produced and hosted multiple programs, including *Catholic Mom TV* and *Making the Grade*, a program aimed at promoting quality Catholic education. Lisa has additionally appeared on EWTN, CatholicTV and as a part of the Momnipotent DVD series. Hendey is a blogger on several sites and also serves as the technology contributor for the *Son Rise Morning Show*. Her articles have appeared in *Catholic Digest*, *National Catholic Register*, and *Our Sunday Visitor*.

Hendey travels internationally giving workshops on faith, family, and Catholic new media topics. She has spoken at the Los Angeles Religious Education Congress, Catholic Marketing Network, the University of Dallas Ministry Conference, National Catholic Youth Conference, the Midwest Family Conference, and the National Council of Catholic Women. In 2013, she was selected as an Egan Journalism Fellow and traveled with Catholic Relief Services in Rwanda to write about the aftereffects of the Rwandan genocide on the eve of its twentieth anniversary. In early 2016, Hendey went to Columbia to see the work of CRS there. She lives with her family in Los Angeles, California.

SARAH A. REINHARD is a Catholic author, blogger, speaker, and freelance writer who has a penchant for coffee and a love of chocolate. She writes at *SnoringScholar.com*.

Reinhard is the author of a number of books, including *A Catholic Mother's Companion to Pregnancy*. She earned a master's degree in marketing and communications from Franklin University and has worked for many years for corporate and nonprofit organizations. She lives in central Ohio with her husband and four children.